D1562741

Personality Disorders

Personality Disorders

Current Research and Treatments

Edited by James Reich

Routledge
Taylor & Francis Group
New York   London

Published in 2005 by
Routledge
Taylor & Francis Group
270 Madison Avenue
New York, NY 10016

Published in Great Britain by
Routledge
Taylor & Francis Group
2 Park Square
Milton Park, Abingdon
Oxon OX14 4RN

Printed in the United States of America on acid-free paper
10 9 8 7 6 5 4 3 2 1

International Standard Book Number-10: 0-415-95074-0 (Hardcover)
International Standard Book Number-13: 978-0-415-95074-9 (Hardcover)

Library of Congress Cataloging-in-Publication Data

Catalog record is available from the Library of Congress

Taylor & Francis Group
is the Academic Division of T&F Informa plc.

Visit the Taylor & Francis Web site at
http://www.taylorandfrancis.com

and the Routledge Web site at
http://www.routledge-ny.com

Contents

About the Editor

James Reich, M.D., M.P.H., is an adjunct associate professor at Stanford Medical School (Psychiatry) and clinical associate professor at UCSF Medical Center (Psychiatry). He is the founder and past president of the Association for Research in Personality Disorders (ARPD). He is currently on the boards of the ARPD and the International Society for the Study of Personality Disorders (ISSPD). He is in clinical practice of psychiatry in San Francisco where he specializes in the treatment of anxiety and personality disorders.

Contributors

David P. Bernstein, Ph.D., is associate professor at the University of Maastricht, Netherlands, in the Department of Medical, Clinical, and Experimental Psychology. He is the president of the Association for Research on Personality Disorders, and a vice president of the International Society for the Study of Personality Disorders. He has published extensively on personality disorders, trauma, and addictions. His current research focuses on developing and testing innovative treatments for personality disorders and for post-traumatic stress disorder.

Ira D. Glick, M.D., is professor in the Department of Psychiatry and Behavioral Sciences at Stanford University School of Medicine. He is an active researcher, teacher, and clinician with extensive publications over a wide variety of topics. His clinical work is not limited to the personality disorders.

Marianne Goodman, M.D., is an assistant professor of psychiatry and the director of the Dialectical Behavioral Therapy (DBT) program at the Mount Sinai School of Medicine. She is an active researcher in the neurobiology of treatment response and is interested in the interface of childhood trauma with emotional dysregulation in personality disorders.

W. John Livesley, M.D., Ph.D., is professor of psychiatry at the University of British Columbia. He is an active teacher, clinician, and researcher and has written extensively on personality disorders. He is editor of the *Journal of Personality Disorders.*

Daniel Mayman, M.D., is a resident, Department of Psychiatry, University of Michigan Health System.

Blair Mullen, B.S., is a clinical research coordinator in the Stanford Department of Psychiatry and Behavioral Sciences.

Antonia New, M.D., is an associate professor of psychiatry at the Mount Sinai School of Medicine. Her research interests include the use of neuroimaging to understand the etiology of impulsive aggression in personality disorders, identifying intermediate endophenotypes of borderline personality disorder and resiliency.

Seth Resnick, B.A., is a graduate of the Mount Sinai School of Medicine and will be pursuing a residency in psychiatry.

Thomas Rinne, M.D., Ph.D., is psychiatrist and senior consultant of the academic psychiatric clinic and associate professor at the Department of Psychiatry of the Leiden University Medical Center. His work is focused on the study of the neuroendocrinology and biological treatment approaches relating to childhood adversity. He has received several awards for his studies of the neuroendocrine alterations in childhood abused female patients with a borderline personality disorder.

Larry Siever, M.D., is a professor of psychiatry at the Mount Sinai School of Medicine, director of the Mood and Personality Disorder Research Group, and director of the VISN 3 MIRECC. He has been involved in the study of the underlying neurobiology of personality disorder for over two decades and is one of the leading experts on schizotypal personality disorder.

Kenneth R. Silk, M.D., is professor of psychiatry, associate chair (Clinical and Administrative Affairs) and director of the personality disorder program at the Department of Psychiatry, University of Michigan Health System. He is an active researcher and a clinician with broad experience in different treatment settings. His practice is not limited to personality disorders.

Per Vaglum, M.D., Ph.D., is a psychiatrist who is a professor in the Department of Behavioral Sciences in Medicine, University of Oslo, Norway.

He also has a part-time psychotherapeutic practice. His main research areas are clinical and epidemiological research on substance abuse, personality disorders, and schizophrenia; clinical communication; and physicians' health.

Introduction

JAMES REICH

The chapters in this book largely come from the conference entitled "Personality Disorders: Update on Research and Treatment," held at Stanford University in June of 2004. This was the third Update conference at Stanford which occurs every two years. This conference was started when members of the Association for Research in the Personality Disorders (ARPD) and members of the Stanford faculty realized that there was an increasing amount of empirical evidence on the personality disorders being produced, and that much of this was changing our conceptions of the personality disorders in a fairly rapid fashion. The conference was conceived as a way to bring together experts to communicate changes in the field to practicing clinicians. This book is intended to bring together some of this same information about research and clinical implications for the professional reading public.

The book is divided into three sections. The first focuses on interesting new research in the area of the personality disorders, the second on clinical aspects of new findings, while the last chapter is a bit of speculation about where we are going from here. To aid the busy reader in finding the sections of most relevance to them, each chapter has a listing of key teaching points (the latter items being a unique feature of the book). While not comprehensive, the book should give the reader a good feel about where some general trends in thinking about personality pathology are headed.

The general theme of the research section of the book is to examine how new empirical findings modify our understanding of clinical phenomena that have been documented for some time. In general, what we observe clinically doesn't change, but our understanding of how it comes about is refined or transformed. The authors use the concept of traits and examining personality pathology at the border with other disorders or fields to advance our knowledge.

Research

The first chapter on *state* personality disorder examines a clinical phenomenon which has been repeatedly observed and documented. That is that many symptoms of personality pathology instead of being life long as earlier theorized can at times be much more transient. Not only has this been documented by clinicians, but also by careful longitudinal research. The state personality chapter wrestles with this information and concludes that by reasonable empirical evidence and standard nosological techniques we do not have two categories of personality disorder, present or absent, but three. These categories are *trait* (early onset long lasting), state (shorter lasting and not necessarily early onset), and *no* personality disorder. This contribution expands our theoretical base to better conform to current empirical data. It is also consistent with other chapters in the book that lean toward viewing personality pathology in a more dimensional and less categorical fashion.

The second chapter also examines our clinical and empirical understanding of personality disorders and also comes to a more elegant theoretical understanding of causation and nosology. Livesley starts with the clinical descriptions of personality disorders such as those found in the DSM descriptions and notes that this type of pathology can be theoretically explained by four higher-order dimensions. He uses these dimensions to explain how *borderline* personality could be explained primarily by the dimension of emotional dysregulation with contributions from submissiveness, insecure attachment, and cognitive distortion. Livesley goes further and argues that these higher-order dimensions are supported by significant genetic evidence for the heritability of personality traits. The role of environment becomes more a matter of whether it triggers or consolidates the inherited personality traits. This is an ambitious and intriguing chapter which conceptualizes personality pathology as a heterogeneous collection of genetically inherited traits.

The third chapter is from a group known for its biological research. This chapter approaches borderline personality disorder by examining biological dimensions of personality. For borderline personality disorder (BPD), it reviews the active investigation of the dimensions of impulsive aggression and affective instability that aim to identify neurotransmitter involvement and regions of brain dysfunction. The authors feel that structural and functional neuroimaging are at the forefront of biological research in BPD and they relate findings from neuroimaging studies in borderline personality disorder implicating dual dysfunction of prefrontal cortex and amygdala. Genetic studies relevant to BPD are reviewed which indicate that polymorphisms of the serotonin system in impulsive aggression suggest only modest genetic contributions. They discuss future biological approaches. Again, the chapter creates further theoretical and empirical underpinnings to our observed clinical phenomena and, again, follows the trait approach.

Few areas are of more clinical interest than that of chronic childhood abuse and borderline personality disorder. In his chapter, Rinne examines this area in detail. Rinne reviews animal and human studies which demonstrate that early and sustained stress alters the function of the hypothalamic pituitary adrenal (HPA) axis and the central seritonergic systems. Moreover, functional neuroimaging studies provide insight in anatomical and functional alterations of the frontolimbic system (crucial for adequate processing of emotional information needed to modulate stress) related to childhood abuse. Other studies indicate an increased central drive of corticotropin releasing hormone (CRH) and argenine vasopressin (AVP) in the hypothalamus is the hallmark of an HPA-axis increased response to stress, which interferes with the functioning of the frontolimbic system and which can render victims (depending on their genetic predispositions) susceptible for stress related psychiatric and somatic disorders. Rinne concludes that sustained traumatic stress during childhood has profound consequences for many brain functions and the development of personality and Axis I psychopathology. Although the prevalence of childhood abuse is considerably increased among borderline personality disorder patients, chronic abuse is not found to be either a necessary or sufficient cause for borderline personality disorder. Rinne is to be congratulated for sorting out the evidence in a difficult area although he does leave us dealing with a great deal of heterogeneity among our patients. This heterogeneity is also found by other authors in this book.

Vaglum's chapter on personality and substance abuse reviews the scientific literature in an area of public health concern. Vaglum reviews the extensive literature on the prevalence of personality disorders in substance abuse populations and finds that it is substantial. The question of the effect of personality pathology on outcome of substance abuse treatment is not quite as clear cut, but the weight of the evidence appears to be that personality pathology can have an effect on substance abuse outcome for good or ill. Vaglum then examines whether the current approaches to personality pathology in this population are adequate. He finds that while some programs do successfully identify and deal with personality pathology, unfortunately many do not. Even of more concern is that even in the programs that do seem to be successful it is not possible with the current state of the art to delineate why they are successful clearly enough to allow their techniques to be replicated elsewhere. Nonetheless, Vaglum feels that the effort should be made by each individual program, as the stakes are high. The chapter brings us up to date in a difficult but clinically and socially important area. It speaks to the heterogeneity of our population, not only within the personality disorders, but also in their border with the Axis I disorders.

Treatment

Fifty years ago the idea of treating personality pathology with drugs could be said to barely even exist. However, currently we have a growing and useful empirical literature on this subject. The chapter on drug treatment of pathological personality traits starts with the conceptual issues involved. It notes that there is not one single accepted model of drug treatment of personality pathology, and reviews a number of possible models that might guide the practitioner, and urges that a model of treatment be kept in mind. Different categories of drug treatment are then reviewed individually. These include traditional neuroleptics, atypical neuroleptics, tricyclic antidepressants, selective seritonergic response inhibitors, monoamine oxidase inhibitors, mood stabilizers, naltrexone, and others. The individual effect of each treatment is described as well as how they might fit into hypothetical cases. Overall we have reached the stage where it is possible to reduce the morbidity load of dysfunctional personality traits in many cases. Once again, the focus is on personality traits rather than disorders.

There is a fair amount of research indicating that personality pathology may be a poor prognostic indicator for the outcome of treatment of Axis I disorders. In particular, there is research that suggests that some clients with personality disorders respond poorly to standard cognitive and behavior treatments for Axis I psychopathology. Clinically, it seems that standard cognitive and behavioral therapy—although powerful treatments —somehow do not always deal with the complexities introduced by the present personality pathology. In the chapter on *schema therapy*, Bernstein discusses a modification of cognitive therapy that holds promise for these difficult patients with seemingly intractable problems. In this chapter the schema therapy conceptual model and treatment approach is reviewed. This approach postulates that there are a finite number of complex behavioral schemas or patterns which can help us understand the behavior in personality pathology cases. Originally these were arrived at by clinical experience and now they have been validated by factor analysis. There are specific techniques for treating the different schema. In a recent randomized clinical trial, schema therapy demonstrated efficacy for reducing both core personality pathology and associated Axis I symptoms in borderline personality disorder clients. These concepts are illustrated with a case example of a female client treated with schema therapy for Dependent Personality Disorder and comorbid major depression. Clearly this technique represents a possible valuable addition to our treatment armamentarium. Its approach, similar to the drug treatment chapter, is to ameliorate traits rather than to treat entire disorders.

A difficult clinical problem faced by clinicians is chronic depression. This is a debilitating disorder that may not respond completely to standard treatments for acute depression. It is an area requiring further understanding. This subject, the relationship between chronic depression and personality disorders, is explored in the chapter by Silk and Mayman. They examine ways in which Axis I and Axis II disorders relate to each other. Models to understand this relationship include one disorder makes a patient more vulnerable to the other disorder; both disorders spring from some common genetic or constitutional substrate or predisposition; or the two disorders are independent but share a number of nonspecific but overlapping criteria. Recent research reveals that depression is more frequently found in cluster C personality disorders than in cluster B personality disorders. Chronic depression may be different from a prolonged major depressive episode. Chronic depression shares many characteristics of how depression often presents itself in patients with personality disorders. When not in a major depressive episode, the depression in personality disordered patients is defined by emptiness, loneliness, fear of abandonment, low self-esteem, negativity, and pessimism. What we view as chronic depression may be aspects of characterological depression that remain or are revealed after the medication-responsive aspects of depression have responded to psychopharmacologic treatment. Treatment of chronic depression in patients with personality disorders involves a thorough evaluation of both axes as well as a careful history of prior treatment successes and failures. Comorbid personality disorder may or may not inhibit recovery from major depression but may impact the persistence of the symptoms of chronic depression. Clearly this chapter does not provide all the answers in this difficult area, but it provides an important update and reasonable approaches to thinking about the phenomenon. As in the chapter by Vaglum, it deals with the difficult area of overlap of Axis I and Axis II pathologies.

The chapter by Glick and Mullen reviews the literature on the role of the family in the understanding and treatment of personality disorder. This is an important area on which relatively little is written. They review the definition of personality disorder in terms of signs and symptoms in the family system, and the etiology, with an emphasis on how "the family" fits into a complex biologic-individual model. Data are accumulating that there are disturbed biological substrates in the patient with personality disorder, and probably in family members as well. There is some suggestive evidence that disturbed biology in combination with a disturbed "bad-fit" family may predispose to borderline pathology. They review the issues of (1) parental pathology, (2) physical and sexual abuse, and (3) neglect and overprotection as related to interactional processes. There is no evidence that pathologic family relationships alone can cause borderline disorder. On the other hand, researchers agree that a family can cause a genetically vulnerable, identified patient great distress, and a very ill identified patient can certainly cause the family great burden.

They stress evaluation of the family is necessary for most patients with personality disorder and describe seven goals of treatment plus enabling factors to allow family participation in treatment. They present a treatment model which includes family psychoeducation, and a systems approach to psychotherapy. They believe that including the family may improve compliance to medication as well as individual intervention. Although there are little hard data available in this area, the authors' conceptualizations help blaze a path for other work to follow. They are examining a different border of personality pathology, that of personality and the family.

Trends for the future

Naturally, in any field where the empirical data are forcing us to reconsider our prior conceptualizations, they also raise the issue of the proper nomenclature for the personality disorders. This is a subject discussed by Silk in his final chapter. He notes that the American psychiatry begins to consider the next iteration of the *Diagnostic and Statistical Manual of Mental Disorders*, or DSM-V. While, as noted above, a nomenclature change may be appropriate at this time, Dr. Silk notes a number of considerations that arise with respect to Axis II, and specifically the personality disorders.

His chapter reviews the development of the DSMs in American psychiatry, beginning with DSM-I in 1952 and ending with DSM-IV in 1996, in relation to the personality disorders. Different personality disorder diagnoses have been added or eliminated over the 40-year history of the DSM, but the greatest change was the development of Axis II as well as the categorical prototypic structure of psychiatric diagnosis that began in DSM-III in 1980. Silk believes that as we look toward DSM-V, particularly with respect to personality disorders, we need to consider the following issues: Should all Axis II disorders be moved to Axis I, or should some Axis II disorders be subsumed under existing Axis I categories of diagnoses? Should Axis II categorical diagnoses be eliminated and replaced by a dimensional system, a system that emphasizes traits and functionality along a continuum? Should some personality disorder diagnoses be changed or eliminated, and should the names of others be changed? What would be the impact upon research efforts and clinical care of these suggested changes? Silk provides a guide to many of the appropriate questions that need to be asked at the time of nomenclature revision.

A Final Note

In sum, the book examines the advancing trends in understanding personality disorders which are tied together by a better understanding of traits, genetics, and biology. Often, by examining personality pathology in its border with other disciplines and disorders, we find the effort valuable in extending our understanding.

PART I

Research

CHAPTER 1

State and Trait in Personality Disorders

JAMES REICH

Key Teaching Points

- Personality disorders (PDs) are currently defined as disorders where the personality pathology is constant and long lasting.
- There is evidence that there are situations where personality pathology may not be enduring and long lasting. This includes remissions with treatment of an Axis I disorder and longitudinal studies of severe personality disorders where some disorders show considerable improvement.
- Proposed is the concept of state personality disorder (SPD), a disorder characterized by fluctuating personality pathology.
- This disorder has been identified in two separate populations, has been distinguished from its near neighbor disorders, and has a possible biological marker.
- State PD may be clinically important as there is less suicidal ideation in state PD than in trait PD. Identifying state PD would therefore help clinicians better identify patients at risk for suicide.
- State PD may also be clinically important in its effect of worsening the outcome of comorbid Axis I disorders such as anxiety and depression.

Introduction

Personality has in the past been considered to be stable, or at the very least, something that changes slowly over time. However, all clinicians can think of a case where there was personality change on a seemingly more rapid basis. Sometimes this is in relation to treatment, sometimes not. It is to this phenomenon that this chapter addresses itself. I propose the concept of a *state* personality disorder (SPD). An SPD would be analogous to the concept of state anxiety, a set of symptoms that appear under certain circumstances and that may remit, perhaps in rapid fashion. In state anxiety these are anxiety symptoms, whereas in state personality these would be symptoms we usually think of as being personality symptoms.

Current Status of the Definition of Personality Disorders

Personality disorders have been conceptualized in different ways by different schools of thought. There is not space here to review all the different conceptualizations of personality disorder, but I will mention two of the current major definitions. The current *Diagnostic and Statistical Manual of Mental Disorders* (4th ed.) (DSM-IV) diagnosis of personality disorder is "An enduring pattern of inner experience and behavior that deviates markedly from the expectations of the individual's culture" (American Psychiatric Association, 1994 and 2000, pp. 630, 681). The pattern is manifested in two or more of the following areas: cognition, affectivity, interpersonal functioning, and impulse control. The pattern is inflexible and pervasive across a broad range of situations, has an early onset, is stable, and leads to significant distress or impairment.

Personality disorders, according to the ICD-10 Classification of Mental and Behavioural Disorders (ICD-10) diagnostic guidelines (World Health Organization, 1992a),

> comprise deeply ingrained and enduring behavior patterns, manifesting themselves in inflexible responses to a broad range of personal and social situations. They represent either extreme or significant deviations from the way the average individual in a given culture perceives, thinks, feels, and particularly, relates to others. Such behavior patterns tend to be stable and to encompass multiple domains of behavior and psychological functioning. They are frequently, but not always, associated with various degrees of subjective distress and problems in social functioning and performance.

The DSM-IV does not allow for the possibility of an SPD. The ICD-10 allows for a personality disorder to be created by stress. An enduring personality change is defined as

> a disorder of adult personality and behavior that has developed following catastrophic or excessive prolonged stress, or following a severe psychiatric illness, in an individual with no previous personality disorder. There is a definite and enduring change in the individual's pattern of perceiving, relating to, or thinking about the environment and the self. The personality change is associated with inflexible and maladaptive behavior that was not present before the pathogenic experience and is not a manifestation of another mental disorder or a residual symptom of any antecedent mental disorder. (WHO, 1992a, 1992b).

The ICD-10 definition does not allow for a stress-created personality disorder to reverse itself.

It is clear that much of the current nomenclature does not have a place for the concept of state and trait personality. (Trait personality or trait PD would be the form of personality dysfunction that is stable over time.)

Some Arguments for the Possibility of an SPD

The two official definitions of personality cited above emphasize the concept of the level of personality functioning being stable over time. However, there is no question that measures of personality characteristics can be elevated if measured when the patient is acutely ill with an Axis I disorder. These measures then return to baseline after resolution of the Axis I disorder (Hirschfeld, Klerman, Clayton, Keller, McDonald-Scott, & Larkin, 1983; Ingham, 1966; Kerr, Schapira, Roth, & Garside, 1970; Reich, Noyes, Coryell, & O'Gorman, 1986; Reich, Noyes, Hirschfeld, Coryell, & O'Gorman, 1987; Reich & Noyes, 1987b; Reich & Troughton, 1988). Although the studies just cited vary in their details, the findings are remarkably similar over several decades and in different populations. That is, that patients who are acutely depressed and patients who are acutely anxious score higher on the same measures of personality than when they are not acutely depressed and not acutely anxious. This would represent one possible model for an SPD. These would be symptoms of personality dysfunction which increase or remit in relatively short periods of time. It certainly demonstrates that clinicians can see more rapid changes in personality than would be expected by current definitions of personality disorder.

An example of this can be seen in Figure 1.1. Here the prevalence of personality disorders in depressed and recovered patients is used (Reich & Noyes, 1987a; Reich & Troughton, 1988). Personality measures in patients were taken when they were acutely ill and from this was subtracted the prevalence when they were in remission from depression. This results in a picture of the personality disorders that have "disappeared." As can be seen in the figure for three different personality instruments the Personality Diagnostic Questionnaire (PDQ), the Millon Clinical Multiaxial Personality Inventory (MCMI), and the Structured Clinical Interview for DSM Personality Disorders (SIDP) (Reich, 1987, 1989) the amount of personality pathology that disappears is large.

One must consider the possibility that this seeming remission of Axis II symptoms with the treatment of an Axis I disorder is a measurement artifact. If this were the case, traits distorted by the presence of an Axis I disorder would have no clinical value (i.e., they would just be "noise" confusing the clinical picture.) However, if the evidence was that SPD can be reliably distinguished from its near neighbors and has important clinical implications, it would clearly be more than noise in the system. The evidence does seem to indicate distinction from near-neighbor disorders and clinical relevance (see sections in this chapter titled "The Disorder Should Be Distinguishable from Its Near-Neighbor Disorders," and "The Concept Should Have Clinical Relevance")

Numerous research reports indicate the phenomena of personality pathology being less than life long. Zanarini, Frankenburg, Hennen, & Silk

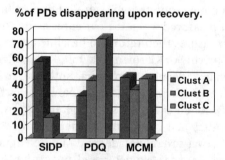

%of PDs disappearing upon recovery.

Figure 1.1 Effect of state. Clusters A, B, and C refer to personality disorders in the DSM Personality A, B, and C clusters. The first cluster, cluster A or the Schizoid cluster, includes the Schizoid, Schizoptypal and Paranoid personality disorders. The second cluster, cluster B or Impulsive cluster, includes Borderline, Histrionic, Antisocial, and Narcissistic PDs. The third cluster, cluster C or the Anxious cluster, consists of the Avoidant, Dependent, and Compulsive PDs. MCMI, PDQ, and SIDP refer to three different personality instruments, The Personality Diagnostic Questionnaire (PDQ), the Millon Clinical Multiaxial Personality Inventory (MCMI), and the Structured Clinical Interview for DSM Personality Disorders (SIDP) (Reich 1987, 1989).

(2003) reported a follow-up of patients diagnosed with borderline personality disorder. Thirty-four and a half percent met criteria for remission at 2 years, 44.9% at 4 years, 68.6% at 6 years, and 73.5% over the entire follow-up. Paris and Zweig-Frank (2001) in a long-term follow-up of 64 borderline patients found that for the 15-year follow-up only five met the criteria for borderline personality disorder. In a 7-year follow-up of borderline patients, Links, Heslegrave, & van Reekum (1998) found that only 47.4% still met the criteria for borderline at the end of the study. In a longitudinal study of schizotypal, borderline, avoidant, and obsessive compulsive personality disorders, the majority did not remain at the diagnostic threshold after 12 months (Shea et al., 2004). Seivewright, Tyrer, & Johnson (2002) in a 12-year follow-up of 202 personality disorder patients also came to the conclusion that the assumption that personality characteristics do not change over time is incorrect. The weight of the empirical evidence is that what we have traditionally diagnosed as personality disorders are clearly not as stable as was once thought.

Other Literature Relevant to the State Personality Concept

Other researchers have speculated about the possibility of state-induced personality disorders. As far back as 1968, Leonhard (1968) theorized about this concept. Mischel (1986) examined the issue and found that while high levels of personality traits could predict behavioral response much of the time, when the personality trait was present at lower levels there was more variability in response. Some of this variability was presumed to be environmental. This conceptualization would fit the concept of stress-induced personality disorders. The high trait (trait PD) would be more predictable in their dysfunctional responses, the very low trait (no PD) would have the greatest adaptive flexibility, and the intermediate group (state PD) would be in between. After a review of the literature on personality and anxiety and depressive disorders, Bronisch and Klerman (1991) concluded that an SPD was a reasonable concept. They referred to the concept as "personality change." They postulated five different areas where fluctuations in personality might occur: mood and affect, impulse control, attitudes toward self, attitudes toward the world, and social and interpersonal behavior.

Other researchers have approached the subject of personality from dimensional and genetic perspectives. Livesley, Jang, Jackson, & Vernon (1993) examined the heritability of personality traits in twin pairs. They found personality traits had varying levels of heritability, some high and some low. They did not see discrete categories of personality, but rather personality traits behaving as dimensionally distributed attributes in the population. For most personality dimensions the best-fitting model specified additive genetic and unique environmental effects. In this model the state personality group would be the middle rank in those who responded to environmental stress. They would be between those who responded maladaptively to minor environmental stress (trait PD) and those who were relatively resilient to environmental stress (no PD.) Although this model would not give clear categorical boundaries, the state personality group would still be of clinical interest.

Tyrer and Ferguson (2000) and Tyrer and Johnson (1996) in the United Kingdom developed an empirically based personality disorder system measured by an instrument called the Personality Assessment Schedule. This system categorizes no personality disorder, subthreshold personality disorder, complex personality disorder, and severe personality disorder. In this system the state personality group might be considered somewhere near the border of subthreshold and the simple personality disorder (Tyrer, personal communication).

Requirements for Validating the Concept of State and Trait Personality Disorders

There are no completely accepted criteria for validating a new psychiatric disorder (Beals et al., 2004). However, the development of diagnostic criteria from other disorders can give us a rough guide. We should be able to distinguish it from near neighbor disorders. We would want it to be associated with an independent measure linking the disorder to its area of hypothesized content. It is useful to have biological, family study, or family history markers. Ideally it should be empirically identified in two or more populations. It should also have clinical relevance.

The Disorder Should Be Distinguishable from Its Near-Neighbor Disorders

No disorder can be considered separate unless it can be distinguished from other disorders with at least some degree of reliability. The ultimate test of this is whether it can be distinguished from its near-neighbor disorders. This does not mean that it does not share symptoms with other disorders, merely that there can be a good differentiation. For example, bipolar disorder and major depression look identical when patients are in the depressed state; however course can distinguish them. Many of the individual personality disorders diagnosed under the DSM system share criteria, but are still considered different constellations of symptoms.

For SPD to meet these criteria it would be necessary to identify groups of patients where there were relatively brief personality fluctuations, and to distinguish this group from trait PD and no PD.

Evidence that This Criterion Is Met. I have now done two empirical studies on SPD. The first (Reich, 1999a) used two measures of personality to identify the groups. One was the Personality Diagnostic Exam (PDE, Loranger, 1988; Loranger, Susman, Oldham, & Russakoff, 1987) which was designed to measure personality dysfunction of longer duration (Loranger et al., 1991). The second instrument was the Personality Diagnostic Questionnaire (PDQ, Hyler, 1987; Hyler, Skodol, Oldham, Kellman, & Doidge, 1992). This instrument was designed in such a way that it would pick up current personality symptoms (Reich, 1987, 1989). Clearly, personality dysfunction and disorders picked up by the PDQ, but not the PDE, would represent a subgroup of patients with relatively brief personality dysfunction. The differences in the two instruments allowed me to identify three groups: no PD (no personality pathology on either instrument); SPD (relatively brief fluctuations in personality pathology indicated by pathology on the PDQ but not the PDE); and trait PD (enduring personality pathology as indicated by the PDE).

The second empirical study (Reich & Hofmann, 2004), using an updated PDQ, followed social phobics over a 12-week course of behavioral treatment. By examining the PDQ-IV scores at baseline and posttreatment, we were able to identify three groups based on the course of their symptoms. There were (1) those with high levels of personality pathology that did not change (trait PD), (2) those with personality pathology which changed over the 12-week treatment (state PD group), and (3) those with consistently low personality scores (no PD group). The state personality group was distinguishable from the other groups by trait anxiety as measured by the State Trait Anxiety scale (Speilberger, Gorsuch, & Lushene, 1970) and by harm avoidance (Cloninger, Przybeck, Svrakic, & Wetzel, 1994). This is shown in Table 1.1.

We now have identified SPD empirically in two populations and in each distinguished it from its near neighbor disorders. This criterion seems to have been met.

There Should Be Some Independent Measure Linking the Identified Group to the Area of Hypothesized Content

Once a group representing a new disorder or category is found, it should have an association with some other measure of a similar concept. This measure, ideally, should not have been used to initially identify the

Table 1.1 Comparison of Personality Groups on Trait Anxiety and Harm Avoidance

Variable	No PD (N = 32)	SPD (N = 33)	Trait PD (N = 28)	p value
State trait Anxiety Scale Trait score	44.5 (SD = 10.1)	51.2 (SD = 12.6)	61.6 (SD = 7.1)	p = 0.0001[a]
Harm Avoidance	19.8 (SD = 5.9)	23.3 (6.7)	26.3 (4.3)	p = 0.0002[a]

[a] Kruskal-Wallis test.

disorder. For example, if a new anxiety disorder was proposed it would strengthen the concept of that disorder if it was associated with other measures of anxiety. In the case of a personality disorder we would want the new group, that is, SPD, to be associated with other established measures of personality.

Evidence that This Criterion Is Met. We do have this evidence on our two empirically identified groups. In the social phobic group (Reich & Hofmann, 2004) the SPD group is separated from the trait personality group by the personality measure harm avoidance. (See Table 1.1.)

In the other identified population drawn from veterans (Reich, 1999a) we have an independent measure, the MCMI version 1, a validated personality instrument. It was available on only part of the subject sample. One scale from the MCMI-I that felt most likely to be relevant was chosen for the comparison. This was the scale which measured cluster B personality pathology. The results obtained by using this scale, were trait PD (75.4, SD = 11.7), SPD (70.6, SD = 6.4) and no PD (55.6, SD = 13.8). Even given the relatively small sample sizes (10, 3, and 5, respectively), Fisher's Exact test indicates a significant difference, p = 0.025. This finding adds an independent personality measure association to the second identified population. (This is currently in press in *Annals of Clinical Psychiatry.*)

Biological, Family Study, or Family History Data to Support the Diagnosis

Biological markers that distinguish the diagnostic group of interest from near-neighbor disorders are a useful validating tool. In most cases they are not available. However, they are present in this situation. The family study method is one such accepted technique. Here relatives of the identified group are diagnosed for psychiatric disorders and compared with relatives of comparison groups. Familial differences are considered as a useful tool in helping to validate a disorder. When the relatives cannot be directly interviewed another method is used where the patients are asked a structured interview about their relatives. This is a valid measure called the family history method (Andreason, Endicott, Spitzer, & Winokur, 1977a, b).

Evidence that This Criterion Is Met. In research on one population of SPD (Reich, 1999a), a validated family history measure of DSM anxiety and personality disorder clusters was used (Reich, 1985; Reich, Crowe, Noyes, & Andreasen, 1985). The personality clusters referred to here are the DSM personality disorder clusters. When the no PD, SPD, and trait PD relatives were compared, we saw significant differences between the groups in all three personality disorder clusters as well as one measure of anxiety, generalized anxiety disorder (GAD). These results can be seen in Table 1.2. The loading of psychopathology is what would be predicted from the model. Relative loading for each of the personality disorder clusters is trait PD>SPD>no PD. The family history measures provide further evidence for the validity of SPD.

The Disorder Should Be Identified in at Least Two Populations

Identifying a potential disorder in a single population is an interesting first step, but as in many interesting first findings, it gains weight with replication. Replicating a potential finding on a new population is a key step toward establishing its validity.

Evidence that This Criterion Is Met. We now have identified an SPD group in two very different populations. The first was a population of veterans in an outpatient clinic (Reich, 1999a), and the second in a group of social phobic patients recruited by advertising in a college setting (Reich & Hofmann, 2004). These two groups were identified by different methods. The

Table 1.2 Family History Measures for Relatives of the Different Groups in Percent

Diagnoses of Relatives	No PD n = 627	SPD n = 430	Trait PD n = 169
GAD	2.2	6.2	11.2 [a]
Schizoid Cluster PD	5.5	8.0	16.5 [b]
Dramatic Cluster PD	21.6	27.2	45.0 [c]
Anxious Cluster PD	11.3	15.6	32.0 [d]

[a] Chi square = 25.9, df = 2, p = 0.0001.
[b] Chi square = 24.2, df = 2, p = 0.0001.
[c] Chi square = 37.2, df = 2, p = 0.0001.
[d] Chi square = 42.9, df = 2, p = 0.0001.

first was identified by the cross-sectional use of two different personality instruments, and the second by following personality symptoms over a period of time with one instrument. Although it would not be expected that the disorder be exactly the same in these two very different populations, that the SPD groups was identified in both contributes to the conclusion that this is a possibly valid disorder requiring further research.

The Concept Should Have Clinical Relevance

Although identifying a new disorder is an intellectually interesting step, of importance in the real world is whether the concept would inform clinical practice. In other words, does it make a difference in how we view a patient and potentially improve our understanding and outcomes.

Evidence that This Criterion Is Met. There are two lines of evidence that SPD might have clinical significance.

Suicide Attempts and Ideation The first area of clinical significance is in the area of suicide impulses or acts. This is a key clinical concern. In both studies of SPD there was evidence that separating the diagnosis of SPD from trait PD increased the ability to predict suicidal ideation.

In the Reich (1999a) study, the subjects were military veterans. The information regarding suicide attempts and impulses was from a structured clinical interview. Here the frequency of making a suicide attempt in their lifetime for the no PD, SPD, and trait PD, respectively, were 5.3, 7.9, and 58.0. This is a significant difference (chi square = 45.2, df = 2, p = 0.001) that indicates that suicide attempts appear much more frequently in the trait PD group than the no PD and SPD groups. The frequency for the no PD and SPD groups appears about the same.

In the second study (Reich & Hofmann, 2004) there is evidence in the same direction. Here a self-report method was used, the PDQ. PDQ item 39 states, "I have tried to hurt or kill myself." We used this item for the comparisons in this population. Here we compared the trait group to the combined no PD and SPD groups. This was due to there being no difference between the SPD and no PD groups on this variable. When all PDQ scores are taken at their highest clinical levels, the trait group had 5 of 28 endorsing this item, while the combined state and no PD group had 0 of 50 (p = 0.005, Fisher's Exact test). Once again there is an indication that there is less suicidal ideation and behavior in the SPD than the trait PD group.

In these two studies we did not find other factors to explain this difference in suicide ideation. Although there are limitations (the second study used only a single variable as a measurement), both studies report similar results. If this finding was further replicated it would be of clinical use. This is because if clinicians could differentiate SPD from trait PD it would help them refine their assessment of which patients are more likely to make a suicide gesture or attempt. This would be clearly an aid to an important clinical decision.

Effect of State PD on the Course of Axis I Illnesses

A second line of evidence is the literature on the effect of personality pathology on the outcome of the treatment of Axis I disorders. Reviews on this subject (Reich & Green, 1991; Reich & Vasile, 1993; Reich, 2003) are extensive. Although there is not complete agreement among all investigators, the weight of the evidence is that personality pathology tends to produce a poorer clinical outcome in these cases. This effect appears to be present whether the personality pathology was measured by a self-report instrument (which would be expected to be measuring more SPD) or by semistructured personality inventories (which would be expected not to be measuring SPD). Although not definitive, it appears that SPD may share with trait PD the ability to be a predictor of poorer outcome for the treatment of Axis I disorders. This would, of course, be of clinical importance.

Clinical Characteristics of State Personality

A Clinical Example of SPD

I suppose that many diagnostic concepts begin with the observation of a clinical case or cases. The first case I saw of this that drew my interest was when I was working in a clinic decades ago. There was a trainee in the clinic not performing well. The trainee appeared to meet all the criteria for a personality disorder. I asked about the trainee from former supervisors and was told that in the past the trainee had performed well and was highly regarded. When the student and I discussed the difficulty, it turned out that there was a major depressive disorder and the student had recently gone off antidepressants. With the resumption of medication, what had clinically appeared to be a personality disorder completely disappeared. This to me became the model of SPD. That is, personality traits which under some sort of stress become temporarily exacerbated and appear on cross-sectional examination to be identical to a personality disorder, but which later go into remission.

Empirical Evidence for Describing Clinical Characteristics of SPD

There is very little empirical evidence on the clinical characteristics of SPD. I have examined this in two different data sets in widely differing populations. One of these was a social-phobic college population (Reich & Hofmann, 2004) and the other was a veteran's population with fairly severe psychopathology (Reich, 1999a). These two populations are different enough that it is unlikely that the results can be combined. This is because the social phobic SPDs demonstrated cluster C pathology while the veterans SPDs demonstrated cluster B pathology.

In the social-phobic population the SPD group differed from the no PD group and the trait PD group by having intermediate levels of trait anxiety, harm avoidance, and the prevalence of the generalized form of social phobia. Numerous variables distinguished the SPD from the trait PD group. Although these varied somewhat, an exploratory logistic regression seemed to indicate that the basic differences might have to do with some aspects of feeling not understood by others (due to paranoia or other reasons) combined with a tendency toward rapid mood shifts and impulsivity. These traits were higher in the trait PD group (Reich & Hofmann, 2004). Although these characteristics do not define a set of clinical criteria they might be somewhat of a guide for those searching for them.

I have more information on the veteran's population with its predominantly cluster B pathology (Reich, 2002). Here, using candidate items from the personality measures (the PDQ and PDE), a logistic regression was able to distinguish SPD from trait PD with a fairly high degree of the variance accounted for. The maximum R squared was 0.63. The most powerful predictors for the presence of trait PD were suicide, reacts to criticism, and needs approval. The specific results of the analysis are shown in Table 1.3, and the full wording of the criteria can be seen in Table 1.4. Although this is only a single sample, the results are intriguing. Clinical variables distinguishing state and trait PD were clearly found and it appears that shame may be a component of SPD in those with cluster B traits.

Of course it is also of interest to know the clinical characteristics that separate SPD from no PD. This is also found in the Reich (2002) report. A logistic regression distinguished the clinical questions that differentiated SPD and no PD in this population. The R squared for this analysis was 0.53, and the maximum R square was 0.71, showing that a good amount of the variance was accounted for. The question whose positive answer showed the greatest predilection for SPD was, "If I don't get my way I get angry and behave childishly." This question was from the self-report in the PDQ, and had an odds ratio of 166. The questions whose negative answer showed the greatest predilection for no PD was, "Some people rarely show

Table 1.3 Logistic Regression Results Comparing Trait and State Groups in a Veterans Population[a,b]

Item	Chi Square	p value	Odds Ratio
Suicide (PDE)	10.2	0.002	41.7
Reacts to Criticism (PDE)	8.9	0.003	37.0
Needs Approval (PDQ)	5.8	0.02	37.0
Ashamed (PDQ)	4.8	0.03	0.006

[a] R squared for this analysis was 0.41, max R square 0.63.
[b] From Reich (2002).

Table 1.4 Definition of Personality Items Used in the Logistic Regression

Item	Text
Suicide	Have you ever threatened to commit suicide? Have you actually made a suicide attempt or gesture?
Reacts to Criticism	Do you ever have a strong reaction to criticism, so that you feel ashamed or humiliated? Does criticism make you feel furious, even when you don't show it?
Fears embarrassment	Are you often afraid of being embarrassed by blushing, crying, or looking nervous when you are in front of other people?
Ashamed	Criticism makes me feel ashamed, inferior, or humiliated.

affection or talk about it. Are you like that? Have people told you that you are not affectionate?" This was from the PDE and had an odds ratio of 0.06.

Although the data available are limited, it does appear that diagnostic criteria for SPD might be developed, although it is possible they might vary somewhat based on the DSM clusters they were describing. It is possible, however, that the key criterion at the end of the day might be the fluctuating course of personality pathology.

An Example of How State Personality Might Inform the Literature of Another Area of Psychiatry: Comorbid Anxiety and Depression

Another question that arises is whether this new conceptualization (SPD) will help inform the psychiatric literature in other areas. One possible way that this concept might have explanatory value is in the area of comorbid anxiety and depression. There is a review which puts forth the main points (Reich, 1999b).

The review points out that there has been long-standing interest in whether comorbid anxiety and depression is qualitatively different from anxiety alone and depression alone. (This is as opposed to two disorders which, from time to time, happen to occur together.) Although there is agreement that this comorbid syndrome presents with a difficult course, nosologic, prospective, factor analytic, family history, and family studies have not definitively answered the question as to whether it is a distinct entity. However, by expanding the investigation of the phenomena between comorbid anxiety and depression to also include personality disorders, we may gain further insight. Clinical studies reveal a strong relationship between comorbid anxiety and depression and personality pathology. Family history studies taken from clinical populations indicate a strong association with personality pathology. Disorders combining anxiety, depression, and personality pathology have an especially virulent course.

It is likely that anxiety/depression/personality disorder represents a distinct clinical entity with its own course, pattern of morbidity, and etiology. If we consider the possibility that SPD is part of the phenomenon, the whole picture becomes clearer. The presence of SPD would likely reduce the odds of the disorder responding to standard treatment, as previously explained. Due to increased personality pathology during times of exacerbation of affective and anxiety symptoms, exacerbations would be particularly nasty and difficult. It would also improve the odds for eventual successful treatment because it would point out the need for treatment or management of personality symptoms. Thus the concept of state PD might add explanatory power, possible new lines of investigation, and treatment to an existing difficult clinical phenomenon.

Future Directions

Clearly, research into SPD is at an early stage. The first order of business would seem to be to identify other populations of SPD. This could be done two ways. A cross-sectional measure of personality pathology could be used over time to identify the different groups as was done in Reich and Hofmann (2004). The second method would be to use an instrument that could assess probable trait PD and to use a cross-sectional personality measure to identify the remaining SPD (Reich, 1999a). I would imagine that initially the most likely populations to study would be clinical psychiatric populations with their presumed high level of personality morbidity. Eventually it would be of interest to examine other populations such as general medical and the general population.

One question that will arise is whether we are examining one disorder or many variants of a disorder. It is possible that some aspects of these phenomena, in cluster B patients for example, would appear different in cluster C patients. This could be because the basic traits in the different clusters are different, but the phenomenon of personality trait variation is the same regardless of the specific traits. Or there might be differences in the phenomena in different types of populations. This is one reason why it would be important to use measures of personality different from those which are used to identify the disorder. Along the same lines, biological markers, either biochemical or of the family study sort, would be useful in further studies.

Earlier, I mentioned that it seemed likely that SPD as well as trait PD would negatively affect the outcome of treatment of Axis I disorders. This is an area which requires significant empirical research.

Summary and Conclusions

In this chapter I have started by reviewing the current official nomenclature for personality pathology. This is a personality disorder characterized by being early onset, long duration, and relatively unchanging personality pathology. I then review the evidence that many patients have personality pathology that bears little resemblance to this picture. Patients may have personality pathology that appears to be mediated by depression or anxiety. Even those patients who appear to have a severe long-lasting borderline personality disorder are often found to be in remission if careful follow-up is performed later. The current diagnostic nosology does not adequately reflect these latter cases.

I have proposed that much of this phenomenon of fluctuating personality pathology might well be explained by creating a new addition to the nomenclature, the concept of an SPD, a personality disorder characterized by more transient personality pathology. The old definition of enduring personality disorder would now define trait PD. This division is analogous to the concepts of state and trait anxiety, an accepted concept. High trait subjects tend to display the symptoms on a regular basis; intermediated trait subjects have a fluctuating course, while low trait subjects seldom evidence the symptoms.

Any new category needs to have some empirical evidence for its existence. In this chapter I have reviewed how this disorder has been identified in two different populations using two different methods. In both cases it could be distinguished from its near neighbors no PD and trait PD. In both cases an independent measure of personality was associated with the SPD group. In one sample there was a biological marker, a family history study of personality clusters, which discriminated the SPD group from trait PD and no PD. Although definite clinical criteria cannot yet be determined, it appears that this will be feasible in the future. In short, there is good preliminary evidence for the validity of SPD.

The clinical phenomenon of comorbid anxiety and depression is discussed to indicate how the concept of SPD might inform other areas of the psychiatric literature. Future work would require replications of identification of the SPD group in different populations. It would also require some longitudinal studies and the determination of other biological markers. I would also include studies to gauge the effect of SPD on the outcome of Axis I disorders.

References

American Psychiatric Association. (1994). *Diagnostic and statistical manual of mental disorders* (4th ed.) Washington, DC: American Psychiatric Association.

American Psychiatric Association. (2000). *Diagnostic and statistical manual of mental disorders,* (4th ed. text revision). Washington, DC: American Psychiatric Association.

Andreasen, N. C., Endicott, J., Spitzer, R. L., & Winokur, G. (1977a). *Family History-Research Diagnostic Criteria (FH-RDC).* Iowa City: Department of Psychiatry, University of Iowa.

Andreasen, N. C., Endicott, J., Spitzer, R. L., & Winokur, G. (1977b). The family history method using diagnostic criteria: Reliability and validity. *Archives of General Psychiatry, 34,* 1229–1235.

Beals, J., Novins, D. K., Spicer, P., Orton, H. D., Mitchell, C. M., Baron, A. E., et al. (2004). Challenges in operationalizing the DSM-IV clinical significance criterion. *Archives of General Psychiatry, 61,* 1197–1208.

Bronisch, T., & Klerman, G. (1991). Personality functioning: Change and stability in relationship to symptoms and psychopathology. *Journal of Personality Disorders, 5,* 307–317.

Cloninger, C. R., Przybeck, T. R., Svrakic, D. M., & Wetzel, R. D. (1994). *The temperament and character inventory (TCI): A guide to its development and use.* St. Louis, MO: Center for Psychobiology of Personality.

Hirschfeld, R. M. A., Klerman, G. L., Clayton, P. J., Keller, M. B., McDonald-Scott, P., & Larkin, B. H. (1983). Assessing personality effects of the depressive state on trait measurement. *American Journal of Psychiatry, 40,* 695–699.

Hyler, S. (1987). *Personality Diagnostic Questionnaire IV (PDQ-R).* New York: New York State Psychiatric Institute.

Hyler, S. E., Skodol, A. E., Oldham, J. M., Kellman., H. D., & Doidge, N. (1992). Validity of the Personality Diagnostic Questionnaire-Revised: A replication in an outpatient sample. *Comprehensive Psychiatry, 33,* 73–77.

Ingham, J. G. (1966). Changes in MPI scores in neurotic patients: A three year follow-up. *British Journal of Psychiatry, 112,* 931–939.

Kerr, T. A., Schapira, K., Roth, M., & Garside, R. F. (1970). The relationship between the Maudsley Personality Inventory and the course of affective disorders. *British Journal of Psychiatry, 116,* 11–19.

Leonhard, K. (1968). *Akzentuirerte Personlichenkeiten.* Berlin: Verlag Volk und Gesundheit.

Links, P. S., Heslegrave, R., & van Reekum, R. (1998). Prospective follow-up study of borderline personality disorder: Prognosis, prediction of outcome, and Axis II comorbidity. *Canadian Journal of Psychiatry, 43,* 265–270.

Livesley, J., Jang, K. L., Jackson, D. N., & Vernon, P. A. (1993). Genetic and environmental contributions to dimensions of personality disorder. *American Journal of Psychiatry, 150,* 1826–1831.

Loranger, A. W. (1988). *Personality Disorder Exam (PDE) Manual.* Yonkers, NY: DV Communications.

Loranger, A., Lenzenweger, M. F., Gartner, A. F., Susman, V. L., Herzig, J., Zammit, et al. (1991). Trait-state artifacts and the diagnosis of personality disorders. *Archives of General Psychiatry, 48,* 720–728.

Loranger, A. W., Susman, V. L., Oldham, J. M., & Russakoff, L. M. (1987). The Personality Disorder Examination: A preliminary report. *Journal of Personality Disorders, 1,* 1–13.

Mischel, W. (1986). *Introduction to personality: A new look* (4th ed.). New York: Holt, Rinehart & Winston.

Paris, J., & Zweig-Frank, H. (2001). A 27 year follow-up of patients with borderline personality disorder. *Comprehensive Psychiatry, 42,* 482–487.

Reich, J. (1985). A family history method for DSM III anxiety and personality disorders. *Psychiatry Research, 26,* 131–139.

Reich, J. H. (1987). Instruments measuring DSM-III and DSM-III-R personality disorders. *Journal of Personality Disorders, 1,* 220–240.

Reich, J. H. (1989). Update on instruments to measure DSM-III and DSM-III-R personality disorders. *Journal of Nervous and Mental Disease, 177,* 366–370.

Reich, J. (1999a). An empirical examination of the concept of "stress induced" personality disorder. *Psychiatric Annals, 29,* 701–706.

Reich, J. (1999b). Comorbid anxiety/depression/personality: Viewed as a possible stress induced personality disorder syndrome. *Psychiatric Annals, 29,* 707–712.

Reich, J. (2002). Clinical correlated of stress-induced personality disorder. *Psychiatric Annals, 32,* 581–589.

Reich, J. (2003). The effect of Axis II disorders on the outcome of treatment of anxiety and unipolar depressive disorders. *Journal of Personality Disorders, 17,* 387–405.

Reich, J., Crowe, R., Noyes, R., & Andreasen, N. (1985). *Family history for DSM III anxiety and personality disorders (FHPD).* San Francisco: Stanford Medical School.

Reich, J. H., & Green, A. I. (1991). Effect of personality disorders on outcome of treatment. *Journal of Nervous and Mental Disease, 179,* 74–83.

Reich, J., & Hofmann, S. (2004). State personality disorder in social phobia. *Annals of Clinical Psychiatry, 16,* 130–144.

Reich, J., & Noyes, R. (1987a). DSM-III personality disorders in unrecovered panic and depressed patients. *Journal of Anxiety Disorders, 1,* 123–131.

Reich, J., Noyes, R., Coryell, W., & O'Gorman, T. (1986). The effect of state anxiety on personality measurement. *American Journal of Psychiatry, 143,* 760–763.

Reich, J., Noyes, R., Hirschfeld, R. P., Coryell, W., & O'Gorman, T. (1987). State effects on personality measures in depressed and panic patients. *American Journal of Psychiatry, 144,* 181–187.

Reich, J., & Troughton, E. (1988). A comparison of DSMIII personality disorders in recovered depressed and panic disorder patients. *Journal of Nervous and Mental Disease, 176,* 300–304.

Reich, J., & Vasile, R. (1993). The effect of personality disorders on the treatment outcome of Axis I conditions: An update. *Journal of Nervous and Mental Disease, 181,* 475–484.

Seivewright, H., Tyrer, T., & Johnson, T. (2002). Change in personality status in neurotic disorders. *Lancet, 359,* 2253.

Shea, M. T., Stout, R., Gunderson, J., Morey, L. C., Grilo, C. M., McGlashan, T., et al. (2004). *American Journal of Psychiatry, 161,* 926–927.

Speilberger, C. D., Gorsuch, R. L., & Lushene, R. E. (1970). *State trait anxiety inventory.* Palo Alto, CA: Consulting Psychologists Press.

Tyrer, P., & Ferguson, B. (2000). Chapter 2, Current classification of personality disorder. In P. Tyrer & T. Johnson (Eds.), *Personality disorders: Diagnosis, management and course* (2nd ed.). London: Arnold.

Tyrer, P., & Johnson, T. (1996). Establishing the severity of personality disorder. *American Journal of Psychiatry, 153,* 1593–1597.

WHO. (1992a, reprinted 1993). *The ICD-10 classification of mental and behavioural disorders: Clinical descriptions and diagnostic guidelines.* Geneva: World Health Organization.

WHO. (1992b) *The international statistical classification of diseases and related health problems (10th rev.), Volume I: Tabular list.* Geneva: World Health Organization.

Zanarini, M. C., Frankenburg, F. R., Hennen, J., & Silk, K. R. (2003). The longitudinal course of borderline psychopathology: 6-year prospective follow-up of the phenomenology of borderline personality disorder. *American Journal of Psychiatry, 160,* 274–283.

CHAPTER 2

The Structure and Etiology of Borderline Pathology

W. JOHN LIVESLEY

Key Teaching Points

- To consider the implications of recent work on the phenotypic structure and genetic architecture for the conceptualization of borderline pathology. Although the DSM-IV definition is consistent with these findings, a more comprehensive definition based on dimensional measures is perhaps a better fit for the data.
- To describe the genetic etiology of borderline pathology and the way genetic factors influence personality structure. Large contributions to overall personality are made by many small contributions of different genetically determined personality traits.
- To discuss the way in which environmental factors contribute to the development of borderline pathology. Environmental factors are quite significant and act by consolidating genetically inherited personality traits and by modifying their expression.
- To discuss the interplay between genes and environment in the development and regulation of the affective core of borderline pathology. As there have been no environmental risks that have

been found to be necessary and sufficient for the production of the borderline personality disorder, the interplay of environment and genes becomes key.

Introduction

Current conceptions of borderline personality disorder, like those of other forms of personality disorder, are largely derived from clinical concepts and observations. Over the last decade or so, however, empirical analyses of the structure of personality disorder and etiological research have begun to offer a new understanding of the structure and origins of personality disorder, including borderline pathology, creating the possibility of developing diagnostic constructs that more closely match empirical findings. The *Diagnostic and Statistical Manual of Mental Disorders* (4th ed.) (DSM-IV) concept of borderline personality disorder as a discrete diagnostic category is challenged by evidence of extensive overlap with other personality disorders. The implication is that DSM-IV concepts of personality disorder do not reflect natural distinctions in the way personality pathology is organized. This assertion is supported by statistical analyses of the descriptive features of the personality disorders that have consistently failed to identify factors that resemble DSM concepts (Austin & Deary, 2000; Ekselius, Lindstrom, von Knorring, Bodlund, & Kullgren, 1994). These findings raise questions about the validity of DSM-IV personality disorder diagnoses, including borderline.

The limited evidential support for the DSM-IV model of personality disorder contrasts with remarkable agreement across studies that four higher-order or secondary dimensions underlie phenotypic variation personality disorder (Mulder & Joyce, 1997). The four factors may be labeled emotional dysregulation or anxious-submissive, dissocial or psychopathic, inhibited or socially withdrawn, and compulsive. These patterns resemble the more prevalent DSM-IV diagnoses of borderline, antisocial, schizoid-avoidant, and obsessive compulsive personality disorders, respectively. They also resemble major dimensions of normal personality, especially the five-factor dimensions of neuroticism, (dis)agreeableness, introversion, and conscientiousness (Widiger, 1998); clinical studies consistently fail to find a fifth component corresponding to the openness domain of normal personality. This agreement suggests that personality disorder is continuous with normal personality variation. This four-factor structure is one of the more robust findings in the study of personality disorder: multiple studies using self-report and interview measures yield the same results (Mulder & Joyce, 1997; Livesley, in press). This chapter examines the implications of both this structure and research on the etiology of personality for the conceptualization of borderline personality disorder. An alternative descriptive model of borderline pathology is proposed based on the findings of nosological and etiological research.

Structure of Borderline Pathology

The current concept of borderline personality disorder derives from two somewhat different traditions (Stone, 1980). The phenomenological description of borderline can be traced to Kraepelin's idea that some personality disorders are attenuated forms of more severe mental disorders, especially schizophrenia. A second influence came from psychoanalytic observations that there were a group of patients in the hinterland between psychosis and neurosis and hence on the borders of analyzability.

The DSM Conception of Borderline Personality Disorder

These origins lead to two distinct uses of the term *borderline* (Spitzer, Endicott, & Gibbon, 1979): a stable set of characteristics that were assumed to be genetically related to schizophrenia, and a constellation of features related to instability and vulnerability as exemplified by the work of Gunderson and Singer (1975) and Kernberg (1967). In an attempt to differentiate the two concepts, Spitzer and colleagues listed the descriptive features of both conditions and asked a panel of psychiatrists to rate two patients they were treating: a patient the psychiatrist considered borderline and a control patient who was moderately to severely ill but did not have a diagnosis of a psychosis or any borderline category. The ratings were examined with factor analysis. A two-factor solution was reported that was used to develop the DSM-III diagnostic criteria for schizotypal and borderline personality disorders. The borderline criteria have undergone only relatively minor change in subsequent versions of the DSM.

Examination of the results of the Spitzer et al. (1979) analysis is instructive. The two-factor solution accounted for a modest 22% of the variance in the factor analysis of ratings of borderline patients, and 33% in the combined analysis of both sets of ratings. Moreover, a five-factor solution appeared to be optimal. The remaining three factors were not described in detail, but apparently they represented affective instability, social isolation, and suspiciousness. Some descriptors of the unstable or borderline pattern that were used as criteria for DSM-III borderline personality disorder had relatively low loadings on the factor, and none had loadings above 0.45 in the borderline sample.

Despite these shaky empirical origins, the concept of borderline personality disorder quickly gained clinical and research attention. The criterion set seemed to capture important aspects of personality pathology. Nevertheless, extensive overlap with other disorders and the failure of multivariate studies to recapture the diagnosis suggest that the diagnosis is not clearly differentiated from other disorders and is not a natural kind that reflects the underlying biological structure of personality. Instead, like other personality disorder categories, it is an artifactual kind of construction used to bring order and meaning to clinical observations about personality disorder.

Multivariate Analyses of Personality Disorder Traits

Factor analyses of personality disorder descriptors suggest that borderline pathology involves a somewhat different set of traits than those proposed by DSM-IV. The first factor extracted in these analyses is consistently defined by an anxious-dependent cluster of traits. The traits defining the pattern are anxiousness, affective lability, submissiveness, insecure attachment, identity problems, cognitive dysregulation, social avoidance, and oppositionality (Livesley, Jang, & Vernon, 1998; see Table 2.1). Narcissism also loads on this factor in some analyses. The factor structure is stable across clinical and general population samples, a finding that also suggests that personality disorder incorporates the extremes of normal variation. The pattern is stable across cultures being reported in studies from Germany (Pukrop, Gentil, Steinbring, & Steinmeyer, 2001), Holland (van Kampen, 2002), China (Zheng, Wang, Huang, Sun, Zhu, & Livesley, 2002), Japan (Ando et al., 2004), and Canada (Livesley et al., 1998). Cross-cultural stability suggests that the pattern may reflect an underlying biological structure.

Table 2.1 Emotional Dysregulation Factor in Clinical and General Population Samples from Livesley, Jang, & Vernon (1998)

Primary Trait	Clinical	General Population
Anxiousness	86	89
Submissiveness	85	84
Social avoidance	76	69
Insecure attachment	70	81
Affective lability	64	78
Cognitive dysregulation	64	75
Oppositionality	64	69

As Table 2.2 shows, this factor bears some resemblance to DSM-IV borderline personality disorder but there are important differences. All DSM-IV criteria for borderline personality disorder are represented. However, the factor also includes traits that are not represented in the DSM-IV criterion set. Although anxiousness has the highest loading, this trait is not prominent in the DSM-IV criteria. It is merely considered a component of affective instability. In the analyses leading to the factorial model, however, anxiousness and affective instability were phenotypically distinctive (Livesley, Jackson, & Schroeder, 1992). Clinical experience with borderline patients is consistent with the factor analytic results: these patients experience intense anxiety; they are often chronic worriers, fearful, ruminative, and expect the worst. At times of crises, they usually experience intense, panic-like anxiety that undermines their coping skills and contributes to the escalation of dyscontrol that often culminates in self-harm. Anxiousness is probably underrepresented in the DSM-IV criteria in an unsuccessful attempt to differentiate the borderline diagnosis from cluster C diagnoses. Similarly, submissiveness is not included in the criteria, although it is also highly salient in empirical analyses because this trait is also a feature of dependent personality disorder. Again, clinical descriptions of these patients often note their intense dependency and difficulty

Table 2.2   Comparison of Emotional Dysregulation and DSM-IV Borderline Personality Disorder

DSM-IV Criteria for Borderline Personality Disorder	Emotional Dysregulation Trait
1. Frantic efforts to avoid abandonment	Insecure attachment
2. Unstable relationships	(No direct equivalent)
3. Identity disturbance	Identity problems
4. Impulsivity	Self-harm
5. Recurrent suicidal behavior	Self-harm
6. Affective instability	Affective lability
	Anxiousness
7. Feelings of emptiness	Identity problems
8. Intense anger	Affective lability
9. Transient psychotic/dissociative features	Cognitive dysregulation
	Not represented in DSM-IV
	Submissiveness
	Social avoidance
	Oppositionality

coping without support. Many are also socially avoidant in the sense that they are a little fearful in social situations.

The results of factor analyses of personality disorder traits suggest that the borderline pattern is organized around affective traits of anxiousness and affective lability. The broad underlying dimension seems to involve emotional dysregulation. This proposal is consistent with Linehan's (1993) contention that borderline personality disorder primarily involves a biological vulnerability to emotional dysregulation that is amplified by psychosocial factors primarily involving invalidating experiences (Linehan & Koerner, 1993). Similarly, Kernberg (1984) suggested that the core of borderline personality organization may be strong inherited aggression associated with an inability to tolerate anxiety. The family history work of Reich (1988) also indicates a relationship between anxiety and cluster B personality pathology.

Anxiousness, along with affective lability, forms an emotional core that influences the expression of other traits in the constellation. Most of these traits incorporate an emotional component. Submissiveness is an important element of dependent behavior that involves problems being assertive, reliance on others for advice and support, and suggestibility. The situations that evoke these behaviors are also likely to evoke anxiety. The second component of dependency is insecure attachment. This trait also has an anxious element: it involves insecurity about attachment relationships including fear of abandonment and separation. Social avoidance is also a salient on this component. Although this trait is usually assumed to be a feature of avoidant or even schizoid personality disorder, it incorporates a fearful element: those at the extremes of this dimension are anxious in social situations. Although borderline individuals are often assumed to be relatively extraverted, many are uncomfortable in social situations. Like avoidant individuals, they all fear rejection and interpersonal hurt. The other traits forming the emotional dysregulation pattern are linked to anxiousness in other ways. Cognitive dysregulation, which involves a tendency for cognitive functions to become disturbed especially at times of stress, is linked to both anxiousness and affective lability because emotional arousal and cognitive performance are inversely related.

Viewed in these terms, these traits form a highly coherent structure that is self-maintaining. In many ways, the pattern represents what might be referred to as "pan-personality disorder." Dysfunction covers a broad array of personality structures and processes. The pervasiveness of this factor accounts for the extensive overlap between borderline and other personality disorders. The interesting question for understanding the origins and pathogenesis of borderline pathology is why personality traits are organized in this way.

Most conceptions of normal and disordered personality, including the DSM-IV, assume that personality phenotypes comprise clusters of covarying traits. Much effort has been expended in identifying and clarifying these clusters. Less attention has been given to the mechanisms that account for trait covariation. It is not clear whether these clusters are the result of environmental factors that repeatedly activate the same trait leading to strong associations among them, or whether these patterns represent genetic influences, or whether a combination of genetic and environmental factors are involved. Explication of the factors involved is fundamental to the development of a cogent theory of borderline pathology. To answer this question we need to consider the etiology of borderline traits.

Etiology

Ideas about the origins of borderline personality have changed in recent years. Early theories, based largely on clinical observation and the treatment of a few selected patients, tended to emphasize the psychosocial origins of the disorder and the importance of traumatic experiences. More recently, this view has been tempered with recognition that genetic predispositions are also important, and that the pathogenesis of the disorder involves the complex interplay of genes and environment. Early etiological studies tended to assume that borderline pathology was caused by factors that had a large effect. The search for major causes has focused on variables ranging from neurotransmitter systems to psychosocial variables such as abuse and trauma. The results have generally been disappointing; thus far, we have not identified a single variable that plays a major role in the development of personality disorder. Instead, multiple biological and psychosocial variables have been identified, each has only a small effect, and none appear to be either necessary or sufficient to cause the disorder. Under these circumstances, it is inappropriate to speak of causes. Rather, it is more appropriate to talk of factors influencing the development of borderline personality disorder. Each variable probably accounts for relatively little outcome variance.

Although etiological research has failed to identify causes of large effect, it has produced a consistent picture of borderline as a psychobiological entity influenced by multiple genetic and environmental factors. This work is also beginning to clarify the role of genetic and environmental influences.

Genetic Influences

Genetic influences on the development of borderline personality have been studied using family and twin studies (Torgersen, 2000). A substantial number of studies have investigated the familial patterns of borderline personality disorder and its cosegregation with other disorders. A review by White, Gunderson, and Zanarini (2003) concluded that there was little evidence of a familial relationship with schizophrenia or schizotypal personality disorder, unconvincing evidence of such a relationship with major depressive disorder, and no evidence of an association with bipolar disorder. There was, however, evidence of increased borderline pathology in the relatives of patients with borderline personality disorder. The results of family studies are, however, difficult to interpret. Studies vary in methodological rigor. Sample sizes are often small. Standardized measures are not always used, and family members may not be interviewed directly. More importantly for understanding the origins of the disorder, evidence of a familial relationship is consistent with both genetic and psychosocial explanations of the origins of the disorder. Twin or adoption studies are needed to unravel genetic and environmental effects. Twin studies suggest that genes and environment each account for about half the variance in both borderline personality disorder, as diagnosed using DSM criteria, and the emotional dysregulation cluster of traits as assessed with self-report scales.

Heritability of Borderline Pathology

A twin study of DSM-III-R personality disorder diagnoses found these disorders were 28 to 79% heritable (Torgersen et al., 2000). The estimate for borderline personality disorder was 57%. Twin studies of personality disorder traits also furnish evidence of a pervasive genetic influence. The heritability of the emotional dysregulation pattern is 53%, and estimates of the heritability of the primary traits in the borderline constellation range from 53% for social avoidance to 44% for anxiousness (Livesley, Jang, Jackson, & Vernon, 1993; Jang, Livesley, Vernon, & Jackson, 1996; see Table 2.3). These estimates are similar to those of normal personality traits. Heritability of the five factors of normal personality assessed with the revised NEO personality inventory (NEO-PI-R) (Costa & McCrae, 1992) ranged from 55 to 37% (Jang, Livesley, & Vernon, 1996; see also Riemann, Angleitner, & Strelau, 1997). The heritability of neuroticism, the dimension of normal personality strongly associated with borderline personality disorder, was 41% when assessed using the NEO-PI-R, and

Table 2.3 Heritability of Emotional Dysregulation Traits (from Livesley, Jang, & Jackson, 1993; Jang, Livesley, Vernon, & Jackson, 1996)

Factor:	
Emotional Dysregulation	53
Primary Trait:	
Anxiousness	44
Submissiveness	45
Social avoidance	53
Insecure attachment	48
Affective lability	45
Cognitive dysregulation	49
Oppositionality	46

36% when the Eysenck Personality Questionnaire was used (Tambs, Sundet, Eaves, Solass, & Berg, 1991). Estimates of the four temperament and three character dimensions of the Temperament and Character Inventory (Cloninger, Przybeck, Svrakic, & Wetzel, 1994) ranged from 34% for novelty seeking to 49% for self-directedness (Ando et al., 2004). It appears that all individual differences in normal and disordered personality are subject to extensive heritable influence.

Twin studies also reveal the importance of environmental factors on personality disorder; more than half the variance in personality disorder traits is due to environmental effects. However, common environmental influences that affect all members of a family in the same way, such as being raised in the same home or receiving similar parental treatment, do not appear to affect the variance of personality traits. Instead, most of the environmental variance arises from nonshared factors that are specific to the individual, such as differential parental behavior and different experiences in peer relationships. Unfortunately, despite extensive investigation, there has been little progress in isolating the actual environmental factors involved.

Although heritability analyses clarify the role of genetic factors in the etiology of borderline pathology, they provide little information on the nature of these effects. Heritability estimates do not tell us whether a single or multiple genetic factors are responsible, or whether the genetic factors influencing a given trait are specific to that trait or shared with other traits. This information is provided by multivariate genetic studies that explore the genetic and environmental factors that account for the covariation among multiple traits (Carey & DiLalla, 1994).

Genetic Architecture of Borderline Pathology

As noted earlier, an important question for understanding the pathogenesis of personality disorder is why personality traits are organized into the four factors identified in factor analyses of personality disorder traits and criteria. Twin studies help us begin to answer this question. Using twin data, it is possible to compute genetic and environmental correlations among traits as well as the usual phenotypic correlations. A genetic correlation estimates the extent to which two traits share correlated genetic influences. Similarly, an environmental correlation indicates the extent to which two traits are influenced by correlated environmental influences. Genetic correlations are useful because they help us to determine the number of genetic factors influencing a set of traits. Matrices of genetic and environmental correlations, like phenotypic correlations, can be examined by factor analysis to determine the number of genetic and environmental dimensions underlying a set of traits—in this case, the traits defining the borderline pattern. By comparing the factor structure underlying matrices of phenotypic, genetic, and environmental correlations, it is possible to evaluate the relative importance of genetic and environmental influences on the structure of borderline traits.

When these analyses are conducted, the results are somewhat surprising: Genetic structure and phenotypic structures are highly congruent (Livesley et al., 1998). Table 2.4 shows the emotional dysregulation factor extracted from phenotypic and genetic correlation matrices. The congruence coefficient computed between these factors was 0.97, indicating high similarity. Similar results were obtained for the remaining three factors of

Table 2.4 Genetic and Phenotypic Structure of the Emotional Dysregulation Factor (from Livesley, Jang, & Vernon, 1998)

	Phenotypic	Genetic
Anxiousness	89	95
Submissiveness	79	91
Identity problems	83	84
Social avoidance	76	76
Oppositionality	69	74
Affective lability	78	69
Cognitive dysregulation	77	66
Insecure attachment	75	64
Narcissism	52	60
Suspiciousness	59	–

dissocial behavior, inhibitedness, and compulsivity. The similarity of phenotypic and genetic structure is not confined to personality disorder. Comparable analyses of the NEO-PI-R also showed high congruence between genetic and phenotypic factors structures (Jang, Livesley, Angleitner, Riemann, & Vernon, 2002).

These findings suggest the presence of a common genetic factor that influences all traits in the borderline cluster. Behavioral genetic methods can only estimate the effects of this genetic component; molecular genetic analyses are required to identify the actual genes involved. This common genetic factor does not appear to be the only source of genetic influence. When the effects of this factor were removed from the primary using regression analyses, a substantial heritable component remained for most traits: namely, submissiveness, identity problems, affective lability, insecure attachment, and social avoidance (Livesley et al., 1998).

These results suggest that there are two kinds of genetic influence on borderline personality: a common genetic factor that influences all borderline traits, and multiple specific factors that influence specific primary traits. The common genetic factor explains much of the covariation among borderline traits, and the congruence of phenotypic and genetic structure suggests that the organization of personality disorder traits into four broad patterns reflects the influence of genetic factors. It might have been expected that environmental factors would modify patterns of covariation among personality traits. This does not appear to be the case: Environmental influences on personality are considerable but they do not appear to change the structural relationships among traits. Personality structure appears to be a self-organizing system that emerges during development under the influence of multiple genetic predispositions. Nevertheless, heritability analyses showed that environmental influences are as large, or even larger, in magnitude than genetic influences. This raises the intriguing question of the nature of environmental influence on personality.

Environmental Influences

Although twin studies point to the importance of nonshared environmental effects, we do not have a clear understanding of the kinds of nonspecific influences that are important. Clinical studies, however, suggest that at least three sets of environmental factors contribute to borderline personality disorder: family factors such as family breakdown, parental loss, and attachment problems; trauma and deprivation; social and cultural factors including societal change (Paris, 2001). None of these factors appear to be specific to borderline personality disorder, none are necessary or sufficient to cause the disorder, and most factors contribute relatively little variance to pathological outcomes.

The effects of psychosocial adversity also appear to depend on preexisting personality characteristics. This is illustrated by studies of the relationship between sexual abuse and the subsequent development of borderline personality disorder. The finding that up to 70% of patients with borderline personality give a history of abuse (Byrne, Cernovsky, Velamoor, Coretese, & Losztyn, 1990; Herman, Perry, & van der Kolk, 1989; Links, Steiner, & Huxley, 1988; Ludolph, Westen, & Misle, 1990; Ogata, Silk, Goodrich, Lohr, Westen, & Hill, 1990; Paris, Zweig-Frank, & Guzder, 1994a, 1994b; Paris & Zweig-Frank, 1992; Perry & Herman, 1993; Westen, Ludolph, Misle, Ruffins, & Block, 1990; Zanarini, 2000; Zanarini, Gunderson, & Marino, 1989; for reviews see Gunderson & Sabo, 1993, Paris, 1994, and Sabo, 1997) prompted the suggestion that trauma is a major etiological factor (Herman & van der Kolk, 1987). Such conclusions do not, however, appear to be supported by the evidence (Paris, 2001; Rutter & Maughan, 1997). A meta-analysis of 21 studies based on 2,479 subjects found only a moderate association between childhood sexual abuse and borderline personality disorder (Fossati, Madeddu, & Maffei, 1999).

Sexual abuse appears to be only one of many risk factors. Nor is it specific to borderline personality disorder. A strong association also occurs with narcissistic, histrionic, sadistic, and schizotypal traits (Norden, Klein, & Donaldson, 1995) and antisocial behavior (Pollock, Briere, Schneider, Knop, Mednick, & Goodwin, 1990). In one study, 73% of patients with borderline personality disorder reported sexual abuse compared with 53% of patients with other personality disorders (Paris et al., 1994a, 1994b). Nor is abuse necessary for the development of borderline personality disorder. After reviewing the literature, Paris (1994, 2001) concluded that about one third of patients with borderline personality disorder report severe abuse; about one third report milder forms of abuse of the type that does not necessarily lead to psychopathology in community samples; and about one third do not report abuse. The fact that many individuals who report abusive experiences do not develop psychopathology and many patients with borderline personality disorder do not have a history of abuse suggests that other factors (probably personality factors) modulate the effects of adversity. Since these variables have a substantial heritable component, a cogent explanation of the development of borderline personality disorder requires an understanding of the interplay between genetic and environmental influence.

Environmental Effects and Gene-Environment Interplay

Although nature seems to be responsible for the major structures that form the personality system and the structural relationships among traits, the effects of nurture are substantial. Environmental factors appear to operate in two ways: at the level of trait structure they consolidate genetic influences on trait structure, and at the primary trait level they influence the way genetic predispositions are expressed.

Environmental Consolidation of Trait Structure

The congruence between phenotype, genetic, and environmental structure suggests that environmental effects operate to consolidate rather than modulate trait structure. This probably occurs as a result of environmental coactivation of traits. Many environmental events are likely to activate several traits simultaneously, especially traits in the same cluster. For example, highly submissive individuals are likely to be anxious and fearful in situations involving the dominance-submission hierarchy. Consequently, life experiences that evoke submissiveness are also likely to evoke anxiousness. Similarly, social situations that activate social apprehensiveness are also likely to evoke anxiousness. Repeated experiences of this type function to consolidate the patterns of trait covariation formed through the effect of common genetic factors.

Borderline patients with extreme levels of traits in the emotional dysregulation cluster also express these traits in rigid and maladaptive ways. They often seem to seek out, or at least frequently find themselves in, situations that encourage maladaptive expression of these traits. For example, many patients with borderline personality disorder and a history of sexual and physical abuse frequently find themselves in abusive relationships. These relationships lead to situations that evoke submissiveness, anxiety, mood changes, and separation anxiety. Hence they provide ample opportunity to consolidate the constellation of traits defined by the disorder.

Environmental Influences on Trait Expression

Environmental factors also have an impact on specific primary traits. They influence the intensity to which genetic predispositions are expressed and shape the behavioral manifestations of primary traits.

Modulation of Trait Intensity

Experience may amplify or dampen the expression of genetic predispositions so that the same level of genetic predisposition may lead to phenotypic differences in trait magnitude in different environments. For a given level of genetic predisposition, there is probably a fixed range over which the phenotype can vary. Within these parameters, variation may arise for several reasons. First, with emotional traits such as anxiousness, some environmental factors may have a direct influence on trait expression. Traumatic events such as childhood sexual abuse may cause lasting biological changes that influence the intensity of affective traits. For example, in patients with borderline personality disorder, a history of childhood sexual abuse is associated with changes in the stress response (Rinne, Westenberg, den Boer, & van den Brink, 2000).

Second, environmental events may affect the intensity of trait expression through their impact on the acquisition of self-regulatory mechanisms. The evidence suggests a close relationship between attachment and affect regulation. Hence in the case of borderline personality, psychosocial factors, especially attachment relationships, are likely to exert a major influence on the expression of the core traits of anxiousness and affective lability through their impact on affect regulation. Sensitive care giving is associated with higher levels of positive affect, lower levels of negative affect, greater self-esteem, and greater social competence in the child, and insensitive care giving is associated with more negative affect (anger and anxiety) and lower social competence and self-esteem (Suess, Grossman, & Stroufe, 1992).

The sensitive caregiver who recognizes and responds appropriately to the child's distress and needs acts as an external regulator of the child's affective state. By responding when the child needs attention, the attachment figure reduces the child's distress and in the process begins to build positive expectations that needs will be met. This sensitivity and these expectations lay the basis for subsequent self-soothing and affect regulation. Over time, these experiences become organized into cognitive and behavioral processes concerned with the regulation of emotions. This means that, given a secure attachment, even a strong genetic propensity toward emotional dyscontrol is likely to be dampened and may not reach levels associated with clinical problems. Poor attachment relationships, on the other hand, are not conducive to the acquisition of emotional self-regulation and may even amplify the expression of genetic predispositions. Attachment relationships also influence the development of cognitive schemata and cognitive processes that are also involved in affect regulation. Cognitive modes such as catastrophizing ways of thinking and tendencies to ruminate over adversity exacerbate emotional dyscontrol and hence influence the expression of other traits in the borderline constellation.

This brief overview illustrates the way genetic and environmental factors combine to determine personality structure and function. It reveals the simplicity of the traditional nature-versus-nurture debate. It is not that some aspects of personality are heritable and others environmental in origin; instead, all aspects of personality arise from the ongoing interplay of genes and environment. Some of the broad features of this interplay are illustrated in Figure 2.1 which shows how nature and nurture affect the expression of the emotional core of borderline pathology. Genetic predispositions toward anxiousness and affective lability under the influence of environmental experiences lead to the core traits that contribute to the affective symptoms of patients with borderline personality disorder. The expression of these traits is governed by affect regulation mechanisms that have biological and cognitive behavioral components. The biological consequences of severe trauma may lead to lasting impairment in the affect regulation and responses to stress (Rinne et al., 2000). Trauma also influences the development of cognitive schemata that affect the way events are perceived and hence the way the individual responds to stress. Other forms of environmental adversity may lead to neuropsychological impairment that may also have an adverse impact on affect and impulse regulation.

Self-regulatory mechanisms develop in the context of attachment relationships. This provides one mechanism whereby psychosocial factors influence the expression of genetic predispositions. But the attachment relationship itself is not immune to genetic influence. The child's and the care-giver's heritable traits also affect the quality of the attachment relationship. Thus, genetic and environmental influences on personality are

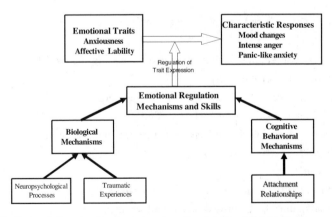

Figure 2.1 Factors influencing the expression of emotional dysregulation traits.

closely intertwined at all levels of the system at all stages of development. Some of the more important factors influencing emotional dysregulation are listed in Table 2.5.

Shaping Trait Expression

Besides modulating the expression of primary traits, environmental factors also influence the actual behaviors through which a trait is expressed. Not all individuals with high levels of stimulus seeking, for example, express this trait in the same way. Some trait expressions will be adaptive, others maladaptive. For example, a successful entrepreneur may use a high level of stimulus seeking adaptively by taking calculated risks that lead to business success. Other individuals may pursue challenging activities such as high-risk sports. In patients with borderline personality disorder, stimulus seeking may lead to a chaotic and reckless life.

Gene-Environment Interplay

The interplay of genes and environment appears to involve two mechanisms: gene-environment interaction, and gene-environment correlation. Gene-environment interaction occurs when the expression of a genetic predisposition differs according to the environment. For example, individuals with differing levels of genetic predisposition toward emotional dysregulation may not differ in levels of psychopathology if raised in a stable and secure attachment relationship, but differ markedly if their attachment relationships are insecure. An example of gene-environment interaction is provided by the work of Caspi, McClay, and Moffitt (2002) on the

Table 2.5 Factors Influencing Emotional Dysregulation

Biological:

　　Genetic predisposition to high levels of anxiousness and affective lability

　　Effects of trauma on stress response

　　Genetic influences on regulation and control mechanisms

　　Genetic influences in attachment relationship

　　Neuropsychological factors influencing the capacity for integration and self-regulation

Environmental:

　　Attachment relationship and effects on emotional regulation

　　Effects of trauma on cognitive processes and schemata

　　Environmental factors influencing affect regulation

　　Environmental influences on trait expression

development of antisocial behavior. They noted that in boys, childhood maltreatment, specifically erratic, coercive, and punitive parenting, is a major risk factor for the development of conduct disorder, antisocial behavior, and violent offending. However, not all maltreated children develop antisocial behavior. Based on observations that the monoamine oxidase A gene (MAOA) is associated with aggressive behavior in mice and, in some studies, humans, they hypothesized that the MAOA genotype can modulate the influence of maltreatment. In a large sample, they found that maltreated children with the genotype that conferred high levels of MAOA expression were less likely to develop antisocial behavior.

Clinical ideas and theories have mainly addressed the interaction between genes and environment; however, gene-environment correlation is also likely to exert a considerable influence on the development of personality. Gene-environment correlation occurs when environment conditions correlate with a genetic predisposition as when individuals seek out environments that are conducive to the expression of their genetic propensities. Three types of gene-environment correlation are usually described (Plomin, DeFries, & Loehlin, 1977; Scarr & McCartney, 1983). The simplest is a *passive* relationship. This occurs because the child shares genes and environments with their parents and may therefore be exposed to environments that are correlated with their genetic predispositions. Consider an aggressive child growing up in an environment that induces aggressive behavior. Here the genotype of the child correlates with the child's environment. This is likely to occur because the child's genotype is influenced by the parent's genotype, which also influences the child's environment. Similarly, affective lability is likely to be increased in children exposed to abusive environments associated with their parent's labile affects.

Reactive genetic predispositions lead to behaviors that evoke responses from others that consolidate these behaviors. The suspicious individual acts in ways that evoke cautious, distrustful responses from others that confirm that individual's suspicions. This phenomenon occurs frequently in patients with borderline pathology who often act in ways that evoke responses from others that confirm fears associated with heritable traits. Thus the insecurely attached individual may act in a clinging, dependent way that often evokes the rejection and separation that they fear.

Finally, *active* gene-environment correlation occurs because people actively select or create environments that provide an outlet for their heritable traits. Thus the impulsive and sensation-seeking child deliberately seeks out risky and exciting situations, and shy inhibited children pursue solitary interests and activities. Similarly the child with a difficult personality is likely to act in ways that evoke negative reactions from others and hence helps to create the environment to which he or she reacts. As the earlier discussion of environmental coactivation of traits showed, gene-environment correlation not only influences the expression of specific primary traits, but also has a powerful influence on the trait structure of personality.

The importance of gene-environment correlations indicates the need to rethink ideas about the environment. Traditionally, clinicians tend to think of the environment as having an independent influence on adjustment. This has often led to the search for environmental correlates for psychopathology using research designs that fail to incorporate individual difference variables. While many environmental circumstances are outside the individual's control, it is clear that many are not. People are not passive; they create the environments in which they interact and even when environmental events are outside their control, the way they perceive and respond to these events is influenced by heritable characteristics.

The impact of gene-environment correlation is not confined to the formative years. These effects operate throughout life and contribute to the stability of trait-based behavior and the maintenance of maladaptive patterns. Although clinicians, especially psychotherapists, seem to assume that maladaptive patterns largely arise from inner structures and processes, environmental contingencies play a critical role and it is rarely sufficient to help the individual to understand and modulate these inner structures; they also need help in managing and changing their environments.

Clinical Implications

These ideas about the genetic basis of personality have several implications for clinical practice. The proposal that emotional dysregulation is the core feature of the disorder suggests that an important treatment strategy, at least during the earlier stages of therapy, is to improve the self-regulation of emotions. The biopsychological nature of this dysfunction suggests that this is best achieved using a combination of medication and psychotherapy. Although medication effects seem modest at present, the evidence suggests that medication is useful in managing affective lability and related symptoms, impulsivity, and cognitive dysregulation (Soloff, 2000). Emotional dysregulation also appears to be amenable to cognitive-behavioral interventions designed to increase affect tolerance, improve affect regulation skills, and modify the maladaptive ways of thinking that are often associated with anxiousness and affective lability (Linehan, 1993; Livesley, 2002, 2003a).

Besides suggesting some broad therapeutic strategies, evidence of a genetic basis for personality has more profound implications for conceptualizing the change process. The biological basis of traits and their consolidation throughout life via gene-environment interplay raises questions about the extent to which change is possible and the kinds of change that can be expected when treating maladaptive expressions of such traits as impulsivity, dependency, anxiousness, and affective lability. Although the fact that these traits are heritable does not mean that they are fixed and cannot be modified with psychotherapeutic interventions, the overall stability of traits suggests that extensive change in the structure of personality traits may not be possible. It seems unlikely that treatments currently available will help an extremely introverted individual to become even a modestly outgoing extrovert, or that the highly emotionally labile individual will ever become calm and phlegmatic. This suggests that an important goal in treating borderline personality disorder should not be to attempt changes in personality structure but rather to help the individual to accept and adapt to their basic traits. Earlier ideas about the way the environment influences personality suggests that this is achieved through interventions that dampen the extreme expression of some traits and by helping individuals to express traits in more adaptive ways. It may also involve supporting patients as they seek environments and life situations that allow them to use their basic traits adaptively and create lifestyles that are compatible with their basic personality style.

Concluding Comments

This chapter offers a tentative reformulation of borderline personality disorder as a disorder of emotional regulation based on empirical analyses of the structure and origins of personality disorder traits. The disorder was described as a cluster of traits that differ a little from those included in the DSM-IV criteria set. This pattern of pathology is not assumed to be a discrete category in the DSM sense. Instead, emotional dysregulation represents the extremes of a broad personality dimension that is continuous with normal personality variation that emerges during development due to the interplay of multiple biological and environmental factors. This means that the pattern is unlikely to have a single cause, have a unified psychopathology apart from emotional dysregulation, or develop along a common pathway.

It should be noted that the traits forming the emotional dysregulation constellation are not all there is to borderline personality disorder. An extreme position on these traits may be necessary for the diagnosis of borderline personality disorder, but it is not sufficient. This is because an extreme trait score or a high genetic liability for a given trait does not invariably indicate disorder. Statistical deviation alone is insufficient for diagnosis (Wakefield, 1992). For this reason, it is useful to think of any form of personality disorder as having two components: (1) a set of core features shared by all forms of personality disorder, and (2) a set of traits that differ across individuals and forms of disorder (Livesley, Schroeder, Jackson, & Jang, 1994; Livesley, 2003b). This chapter has focused on the second component: the traits delineating the borderline pattern. However, extreme levels of these traits only indicate personality disorder when the individual displays the global features of personality disorder. These involve the failure to develop a cohesive and adaptive self-structure and the failure to function effectively in either intimate attachment relationships or in the broader context of societal relationships (Livesley, 2003b). Trait extremity increases the probability of these global dysfunctions, but they do not invariably indicate the presence of disorder.

References

Ando, J., Suzuki, A., Yamagata, S., Kijima, N., Maekawa, H., Ono, Y., et al. (2004). Genetic and environmental structure of Cloninger's temperament and character dimensions. *Journal of Personality Disorders, 18*(4), 379–393.

Austin, E. J., & Deary, I. J. (2000). The "four As": A common framework for normal and abnormal personality? *Personality and Individual Differences, 28*, 977–995.

Byrne, C. P., Cernovsky, A., Velamoor, V. R., Coretese, L., & Losztyn, S. (1990). A comparison of borderline and schizophrenic patients for childhood life events and parent child relationships. *Canadian Journal of Psychiatry, 35*, 590–595.

Carey, G., & DiLalla, D. L. (1994). Personality and psychopathology: Genetic perspectives. *Journal of Abnormal Psychology, 103*(1), 32–43.

Caspi, A., McClay, J., & Moffitt, T. (2002). Role of genotype in the cycle of violence in maltreated children. *Science, 297*(5582), 851–854.

Cloninger, C. R., Przybeck, T., Svrakic, D., & Wetzel, R. D. (1994). *The temperament and character inventory (TCI): A guide to its development and use.* St. Louis, MO: Washington University, Center for Psychobiology and Personality.

Costa, P. T., & McCrae, R. R. (1992). *The revised NEO personality inventory (NEO-PI-R) and the NEO five-factor inventory (NEO-FFI) professional manual.* Odessa, FL: Psychological Assessment Resources.

Ekselius, L., Lindstrom, E., von Knorring, L., Bodlund, O., & Kullgren, G. (1994). A principal component analysis of the DSM-III-R Axis II personality disorders. *Journal of Personality Disorder, 8*, 140–148.

Fossati, A., Madeddu, F., & Maffei, C. (1999). Borderline personality disorder andchildhood sexual abuse: A meta-analytic study. *Journal of Personality Disorders, 13*(3), 268–280.

Gunderson, J. G., & Singer, M. T. (1975). Defining borderline patients: An overview. *American Journal of Psychiatry, 132*(1), 1–10.

Gunderson, J. G., & Sabo, A. N. (1993). The phenomenological and conceptual interface between borderline personality disorder and PTSD. *American Journal of Psychiatry, 150*(1), 19–27.

Herman, J. L., Perry, J. C., & van der Kolk, B. A. (1989). Childhood trauma in borderline personality disorder. *American Journal of Psychiatry, 146*, 490–495.

Herman, J. L., & van der Kolk, B. A. (1987). Traumatic antecedents of borderline personality disorder. In B. A. van der Kolk (Ed.), *Psychological trauma* (pp. 111–126). Washington, DC: American Psychiatric Publishing, Inc.

Jang, K. L., Livesley, W. J., Vernon, P. A., & Jackson, D. N. (1996). Heritability of personality disorder traits: A twin study. *Acta Psychiatrica Scandinavica, 94*, 438–444.

Jang, K. L., Livesley, W. J., Angleitner, A., Riemann, R., & Vernon, P. A. (2002). Genetic and environmental influences on the covariance of facets defining the domains of the five-factor model of personality. *Personality & Individual Differences, 33*(1), 83–101.

Jang, K. L., Livesley, W. J., & Vernon, P. A. (1996). Heritability of the big five personality dimensions and their facets: A twin study. *Journal of Personality, 64*(3), 577–591.

Kernberg, O. (1967). Borderline personality organization. *Journal of the Psychoanalytic Association, 15*, 641–685.

Kernberg, O. F. (1984). *Severe personality disorders*. New Haven, CT: Yale University Press.

Linehan, M. M. (1993). *Cognitive-behavioral treatment of borderline personality disorder*. New York: Guilford Press.

Linehan, M. M., & Koerner, K. (1993). A behavioral theory of borderline personality disorder. In J. Paris (Ed.), *Borderline personality disorder* (pp. 103–121). Washington, DC:American Psychiatric Publishing, Inc.

Links, P. S., Steiner, M., & Huxley, G. (1988). The occurrence of borderline personality disorder in the families of borderline patients. *Journal of Personality Disorders, 2*, 14–20.

Livesley, W. J. (2002). Treating the emotional dysregulation cluster of traits. *Psychiatric Annals, 32*(10), 601–607.

Livesley, W. J. (2003a). *Practical management of personality disorder*. New York: Guilford Press.

Livesley, W. J. (2003b). Diagnostic dilemmas in the classification of personality disorder. In K. Phillips, M. First, & H. A. Pincus (Eds.), *Advancing DSM: Dilemmas in psychiatric diagnosis* (pp. 153–189). Arlington, VA: American Psychiatric Publishing, Inc.

Livesley, W. J. (in press). Behavioral and molecular genetic contributions to a dimensional classification of personality disorder. *Journal of Personality Disorders*.

Livesley, W. J., Jackson, D. N., & Schroeder, M. L. (1992). Factorial structure of traits delineating personality disorders in clinical and general population samples. *Journal of Abnormal Psychology, 101*, 432–440.

Livesley, W. J., Jang, K. L., Jackson, D. N., & Vernon, P. A. (1993). Genetic and environmental contributions to dimensions of personality disorder. *American Journal of Psychiatry, 150*, 1826–1831.

Livesley, W. J., Jang, K. L., & Vernon, P. A. (1998). Phenotypic and genetic structure of traits delineating personality disorder. *Archives of General Psychiatry, 55*, 941–948.

Livesley, W. J., Schroeder, M. L., Jackson, D. N., & Jang, K. L. (1994). Categorical distinctions in the study of personality disorder: Implications for classification. *Journal of Abnormal Psychology, 103*, 6–17.

Ludolph, P. S., Westen, D., & Misle, B. (1990). The borderline diagnosis in adolescents: Symptoms and developmental history. *American Journal of Psychiatry, 147*, 470–476.

Mulder, R. T., & Joyce, P. R. (1997). Temperament and the structure of personality disorder symptoms. *Psychological Medicine, 27*, 1315–1325.

Norden, K. A., Klein, D. N., & Donaldson, S. K. (1995). Reports of the early home environment in DSM-III-R personality disorders. *Journal of Personality Disorders, 9*(3), 213–223.

Ogata, S. N., Silk, K. R., Goodrich, S., Lohr, N. E., Westen, D., & Hill, E. M. (1990). Childhood sexual and physical abuse in adult patients with borderline personality disorder. *American Journal of Psychiatry, 147*, 1008–1013.

Paris, J. (1994). *Borderline personality disorder: A multidimensional approach*. Washington, DC: American Psychiatric Publishing, Inc.

Paris, J. (2001). Psychosocial adversity. In W. J. Livesley (Ed.), *Handbook of personality disorders* (pp. 231–241). New York: Guilford Press.

Paris, J., & Zweig-Frank, H. (1992). A critical review of childhood sexual abuse in the etiology of borderline personality disorder. *Canadian Journal of Psychiatry, 37*, 125–128.

Paris, J., Zweig-Frank, H., & Guzder, J. (1994a). Psychological risk factors for borderline personality disorder in female patients. *Comprehensive Psychiatry, 35*, 301–305.

Paris, J., Zweig-Frank, H., & Guzder, J. (1994b). Risk factors for borderline personality in male outpatients. *Journal of Nervous and Mental Disease, 182*, 375–380.

Perry, J. C., & Herman, J. L. (1993). Trauma and defence in the etiology of borderline personality disorder. In J. Paris (Ed.), *Borderline personality disorder, etiology and treatment.* Washington, DC: American Psychiatric Publishing, Inc.

Plomin, R., DeFries, J. C., & Loehlin, J. C. (1977). Genotype-environment interaction and correlation in the analysis of human behavior. *Psychological Bulletin, 84,* 309–322.

Pollock, V. E., Briere, J., Schneider, L., Knop, J., Mednick, S. A., & Goodwin, D. W. (1990). Childhood antecedents of antisocial behavior: Parental alcoholism and physical abusiveness. *American Journal of Psychiatry, 147*(10), 1290–1293.

Pukrop, R., Gentil, I., Steinbring, I., & Steinmeyer, E. (2001). Factorial structure of the German version of the dimensional assessment of personality pathology-basic questionnaire in clinical and nonclinical samples. *Journal of Personality Disorders, 15,* 450–456.

Reich, J. (1988). DSM-III personality disorders and family history of mental illness. *Journal of Nervous and Mental Disease, 176,* 45–49.

Riemann, R., Angleitner, A., & Strelau, J. (1997). Genetic and environmental influences on personality: A study of twins reared together using the self- and peer-report NEO-FFI scales. *Journal of Personality, 65,* 449–475.

Rinne, T., Westenberg, H. G. M., den Boer, J. A., & van den Brink, W. (2000). Serotonergic blunting to meta-chlorophenylpiperazine (m-CPP) highly correlates with sustained childhood abuse in impulsive and autoaggressive female borderline patients. *Biological Psychiatry, 47,* 548–556.

Rutter, M., & Maughan, B. (1997). Psychosocial adversities in childhood and adult psychopathology. *Journal of Personality Disorders, 11,* 4–18.

Sabo, A. N. (1997). Etiological significance of associations between childhood trauma and borderline personality disorder: Conceptual and clinical implications. *Journal of Personality Disorders, 11*(1), 50–70.

Scarr, S., & McCartney, K. (1983). How people make their own environments: A theory of genotype-environment effects. *Child Development, 54,* 424–435.

Soloff, P. H. (2000). Psychopharmacology of borderline personality disorder. *Psychiatric Clinics of North America, 23,* 169–190.

Spitzer, R., Endicott, J., & Gibbon, M. (1979). Crossing the border into borderline personality disorder and borderline schizophrenia: The development of criteria. *Archives of General Psychiatry, 36,* 17–24.

Stone, M. H. (1980). *The borderline syndromes.* New York: McGraw-Hill.

Suess, G. J., Grossman, K. E., & Stroufe, L. A. (1992). Effects of infant attachment to mother and father on quality of adaptation in preschool: From dyadic to individual organization of the self. *International Journal of Behavioral Development, 15,* 43–65.

Tambs, K., Sundet, J. M., Eaves, L., Solass, M. H., & Berg, K. (1991). Pedigree analysis of Eysenck Personality Questionnaire (EPQ) scores in monozygotic (MZ) twin families. *Behavior Genetics, 21*(4), 369–382.

Torgersen, S. (2000). Genetics of patients with borderline personality disorder. *The Psychiatric Clinics of North America, 23*(1), 1–9.

Torgersen, S., Lygren, S., Oien, P. A., Skre, I., Onstad, S., Edvardsen, J., et al. (2000). A twin study of personality disorders. *Comprehensive Psychiatry, 41,* 416–25.

van Kampen, D. (2002). The DAPP-BQ in the Netherlands: Factor structure and relationship with basic personality dimensions. *Journal of Personality Disorders, 16,* 235–254.

Wakefield, J. C. (1992). Disorder as harmful dysfunction: A conceptual critique of DSM-III-R's definition of mental disorder. *Psychological Review, 99*(2), 232–247.

Westen, D., Ludolph, P., Misle, B., Ruffins, S., & Block, J. (1990). Physical and sexual abuse in adolescent girls with borderline personality disorder. *American Journal of Orthopsychiatry, 60,* 55–66.

White, C. N., Gunderson, J. G., & Zanarini, M. C. (2003). Family studies of borderline personality disorder: A review. *Harvard Review of Psychiatry, 11*(1), 8–19.

Widiger, T. A. (1998). Four out of five ain't bad. *Archives of General Psychiatry, 55,* 865–866.

Zanarini, M. C. (2000). Childhood experiences associated with the development of borderline personality disorder. *Psychiatric Clinics of North America, 23,* 89–101.

Zanarini, M. C., Gunderson, J. G., & Marino, M. F. (1989). Childhood experiences of borderline patients. *Comprehensive Psychiatry, 30,* 18–25.

Zheng, W., Wang, W., Huang, Z., Sun, C., Zhu, S., & Livesley, W. J. (2002). The structure of traits delineating personality disorder in China. *Journal of Personality Disorders, 16*(6), 477–486.

CHAPTER 3

The Biology of Borderline Personality Disorder: Recent Findings and Future Approaches to the Study of Impulsive Aggression and Affective Instability

SETH RESNICK, MARIANNE GOODMAN, ANTONIA NEW,
AND LARRY SIEVER

Key Teaching Points

- The biological underpinnings of personality disorders are best approached from a dimensional perspective.
- These dimensions include impulsivity, aggression, affective instability, and cognitive disorganization.
- The role of a hypofunctioning serotonin system in impulsive aggression is supported by metabolite and challenge studies.
- Neuroimaging, including MRI, PET, SPECT, and fMRI, has forwarded our understanding of BPD pathology.
- The "dual brain" hypothesis suggests that dysfunction in the regions of prefrontal cortex and amygdala may be implicated in BPD.

- Polymorphisms related to gene products involved in serotonin synthesis, reuptake, metabolism, and receptors have been identified.
- In subjects with impulsive aggression, the following polymorphisms have been studied: tryptophan hydroxylase, 5-HT1B receptor, 5-HT2A, and serotonin transporter. To date, these studies suggest only modest contributions to impulsive aggressive behavior.

Introduction

This chapter will introduce strategies and review recent findings for a neurobiological approach to the study of personality disorders, focusing primarily on borderline personality disorder (BPD). While there have been important neurobiological studies on other personality disorders including the cluster A disorder of schizotypy, the overwhelming majority of empirical data involves the cluster B diagnosis of BPD. This chapter will discuss a dimensional model of personality, arguing for investigations geared at symptom dimensions rather than the Axis II disorder as a whole. For BPD, the dimensions discussed in this chapter will be impulsive aggression and affective instability, two hallmarks of BPD symptomatology. Research strategies for elucidating the biological underpinnings of these two dimensions will be described in detail. These strategies include neuroimaging and genetics, and pertinent literature will be reviewed.

Instability of BPD Diagnosis

Recent research brings into question the stability of the borderline diagnosis and argues for the use of a dimensional approach for the domains of BPD. Factor analyses of the phenomenology of BPD suggest that a dimensional approach may be more appropriate, with impulsive aggression, affective instability, and identity disturbance as core dimensions of the disorder (Blais, Hilsenroth, & Castlebury, 1997). Moreover, a retrospective chart review assessing criteria for BPD defined three independent domains: (1) identity and interpersonal instability, (2) impulsivity, and (3) affective instability (Blais et al., 1997). Another approach using emotional responsiveness in a laboratory to a story suggested that affective instability as demonstrated by the intensity of emotional responses to a story was highly associated with measures of impulsive behavior (Herpertz, Gretzer, Steinmeyer, Muelbaver, Schuerkens, & Sass, 1997). A group of hospitalized women with BPD were assessed with a laboratory assessment for aggressive responding, the Point Subtraction Aggression Paradigm (PSAP), a well-validated tool to assess impulsive aggression. This model uses monetary reinforcement and provokes aggressive responses in subjects by subtracting money, which is blamed on a fictitious other participant. An aggressive response is defined by the subject subtracting money from the fictitious participant. Borderline patients demonstrate a high degree of aggressive responses compared to normal controls (Dougherty, Bjork, Huckabee, Moeller, & Swann, 1999).

Studies of the diagnostic stability of BPD in a nonclinical sample show only moderate stability over a 2-year period of time (0.28– 0.62) (Trull et al., 1998). The same study indicated greater stability for self-report measures assessing features of borderline personality disorder than for semistructured interviews for the disorder. The self-report measures, however, were more subject to instability over time related to changes in the level of "negative affect," which was interpreted as a change in self-report related to acute current affective state of the subject. Another complexity in the assessment of BPD relates to comorbidity with other personality disorders.

Comorbidity studies among personality disorders show a high degree of comorbidity between personality disorders, and specifically high levels of comorbidity between BPD and paranoid personality disorder (14.5%), schizotypal personality disorder (14.3%), histrionic (13.5%), narcissistic (16.0%), and passive aggressive (13.4%). The comorbidity between clusters also undercuts the distinctness of the three personality disorder cluster described in the *Diagnostic and Statistical Manual of Mental Disorders* (4th ed.) (DSM-IV) (Watson & Sinha, 1998).

Our research group in mood and personality disorders conducts an extensive diagnostic evaluation of each subject including an assessment of personality disorder diagnoses with the Structured Interview for Personality Disorders-IV (SIPD-IV) (Pfohl, Blum, & Zimmerman, 1997). In our sample, patients with BPD meet on average 3.2 personality disorder diagnoses, and these cut across the three clusters.

Biological Findings Argue for a Dimensional Approach

In addition, the neuroendocrine and heritability findings have not been specific to personality disorder diagnoses, but rather have conformed to the dimension of impulsive aggression. Heritability data also argue for the dimensional approach, in that monozygotic-dizygotic twin studies suggest that while the personality disorder diagnoses are not heritable, the traits of impulsive aggression or assertive aggressiveness are significantly heritable (Alnaes & Torgersen, 1989; Coccaro, Bergman, & McLean, 1993; Torgersen, 1992). Studies of adoptees with biological parents with anti-social personality disorder demonstrated a genetic contribution to the development of antisocial PD characterized by antisocial aggressive behavior (Cadoret, O'Gorman, Troughton, & Heywood, 1985; Crowe, 1974), and this heritable tendency appeared to be brought out by adverse home environment (Cadoret, Yates, Troughton, Woodworth, & Stewart, 1995). Preliminary data from candidate gene studies suggest a relationship between genotype and impulsive aggression; for example, the "LL" allele of tryptophan hydroxylase may be associated with a risk for aggression (New et al., 1998).

Dimensional Approach

In a landmark paper, Siever and Davis (1991) outline a dimensional approach to the study of personality dysfunction. Core biological vulnerabilities in personality include dimensions of affective instability/sensitivity, impulsivity, aggression, cognitive/perceptual, and pain sensitivity domains. Current understanding of involved neuroanatomic circuitry and neuromodulators are described in Figure 3.1. The dimensions of impulsivity, aggression, and affective instability have been studied most extensively, and current developments will be described in this chapter.

The Serotonin Hypothesis and Early Research on Metabolite and Neuroendocrine Challenge Studies

While many other neurochemical factors seem to interplay in the pathophysiology of the underlying dimensions of BPD, including norepinephrine, dopamine, acetylcholine, GABA, vasopressin, opiates, nitric oxide, testosterone, and leptins and cholesterol, the clearest connection is to serotonin (5-HT). Neuroendocrine response to 5-HT challenge studies have played a key role in both linking the serotonergic and HPA axis systems and firmly

Dimension	Neuroanatomic Circuitry	Neuromodulator
Impulsivity / Aggression	OFC / Cingulate/ Amygdala	Serotonin
Anxiety	PFC / Amygdala	GABA / NE
Affective Instability	Amygdala / Enterorhinal Cortex	GABA / Glutamate
Cognitive Disorganization	PFC / Striatum	Dopamine

Figure 3.1 Brain systems in personality disorders.

establishing 5-HT hypofunction in the pathophysiology of BPD characteristics, including impulse dysregulation, autoaggressive behavior, and affective instability. The earliest challenge studies measured plasma levels of prolactin, a hormone known to be released from the hypothalamus in response to 5-HT stimulation, after administration of a 5-HT agonist, usually d-fenfluramine, and found the response to be blunted specifically in personality disordered patients with impulsive aggression and assaultiveness (Siever & Trestman, 1993) as well as in subjects with a history of attempted suicide (Coccaro et al., 1989). New et al. (1997) found this blunted response to be specific to personality disordered patients not only with suicidality but also with other forms of self-directed aggression, such as self-injurious behavior, compared to those without such a history. Treatment studies with selective serotonin reuptake inhibitors (SSRI) not only corroborated a suspected underlying biochemical pathophysiology in BPD, but also showed a correlation with pathological behaviors in their efficacy in treating them. Later studies using d, fenfluramine, in addition to confirming the hypothesis of 5-HT hypofunction, sought the relationship between this finding and impulsive aggression using instruments measuring behavior. The relationship of a blunted prolactin response in impulsive aggressive personality disordered subjects to validated questionnaires and interviews assessing impulsive aggressive behavior, namely, the Buss-Durkee Hostility Inventory (BDHI), Lifetime History of Aggression, the Brown-Goodwin Aggression Scale, and the Barratt Impulsivity Scale (BIS), consistently confirmed a direct correlation. However, the intercorrelation with other paradigms being studied at the time, including the cerebral spinal fluid (CSF) levels of the serotonin metabolite 5-HIAA (Coccaro, Kavoussi, Cooper, & Hauger, 1997), prolactin response to m-chlorophenylpiperazine (m-CPP) (Coccaro, Kavoussi, Trestman, et al., 1997), prolactin response to ipsapirone, another 5-HT agonist that is selective for the 5-HT1A receptor (Coccaro, Kavoussi, & Hauger, 1995), and the Point-Subtraction Aggression Paradigm (PSAP), a laboratory simulation whereby subjects work to earn points that have a monetary reward value and assesses aggression by their measured response to having them taken away by a confederate subject (Coccaro, Berman, Kavoussi, & Hauger, 1996), proved to be more complicated than a simple direct relationship. Despite this, a connection does exist between the responses to a 5-HT challenge and treatment study. Specifically, there is a direct correlation between efficacy of an SSRI, fluoxetine, in treating aggression, as measured by improvement on the Overt Aggression Scale-Modified (OAS-M), and pretreatment prolactin responses to fenfluramine, suggesting that its antiaggressive effects are directly dependent on the extent of the physiologic responsiveness of 5-HT synapses.

While these important findings implicating hypofunctioning of the serotonin system through various challenge paradigms have advanced our understanding of the underlying pathology of impulsive aggression in personality disorders, there are limitations to studying serotonin metabolites as a reflection of central nervous system dysfunction, and recent human subject research concerns have limited the utility of the "endocrine challenge" approach. Exciting new strategies, including the ability to visualize the brain both at rest and while it is functioning, have evolved. These foster new avenues of inquiry and a means to deepen our understanding of how serotonin dysfunction is implicated in BPD.

Neuroimaging

Current research on the biology of personality disorders seeks to localize regions of the brain that are responsible for modulating various affective and behavioral traits, an area that may be disrupted in patients with personality disorders. Progress in neuroimaging has allowed researchers to move beyond identifying *what* biochemical disturbances might be involved in a particular dimension of a personality disorder, providing a way to investigate *where* in the brain these disturbances may be taking place. As technology improves, the brain and its subregions can be viewed with finer resolution and greater detail. A major advance in imaging of the brain for research has been functional imaging that enables observation and localization of processes going on in the brain. This has allowed scientists to investigate the "what" and the "where" simultaneously by viewing biochemical processes being carried out in various brain regions.

Structural Neuroanatomy

Observation of the structural anatomy of the brain yields important information about the size, volume, and structure of various brain regions at rest. Since changes in the physical substance of the brain generally occur over the course of months or years, a single snapshot is a valid representation of structural neuroanatomy over that time course. Imaging modalities used to view the structural anatomy of the brain require only a still picture of the brain at one time point. The quality of the image depends on its resolution. Advances in technology for structural imaging have provided finer resolution and the ability to view greater detail.

Radiography is relatively new in the long history of medicine. More recent still are neuroimaging and the application of radiographic techniques in psychiatric research. Previously, study of the neuroanatomy associated with psychiatric symptoms and disorders depended on case studies.

Involvement of the prefrontal cortex in controlling impulsivity and aggression was discovered in the 1800s with the case of Phineas Gage. Phineas Gage was a railroad worker who sustained an injury to his frontal cortex in the 1800s when using a tamping iron. The rod kicked back with such force that he lost grip of it and it shot clear through his skull, entering inferiorly through his mandible, passing through his prefrontal cortex, and exiting superiorly through his cranium. Through computerized reconstruction of his skull (Damasio, Grabowski, Frank, Galaburda, & Damasio, 1994), this was more precisely identified to include the anterior and medial aspects of the region bilaterally, but predominantly the left (dominant) hemisphere. Fortunately for him and for neuroscience, but perhaps not for those with whom he was acquainted, Mr. Gage survived the accident but subsequently underwent a radical change in personality, including a drastic increase in hostility, irritability, and impulsiveness, and a tendency to engage in verbal aggression with profanity. Other anecdotal reports of such lesions have noted postinjury alterations in personality characteristics, particularly in the ability to control aggression and impulsivity (Max et al., 1995; Relkin, Plum, Mattis, Eidelberg, & Tranel, 1996). These cases suggest a critical role of the orbital frontal cortex in the regulation of aggression (Brickner, 1934; Damasio & Van Hoesen, 1983; Grafman et al., 1996; Grafman, Vance, Weingartner, Salazar, & Amin, 1986; Volavka, Mohammad, Vitrai, Connolly, Stefanovie, & Ford, 1995).

The amygdala is another brain region implicated in the development of impulsive aggressive symptomatology. Animal lesion studies have consistently associated impulsive aggressive traits with the amygdala and certain regions of the temporal lobes (Spoont, 1992). Case reports of violent and aggressive behavior in patients with temporal lobe tumors and lesions (Martinius, 1983), and studies showing numerous anterior and inferior temporal lobe tumors in violent patients (Tonkonogy, 1991; Tonkonogy & Geller, 1992), suggest a susceptibility to violence in patients with temporal lobe lesions. Manipulation of the amygdala has led to its implication in the regulation of aggression as a result of findings from both electrical stimulation which has been associated with rage attacks, and amygdolotomy (Mark & Ervin, 1970) which, in fact, has been associated with reduced aggressive outbursts in patients with intractable aggression (Lee et al., 1998), and has led to destructive behaviors in the context of coagulation (Hichcock & Cairns, 1973).

Computed Tomography (CT)

The first radiographic technique for viewing the brain that was of clinical use was computed tomography, or CT scan. CT is a series of x-rays taken at regular spatial intervals. It involves exactly the same mechanism as the x-ray, the most basic and paradigmatic radiological procedure. X-rays are a form of radiation, like light or radio waves, which can be focused into a beam, much like a flashlight beam. Unlike a beam of light, however, x-rays can pass through most objects, including the human body. When x-rays strike a piece of photographic film, they can produce a picture of the shadows cast by body structures of different density that block or absorb the x-ray beams to varying degrees. With CT, x-ray beams are passed through the body tissue at different angles, and special sensors measure the amount of radiation absorbed by different tissues traversed along the beam's trajectory from its source to the sensor. A computer then processes the information from up to a thousand points to create a series of cross-sectional images at small regular intervals along the axis of the study.

While it continues to have diverse clinical applications, CT has only sparsely been used as a neuroimaging modality for research in psychiatry because of its relatively poor resolution that is so fundamental for studying structural neuroanatomy. Conversely, any findings detected using this crude technique are likely to be significant. For example, lateral and third ventricle enlargement and frontal cortical atrophy have been identified in individuals with schizophrenia.

While early notions of BPD did frame the disorder at the border between psychosis and neurosis, and in the schizophrenia spectrum disorders, CT scans of BPD subjects have consistently found no difference in lateral and third ventricle size as compared to healthy controls (Goyer et al., 1994; Lucas, Gardner, Cowdry, & Pickar, 1989; Schulz, Koller, Kishore, Hamer, Gehl, & Friedel, 1983; Snyder, Pitts, & Grustin, 1983). However, one study evaluating brain function in a small sample of four psychiatric patients with histories of repetitive violent behavior, and unclear Axis II diagnoses, found generalized cortical atrophy on CT and spiking activity in the left temporal regions on the EEG of three of the subjects (Volkow & Tangreti, 1987).

Magnetic Resonance Imaging (MRI)

With the advent of MRI, structural neuroimaging has taken on new vigor. MRI provides clear and detailed pictures of internal organs and tissues by using radio frequency waves and a strong magnetic field rather than x-rays. Moreover, it does not rely on ionizing radiation. Instead, radio frequency waves are directed at protons, the nuclei of hydrogen atoms, in a strong magnetic field. The protons are first "excited" and then "relaxed," emitting radio signals that can be computer-processed to form an image. In the body, protons are most abundant in the hydrogen atoms of water, so an MRI image shows differences in the water content and distribution in various body tissues. Even different types of tissue within the same organ, such as the gray and white matter of the brain, can easily be distinguished.

Studies using MRI to identify structural brain pathology in BPD have localized differences compared to healthy controls at various sites (see Table 3.1). Recent reviews of findings of neuroimaging in BPD categorized it as a disorder of "dual brain pathology" (Bohus, Schmahl, & Lieb, 2004). The abnormalities fall in two general regions of the brain. There is dysfunction and resultant structural abnormality in the prefrontal cortex (PFC), a site that has been historically recognized to give rise to impulse dyscontrol and aggression when damaged, as well as the limbic region, the purported locus of emotional regulation.

Similar to the use of CT, an MRI study was undertaken to corroborate the hypothesis that BPD was similar to schizophrenia by seeking to find the same neuroanatomical abnormalities found in individuals with schizophrenia in BPD patients. Conversely, it found subjects with BPD to have smaller frontal lobe volumes, and no difference in the temporal lobes or lateral ventricles, compared to healthy controls (Lyoo, Han, & Cho, 1998).

Table 3.1 MRI in Borderline Personality Disorder

Author	N Study Design	Findings
Lyoo et al., 1998	25 BPD/ 25 control, methodological limitations	Smaller frontal lobes in subjects with BPD
Driessen et al., 2000	21 BPD with early traumatization/21 control High-resolution structural MRI	16% smaller hippocampus and 8% smaller amygdala in BPD Unclear association of volume loss with trauma
Schmahl et al., 2003	10 BPD with child abuse/23 control	23% reduction in amygdala and 13% reduction in hippocampus in BPD with abuse
van Elst et al., 2003	8 BPD/8 control- subgroup of Rusch study, theorizing frontolimbic dysfunction	Confirmed hippocampal and bilateral loss findings but also noted left orbital frontal cortex 24% decrease and right anterior cingulate cortex loss of 26%
Rusch et al., 2003	20 female BPD/21 control, voxel-based morphometry (VBM)- (localizes changes in gray and white matter)	Gray matter volume loss in left amygdala, no prefrontal structural alterations found

However, this is the only structural neuroimaging study in BPD with isolated frontal lobe findings, and it suffered from overly strict inclusion and exclusion criteria.

Another MRI study found temporal, but no frontal, volume differences between personality disorder subjects with and without impulsive aggression and controls (Dolan, Deaking, Roberts, & Anderson, 2002). Although no imaging studies to date have reported a direct relationship of amygdala activity to aggression, it has been suggested that the extensive amygdalo-prefrontal connections represent an inhibitory influence of the frontal cortex on the amygdala (Porrino & Goldman-Rakic, 1982).

There has been little or no work on the neuroanatomic correlates of affective instability, but there have been several studies in the borderline population of limbic structures, which are typically associated with emotional regulation, and, in fact, most of the more recent studies of structural neuroanatomy in BPD using MRI have looked at this region (see Table 3.1): Three studies have found significantly smaller amygdala volumes, one of which specifically found gray matter reductions in the left amygdala and no PFC abnormalities (Rusch et al., 2003). The other two additionally cited corresponding reductions in hippocampal size that, furthermore, correlated with extent and duration of trauma (Driessen et al., 2000) in borderline women with histories of childhood abuse (Schmahl, Vermetten, Elzinga, & Bremmer, 2003). These results concur with data from patients with post-traumatic stress disorder (PTSD) secondary to childhood abuse, suggesting that the decrease may correlate with traumatic experience rather than BPD per se (Bremner et al., 1997). Findings of reductions in hippocampal size in major depressive disorder (MDD) as well further corroborate the involvement of these limbic structures in affective instability (Bremner et al., 2000).

Structural abnormalities at either one of these two loci are relatively nonspecific and are known to be associated with a number of psychiatric disorders. However, disturbance in both of these regions simultaneously is much less common and might be a signature of BPD pathology. In one study, this frontolimbic pattern of volume loss in BPD patients included a decrease in size of the left orbitofrontal cortex, the right anterior cingulate cortex, the hippocampus, and the amygdala, but also included a correlation between the volumes of structures in these two regions, namely, the amygdala and the left orbital frontal cortex (van Elst et al., 2003).

Diffusion tensor imaging (DTI) is a relatively new MRI modality that provides information on the directionality and coherence of the self-diffusion of water. This may have implications for representations of the anatomical organization of structural elements of neurons (e.g., axons and myelin) that are responsible for connectivity. DTI has been shown to provide valid measures of white matter integrity. Amongst many other factors that have been shown to be associated with aggression in schizophrenia (Cheung & Schweitzer, 1998), a study using DTI has shown that, in the right inferior frontal white matter of subjects with schizophrenia, decreased fractional anisotropy (FA) is associated with higher motor impulsiveness, and higher trace is associated with aggressiveness (Hoptman et al., 2002). Future studies in personality disorder dysfunction will likely be employing this technique.

Functional Neuroanatomy

Functional imaging provides a means of observing underlying chemical processes occurring over the period of time that the study is being performed. These methods can be applied to search for differences in regional brain activity between normality and the various personality disorders, and among the personality disorders themselves.

Positron Emission Tomography (PET)

PET was one of the earliest neuroimaging modalities available, but quickly fell out of favor when CT became available due to its poor resolution and relatively narrow range of clinical purposes. However, in psychiatric research, PET has found promising application as it permits visualization of brain activity by locating the distribution of radiolabeled compounds in the brain. Briefly, before the examination begins, a radioactive substance is produced in a machine called a cyclotron and attached, or tagged, to a natural body compound, most commonly glucose, but sometimes water or ammonia. Once this radioactive substance is administered to the patient, it emits positrons, tiny particles that are localized as areas of radioactivity in particular areas in the body and detected and represented in a streaming image produced by the PET scanner.

The major advantage of PET scan is that it provides a picture of the working brain, as opposed merely to its structure. One can see how the brain functions (or malfunctions) at any given time. It theoretically gives insight into the diverse responses of a brain in a given instant, rather than structural imaging, which will essentially only show differences in brains after chronic long-term changes due to exposure to altered functioning over a period of time. One of the most commonly measured parameters in PET is regional cerebral blood flow (rCBF) which can be measured by several different tagged compounds.

To study impulsive aggression, PET has been utilized in various populations including aggressive combat veterans with PTSD, violent psychiatric patients, and individuals with personality disorders. Amongst the various PTSD traits in combat veterans, impulsive aggression, in particular, had a functional correlate in the brain, which was increased rCBF in the projection area to the nucleus accumbens. Moreover, the use of PET to measure the rCBF of psychiatric patients with histories of violence, found decreased activity in the left temporal lobes in all subjects and decreased activity in the frontal lobes in half of the subjects (Volkow & Tancredi, 1987). Similar findings were found in a study of glucose metabolism, another commonly measured parameter in PET imaging. This larger study showed decreased 2-deoxy-2 fluorodeoxy glucose (FDG), in the medial temporal and prefrontal cortices of patients with a history of repetitive violent behaviors (Volkow et al., 1995). Another study performed with a sample of criminals convicted of murder demonstrated decreased regional cerebral metabolic rate of glucose (rCMRG) not only in the lateral and medial PFC (Raine et al., 1994), but also in the amygdala, and found that it was those who had committed impulsive (Raine, Buchsbaum, & LaCasse, 1997), as opposed to premeditated, murders who showed reductions in the lateral PFC (Raine et al., 1998).

Early PET studies in the BPD population utilized measurement of glucose metabolism, using FDG. Three studies were performed, originally to address speculations about an organic etiology of BPD due to its clinical similarities to patients with chronic partial seizures in both the frontal (Gedye, 1989; Williams, 1969) and temporal lobes (Devinsky & Bear, 1984) who may also present with aggressive behavior. Glucose metabolism was found to inversely correlate with a life history of aggression and impulse difficulties in all subjects with personality diagnoses, and to be decreased in subjects with BPD in certain regions of the frontal cortex (Goyer et al., 1994) in Brodmann areas (BA) 46 and 6, which correspond with the prefrontal, premotor, and cingulate cortices, and the thalamic, caudate, and lenticular nuclei (De La Fuente et al., 1997). After more definitively delineating the specific brain regions associated with impulsive aggression, an additional study has since more rigorously confirmed significant metabolic reductions bilaterally in the orbital frontal cortex (Brodmann areas 9, 10, and 11) in impulsive aggressive subjects with BPD (Soloff et al., 2003) (see Table 3.2). One study, however, found hypermetabolism in frontal and prefrontal areas in hospitalized females with BPD (Juengling et al., 2003). This is the only study to date using PET which has noted *hyper*metabolism of prefrontal areas. Perhaps the study of

Table 3.2 PET Scans in Borderline Personality Disorder

Author	N Study Design	Findings
De La Fuente et al., 1997	10 BPD/10 control resting, mixed gender, 6 of 10 recent abuse	Dec. metabolism in prefrontal, premotor, anterior cingulate, thalamic, caudate, and lenticular nuclei
Juengling et al., 2003	12 BPD/12 control, resting, all hospitalized female	Inc. metabolism frontal and prefrontal areas, dec. hippocampus and cuneus
Soloff et al., 2003	13 female BPD with impulsivity/9 control resting scan	Dec. metabolism in Brodmann areas 9, 10, 11 in bilateral medial prefrontal cortex
Siever et al., 1999	6 IED (4 BPD)/5 control fenfluramine challenge (5-HT agonist)	Blunted response left lateral orbital and right dorsolateral cortex, ventral medial frontal cortex, and cingulate gyrus
Soloff et al., 2000	5 BPD/8 control fenfluramine challenge	Blunted response in medial and orbital regions of prefrontal cortex, left middle and superior temporal gyrus, left parietal lobe and left caudate body
New et al., 2002	13 BPD /13 control m-CPP challenge mixed gender, BPD with impulsive aggression	Blunted response in left medial frontal cortex and anterior cingulate gyrus
Leyton et al., 2001	13 BPD/11 control alpha-[11C]methyl-L-tryptophan trapping (measures presynaptic synthesis of 5-HT)	Females: lower trapping right temporal gyrus, and right dorsal cingulate gyrus Males: lower trapping in cortico-striatal sites: medial prefrontal cortex, anterior cingulate, superior temporal gyrus, and corpus striatum
Schmahl et al., 2003	20 female with childhood physical/sexual abuse compared BPD with non-BPD PET scans to autobiographical trauma script	In abused BPD dec. activation in right cingulate and left orbital frontal cortex

hospitalized patients may include potential confounds such as comorbid-ity or medication use.

There exist reviews of functional neuroimaging studies in impulsive aggressive populations related to BPD. These reviews have emphasized the central importance of the prefrontal cortex in controlling aggression (Lee & Coccaro, 2001), but implicate the limbic, temporal, and frontal cortices as well (Garza-Trevion, 1994).

Challenge Studies Using PET

Another advantage of PET imaging, and functional imaging in general, is that it provides relatively real-time images of the chemical processes in the brain. This characteristic has been utilized in combination with the neuro-chemical challenge paradigm to understand where and under what condi-tions in the brain biochemical responses are altered.

It has become increasingly clear that the central role of the prefrontal cortex (particularly the orbital frontal cortex and the adjacent ventral medial cortex) in regulating aggression is modulated by ascending sero-tonergic tracts from midbrain raphe nuclei where 5-HT cell bodies are located. These cell bodies synapse on various receptors in the neocortex, and in particular, likely involve the 5-HT2A receptor. Challenge paradigms coupled with functional neuroimaging enable investigators to study the role of 5-HT dysfunction in impulsive aggression *at the level of the receptor.*

However, the earliest functional studies of neurotransmitters in the human brain did not involve neuroimaging. Instead, less direct means were utilized with the measurement of CSF serotonin metabolite levels. In patients with brain contusions, levels were found to be significantly lower in subjects with frontotemporally localized lesions as compared to those with more diffuse injuries (Van Woerken, Teelken, & Minderhoud, 1977). Later postmortem studies used techniques allowing measurement of par-ticular types of serotonin receptors in the brain. In human suicide victims, such studies showed high concentrations of both 5-HT2 and 5-HT1A receptors and 5-HT transporter sites in the prefrontal cortex (Arango, Ernsberger, Sved, & Mann, 1993). Moreover, impulsivity and aggression, as well as suicidal behavior and depression, correlated with regional differ-ences in 5-HT activity (Arango, Underwood, & Mann, 1992). In primates, the number of 5-HT2A receptors in posterior orbital frontal cortex, medial frontal cortex, and amygdala was inversely correlated with aggres-sive behavior in monkeys (Raleigh & Brammer, 1993).

Similar to the aforementioned postmortem studies, the first 5-HT chal-lenge studies with neuroimaging in impulsive aggressive individuals with neuroimaging also included individuals with depression. Individuals with depression, similar to controls, demonstrated an increase in left cingulate gyrus and prefrontal cortex metabolism to d,l fenfluramine (Meyer et al., 1996). However, a hypometabolic response to fenfluramine was seen specifically in patients with a history of suicide attempts (Mann, Malone, Diehl, Perel, Cooper, & Mintun, 1996; Mann, Malone, Diehl, Perel, Nichols, & Mintun, 1996). Additionally, high-lethality suicide attempters had lower activation in ventral, medial, and lateral prefrontal cortex than low-lethality attempters, a difference that was more pronounced after fenfluramine administration. Also, lower ventromedial PFC activity was associated with lower lifetime impulsivity, but higher suicidal intent (planning), and higher-lethality suicide attempts (Oquendo et al., 2003). These results suggest that there are neurobiological differences in depressed patients that commit suicide and those depressed individuals who do not. Suicide attempters share characteristics with populations of impulsive aggressive subjects. It is therefore the aggressive act of suicide, not depression, that is suggestive of serotonergic dysfunction and hypofunction in prefrontal regions in the brain.

Similar findings have also been noted in an impulsive aggressive alcoholic population using a serotonergic challenge with m-CPP. Aggressive alcoholics displayed blunted glucose metabolic responses to m-CPP in the right orbital frontal cortex, left anterolateral prefrontal cortex, posterior cingulate cortex, and the thalamus (Hommer et al., 1997).

Two studies have been performed looking specifically at personality disordered subjects with impulsive aggression. One study using fenfluramine found increased glucose metabolic responses amongst healthy volunteers in the orbital frontal, ventral medial, and anterior cingulate cortices, and inferior parietal lobe. However, impulsive aggressive personality disordered subjects demonstrated significantly blunted responses in each of these areas except for the inferior parietal lobe (Siever et al., 1999). In a related study using mCPP, patients with impulsive aggression, unlike normal subjects, did not show activation specifically in the left anteromedial orbital cortex in response to m-CPP, and deactivated the anterior cingulate, which is normally activated by m-CPP. In contrast, the posterior cingulate gyrus was activated in patients and deactivated in controls (New et al., 2002). These findings suggest that the decreased activation of inhibitory regions, such as the PFC, in patients with impulsive aggression in response to a serotonergic stimulus, may contribute to their difficulty in modulating aggressive impulses which perhaps, themselves, stem from the amygdala.

One FDG PET challenge study, targeting in BPD specifically, supported previous findings implicating diminished activation of key brain inhibitory regions in the prefrontal cortex. In the placebo condition, greater FDG uptake was noted in large areas of the prefrontal cortex including medial and orbital regions bilaterally (BA 10 to 11), left superior temporal gyrus, and right insular cortex in healthy controls compared to BPD subjects. In the fenfluramine condition, greater uptake of FDG in medial and orbital regions of right prefrontal cortex (BA 10), left middle and superior temporal gyri (BA 22 to 23), left parietal lobe (BA 40), and left caudate body was found in controls compared to blunted responses in these areas for BPD subjects (Soloff, Meltzer, Greer, Constantine, & Kelly, 2000).

There have been other neuroimaging challenge paradigms for studying the relationship between 5-HT and impulsive aggression in the brain and identifying the components of the 5-HT system leading to hypofunction. Possibilities include decreased production of 5-HT, decreased transmission, increased metabolism, or some combination of these factors.

PET has been used to measure 5-HT synthesis in the brain with trapping of the tracer alpha-[11C] methyl-L-tryptophan (alpha-[11C]MTrp) as an index. This was found to be lower in subjects with BPD compared to controls in certain corticostriatal sites (Leyton et al., 2001). These findings were more pronounced in males compared to females, likely due to lower basal levels in men of plasma-free tryptophan, the chemical precursor in the synthesis of 5-HT (Young, Leyton, & Benkelfat, 1999). This same study also noted that diminished levels of alpha-[11C]MTrp inversely correlated with measures of impulsivity, suggesting that degree of 5-HT synthesis may contribute to the impulsivity dimension of BPD (Leyton et al., 2001). Interestingly, in this study the measurement of impulsivity used self-report measures but also a neuropsychological task. Impulsivity or behavioral disinhibition was measured as errors committed on a go/no-go task. It should be noted that some PET studies typically use an auditory CPT to ensure a sufficient metabolic signal in the brain, including two studies that were previously mentioned (Goyer et al., 1994; Raine et al., 1994).

As compared to research on impulsive aggression, there is minimal neuroimaging data available on the substrates of affective instability and its underpinnings in BPD. The data that do exist utilize paradigms involving the performance of neuropsychological or mood induction tasks, and many of the studies use normal populations. One such example is a PET study in healthy subjects during film-and-recall emotion induction which found correlations of activation in Brodmann area 24 (the anterior cingulate cortex) with scores on the Level of Emotional Awareness Scale. This scale assesses individual differences in the capacity to experience emotion in a differentiated and complex way. This finding suggests that the anterior cingulate cortex, a structure of the limbic system, may be responsible for the experiential processing and response to emotion cues, in addition to its involvement in attention and response selection (Lane et al., 1998).

Affective instability has been investigated using PET in several other axis I disorders which may overlap with BPD. There are data supporting the existence of an important link between BPD and MDD (Koenigsberg et al., 1999) and evidence from PET studies that abnormalities in the cingulate and dorsal lateral cortex may be involved in depression (Baxter et al., 1989; George et al., 1997; Ketter, George, Kimbrell, Benson, & Post, 1996; Mayberg et al., 1997). The neurobiology of BPD and MDD may share common elements, but the precise mechanisms differentiating the two disorders remain to be clarified.

Affective instability has also been examined in BPD within the context of post-traumatic stress disorder. This follows a recent conceptualization of BPD as trauma spectrum disorder or as a *complex PTSD* subtype. PET studies during script-induced recall of traumatic or abandonment memories target the dimension of affective instability. Two such PET studies on females with childhood physical or sexual abuse compared BPD with nonBPD samples during recall of abandonment memories (Schmahl et al., 2003) and memories of childhood abuse. In both studies, traumatized females with BPD, but not traumatized females without BPD, demonstrated dysfunction in the dorsal lateral prefrontal cortex and anterior cingulate regions. The authors posit that brain dysfunction in these areas, known to be involved in impulsive aggression, might also mediate other trauma-related symptoms in BPD, including affective instability and dissociation.

There is growing consensus that BPD may involve a dual-brain pathology involving both the prefrontal and limbic regions. PET imaging to date in BPD has most consistently noted hypofunctioning of prefrontal cortex regions in impulsive aggression, and some data exist suggesting an inability to dampen emotional stimuli from the amygdala. This network of brain regions is also implicated in emotion regulation which is the core dysfunctional pathway that is common to the various clinical phenotypes of BPD (Johnson et al., 2003).

Single Photon Emission Computed Tomography (SPECT)

In SPECT, internal radiation is administered by means of a pharmaceutical which is labeled with a radioactive isotope. This tracer is injected, ingested, or inhaled. The radioactive isotope decays, resulting in the emission of gamma rays. These gamma rays provide a picture of what is happening inside the patient's body. The main difference between SPECT and PET is that SPECT looks at only one photon from each radioactive emission. As a result, it cannot give a map as accurate as with PET. However, depending upon what is being studied, the information obtained from SPECT may be sufficient. SPECT also uses other types of radioactive tracers that are less expensive. As such, it is less costly and more widely available than PET.

Neuroimaging provides the unique possibility of directly viewing 5-HT activity in the brain. Before advances in technology and resolution in neuroimaging, as previously discussed in this chapter, 5-HT activity could only be measured indirectly through measurement of tracers of surrogate compounds in the blood or CSF. The problem that became apparent with this paradigm was that too many things happen to a compound between its production and activity in the brain and its ultimate transport through the bloodstream. Therefore, blood levels representing some measurement of neural activity are confounded, and sorting it out has posed a complicated challenge. The advent of compounds such as [123I] beta-CIT have allowed direct visualization of receptor binding in the brain and limited the need to rely on metabolite measurements. [123I] beta-CIT has been found to be useful in the brains of mammals, nonhuman primates, and in humans, as a tracer of the 5-HT transporter (5-HTT) with SPECT.

In one study in young rhesus monkeys, higher beta-CIT binding to 5-HTT, and therefore, lower 5-HT availability both at the synapse and for turnover, was associated with greater aggressivity and diminished sensitivity to alcohol-induced intoxication (Heinz, Higley, et al., 1998). A study in humans noted decreased beta-CIT binding in alcoholics, and concluded that this represents decreased 5-HTT availability, and not increased 5-HT tone (Heinz, Ragan, et al., 1998). However, a study that found 5-HT specific binding of [123I]beta-CIT in the brainstem raphe, the origin of central serotonergic projections, to be lower in violent offenders than in healthy controls and in nonviolent alcoholics, concluded that hyposerotonergia is associated with impulsive aggression, rather than alcoholism (Tiihonen et al., 1997). This is perhaps the most direct evidence to date that habitual impulsive aggressive behavior in humans is associated with a decrease in 5-HTT density. However, the relationship between alcoholism and impulsive aggression remains to be clarified.

The study of emotional processing using SPECT includes one study examining the differences between psychopathic and nonpsychopathic substance abusers. A lexical decision task contrasting the processing of emotional and neutral words was performed. Results indicated that psychopathic individuals displayed different patterns of rCBF in the frontal temporal and medial frontal regions when processing emotional and neutral words (Intrator et al., 1997). There have been no SPECT studies to date directly assessing the dimension of affective instability.

Functional Magnetic Resonance Imaging (fMRI)

Functional MRI (fMRI) is a functional modality that takes advantage of the fact that MRI technology can detect the rapid changes in local blood flow. This is possible because the velocity of blood flow and oxygenation directly affects signal strength since deoxygenated hemoglobin (Hb) is a paramagnetic substance. This can be applied to functional imaging of the brain since increases in both blood flow and deoxygenation of Hb are seen with neuronal activity. One major advantage of fMRI over other functional imaging modalities is that it does not require the use of contrast agents or involve radiation exposure.

For the dimension of impulsive aggression, the only study using fMRI used a go/no-go task to show that subjects with BPD activated different neural networks during response inhibition. BPD subjects activated a pattern with bilateral involvement of the frontal lobe including medial, superior, and inferior gyri. In contrast, normal controls activated regions of the left orbitofrontal and right dorsolateral cortex (Vollm et al., 2004).

FMRI has been extensively used in the study of the dimension of affective instability. Studies involving mood induction tasks with fMRI suggest that limbic hypersensitivity is the neurofunctional correlate of emotional vulnerability that Linehan (1993) describes as the core feature of BPD, involving high sensitivity to emotional stimuli, high emotional intensity, and slow return of emotional arousal to baseline. There have been three fMRI studies involving mood induction in BPD subjects. One study measured regional blood oxygenation level dependent (BOLD) response to International Affective Picture Series (IAPS) slides that were emotionally aversive as compared to those that were neutral. It demonstrated bilaterally elevated response in the amygdala, fusiform gyrus (which processes complex visual features), the orbital frontal cortex, and anterior cingulate in BPD, but not control subjects, and in the temporal-occipital region in both groups. This suggests that the amygdala may modulate perceptual processing in borderline individuals, resulting in preferential attention to environmental stimuli that are emotionally relevant (Herpertz et al., 2001). Similarly, a second study viewing IAPS slides in 11 subjects with BPD and control subjects noted differing patterns of activation, with BPD subjects showing activation in the ventrolateral prefrontal cortex and controls activating dorsolateral prefrontal cortex (Koenigsberg et al., 2004). As one of the functions of the ventrolateral prefrontal cortex is to inhibit the amygdala, the authors propose that BPD subjects are requiring increased frontal activation to modulate negative emotion (see Table 3.3).

Another study revealed an increase in left amygdala activation compared to controls during observation of Ekman slides of facial expressions of emotion while undergoing fMRI in subjects with BPD. Furthermore, some of the BPD subjects reported having difficulty disambiguating or being threatened by neutral faces, perhaps pointing to a neurofunctional correlate for the effect of emotional dysregulation on interpersonal relationships which are often disturbed in BPD (Donegan et al., 2003).

A model for emotional modulation has been postulated by Davidson, Putnam, and Larson (2000) involving specific brain regions including the anterior cingulate, orbital frontal cortex, ventral medial cortex, and dorsal lateral prefrontal cortex. The anterior cingulate may play a role in the cognitive processing and evaluation of mood and affect regulation as well as responses to conflict. The orbital frontal cortex appears to inhibit impulsive aggression by regulating the amygdala, the dorsal lateral prefrontal cortex may integrate emotions with cognition, and the ventral medial prefrontal cortex may involve the general processing of emotions. This neural

Table 3.3 FMRI Scans in Borderline Personality Disorder

Author	N Study Design	Findings
Herpertz et al., 2001	6 BPD/6 controls emotional stimulation paradigm emotionally aversive pictures (IAPS)	Increased signal bilateral amygdala and in 50% of subjects—also in medial and inferolateral prefrontal cortex
Donegan et al., 2003	15 BPD/15 controls BPD on medications and sign comorbid Axis 1 20-second blocks of neutral, happy, sad, and fearful faces	Increased left amygdala activation to facial expression
Koenigsberg et al., 2004	11 BPD/9 controls IAPS pictures (negative vs. positive)	Increased activation in BPD for BA 9, 10, and 47; right ventral inferior frontal gyrus, left middle and superior frontal gyri
Vollm et al., 2004	8 BPD or antisocial PD/8 controls go/no-go task	Bilateral activation in BPD in superior, inferior, and medial frontal gyri compared to controls who activated regions of prefrontal cortex

circuitry of emotion is actively being studied, and growing evidence suggests that threatening or aversive stimuli activate the amygdala, which in turn activates the anterior cingulate and prefrontal cortex. These regions may play a role in modulating amygdala-driven emotional behavior via serotonergic neurotransmission (Davidson et al., 2000). Future studies will continue to clarify the patterns of connectivity between brain regions and putative mechanisms for dysfunction and symptom production.

Magnetic Resonance Spectroscopy (MRS)

Magnetic resonance spectroscopy (MRS) is a new neuroimaging technique that allows localization of specific neurochemical processes. Prior to the use of MRS, functional imaging was limited to localization of general metabolic processes by measuring various parameters. In order to be more precise, however, it would be useful to be able to describe what particular activity was being carried out in the brain that entailed a change in metabolism. MRS takes advantage of the unique structures of a given chemical to allow its activity to be viewed. This allows imaging of a broad array of substances that may be more directly related to the object of study. For brain imaging, this modality has the potential to provide imaging of the activity of specific substances directly related to the nervous system, including various neurotransmitters.

The only MRS study in BPD used hydrogen-1 MRS ([1H]MRS), one of the most sensitive techniques for the assessment of subtle neuronal dysfunction. A significant reduction of absolute N-acetylaspartate (NAA) concentrations in the dorsolateral prefrontal cortex was found. This is generally thought to reflect either disturbed neuronal metabolism caused by reversible mechanisms such as genetic defects or toxic substances, or an underlying disturbance in the microstructure of the neuron, such as a decrease in density, as a result of pathological development of certain subregions of the brain. These hypotheses are supported by the fact that BPD symptoms are present at a very young age and do not worsen over time (van Elst et al., 2001) (see Table 3.4).

Table 3.4 MR Spectroscopy in Borderline Personality Disorder

Author	N Study Design	Findings
van Elst et al., 2001	12 BPD/14 controls all females orbital frontal and cingulate regions not studied	19% decreased NAA concentration in BPD in dorsolateral prefrontal cortex = reflection of neuronal dysfunction

Neuroimaging has proven to be a powerful modality in which to deepen our understanding of brain pathology and for clarifying the underlying biological mechanisms for the dimensions of impulsive aggression and affective instability. Future work will continue to be derived from these techniques and with continuing improvements in resolution, visualization of smaller brain structure and a better understanding of the pathways connecting these structures will be possible. Future development of receptor ligands for various serotonin receptor subtypes (several already exist) will enable quantification of receptor number *in vivo*.

Genetics of Impulsive Aggression in Personality Disorders

Twin and family studies suggest a partially heritable basis for impulsive aggression (Bohman, Cloninger, von Knorring, & Sigvardsson, 1984; Coccaro, Bergman, & McLean, 1993; Coccaro, Silverman, Klar, Horvath, & Siever, 1994). Preliminary data from monozygotic-dizygotic twin studies suggest that while the personality disorder diagnoses are not heritable, the traits of impulsive aggression or assertive aggressiveness are significantly heritable (Alnaes & Torgersen, 1989; Coccaro et al., 1993; Torgersen, 1992). Studies of adoptees with biological parents with antisocial personality disorder demonstrated a genetic contribution to the development of antisocial personality disorder characterized by antisocial aggressive behavior (Cadoret et al., 1985; Crowe, 1974), and this heritable tendency appeared to be brought out by adverse home environment (Cadoret et al., 1995).

The well-established serotonergic abnormalities associated with aggression and the apparent heritable contribution to these behaviors compel genetic studies of 5-HT–related genes and impulsive aggression. The approach of identifying the relationship between candidate genes and impulsive aggressive behavior is promising in that it may elucidate the mechanism underlying the susceptibility to impulsive aggression. Polymorphisms related to gene products involved in 5-HT synthesis, reuptake, metabolism, and receptors have been identified in nonhuman primates and in human subjects. In subjects with impulsive aggression and related disorders, the following polymorphisms have been studied: tryptophan hydroxylase (TPH; A779C substitution), 5-HT1B receptor (G861C allele), 5-HT2A (T102C and 1438G/A alleles), and serotonin transporter (5-HTT; 5-HTTLPR allele).

Tryptophan hydroxylase (TPH), the first enzyme involved in the synthesis of 5-HT, demonstrated two polymorphic sites: A218C and A779C. The A779A/A218A corresponds to "U" and the A779C/A218C to "L"

(Nielsen, Jenkins, Stefanisko, Jefferson, & Goldman, 1997). There is an association between the "L" (218C/779C) allele and suicidal behavior, at times a form of impulsive behavior (Nielsen et al., 1994). In data from our group for 21 male Caucasian personality disorder patients, the "LL" genotype was associated with significantly higher total and irritability/assaultiveness composite subscale scores on the Buss-Durkee Hostility Inventory (BDHI) compared to Caucasian males with the "UL or "UU" genotypes. No significant association was found between the "LL" genotype and a history of suicide attempt or impulsive borderline personality disorder traits in this sample. Females with the "LL" genotype did not demonstrate higher BDHI scores or a blunted prolactin response to fenfluramine (New et al., 1998). These results have been replicated in one study (Staner et al., 2002) but in another, the "UL" and "UU" genotypes were associated with an attenuated prolactin response to fenfluramine in male but not in female community volunteers (Manuck et al., 1999).

The serotonin 1B receptor is a terminal autoreceptor involved in the regulation of 5-HT synthesis and release. Increased aggression has been demonstrated in mice lacking the 5-HT1B receptor (Saudou et al., 1994). In human studies of personality disordered patients, the "G" allele has been associated with a history of suicide attempts but not with self-report measures of impulsive aggression (New et al., 2001). However, these findings were not replicated in another study (Rujescu, Giegling, Sato, & Moller, 2003).

The 5-HT2 class of receptors, including 5-HT2A and 2C, appear to be centrally related to the pharmacology of antidepressants, and mediate the prolactin response to fenfluramine, which has been shown to be blunted in personality disorder patients with impulsive aggressive symptoms. Findings are inconsistent across studies. Problems with impulsivity (Bjork et al., 2002) and behavioral problems in alcoholics (Hwu & Chen, 2000) have been associated with the T102C allele, while another study found no associations with either the T102C or 1438G/A alleles and personality function in normal subjects (Kusumi et al., 2002). Moreover, some (Arias et al., 2001) but not all studies (Arango, Huang, Underwood, & Mann, 2003; Bondy et al., 2000) have noted an association between suicide and the T102C allele. Criminals demonstrate lower "GG" levels but no significant associations with the Korslinka Scale of Personality (Berggard et al., 2003). As these data indicate, clarification of the role of the 5-HT2A receptor in impulsive aggression is needed.

The serotonin transporter (5-HTT) is important in serotonergic functioning in that it plays a central role in the termination of 5-HT neurotransmission by the presynaptic reuptake of 5-HT, and represents a site of antidepressant activity (Amara & Kuhar, 1993). Twin studies suggest that platelet 5-HT uptake, mediated by the 5-HTT, may be partially genetically controlled (Meltzer & Arora, 1986). While the 5-HTT on the human platelet has been shown to be identical to the 5-HTT in the human brain (Lesch, Wolozin, Murphy, & Reiderer, 1993), a recent PET study in humans showed no association between the genotype of the promoter region and 5-HTT binding (Shioe et al., 2003).

A polymorphism in the promotor region of the 5-HTT gene (SLC6A4) has been identified; this polymorphism has demonstrated functional significance in coding for high and low transporter production. Evidence suggests that the "s" allele may be associated with increased measures of harm avoidance, impulsivity (Costa & McCrae, 1997; Gorwood, Batel, Ades, & Hamon, 2003; Lesch et al., 1996), and suicidality (Gorwood, Batel, Ades, Hamon, & Boni, 2000), although other studies did not replicate these findings (Ebstein et al., 1997; Gelernter, Kranzler, & Cubells, 1997; Patkar et al., 2002; Umekage et al., 2003). Another study has reported that the "s" allele may confer susceptibility to severe alcohol abuse (Sander et al., 1997).

The studies of serotonin-related genes to date suggest only modest contributions to impulsive aggressive behavior. While additional replication studies of larger power are necessary, such studies are further complicated by the marked population variability and molecular complexity of these genes (Glatt, Tampilic, Christie, DeYoung, & Freimer, 2004).

Summary

In summary, the biological study of personality disorder is best conducted by examining dimensions of personality. For BPD, the dimensions of impulsive aggression and affective instability are under active investigation with efforts to identify the neurotransmitter involvement and regions of brain dysfunction. With advancing technologies, analytic techniques, and constant improvements in visual resolution, structural and functional neuroimaging are at the forefront of biological research in BPD. Important findings implicating dual dysfunction of prefrontal cortex and amygdala are advancing our understanding of the etiology of this disorder. The study of genetics, another important research strategy, and future research direction of the field, to date has focused on polymorphisms of the serotonin system in impulsive aggression. While the findings to date only suggest modest contributions, advances in methodology and identification of more intermediate expressions of the BPD disorder, or endophenotypes, will forward this endeavor.

The evolving understanding of the neurobiology of BPD in particular, and personality disorders in general, offers great promise and hope for the individuals afflicted. Future directions will hopefully translate this understanding into more effective treatment strategies.

References

Alnaes, R., & Torgersen, S. (1989). Clinical differentiation between major depression only, major depression with panic disorder and panic disorder only: Childhood, personality and personality disorder. *Acta Psychiatrica Scandinavica, 79*(4), 370–377.

Amara, S., & Kuhar, M. (1993). Neurotransmitter transporters: Recent progress. *Annual Review of Neuroscience, 16*, 73–93.

Arango, V., Ernsberger, P., Sved, A. F., & Mann, J. J. (1993). Quantitative autoradiography of alpha 1- and alpha 2-adrenergic receptors in the cerebral cortex of controls and suicide victims. *Brain Research, 630*(1–2), 271–282.

Arango, V., Huang, Y. Y., Underwood, M. D., & Mann, J. J. (2003). Genetics of the serotonergic system in suicidal behavior. *Journal Psychiatric Research, 37*(5), 375–386.

Arango, V., Underwood, M. D., & Mann, J. J. (1992). Alterations in monoamine receptors in the brain of suicide victims. *Journal of Clinical Psychopharmacology, 12*(2 Supplement), 8S–12S.

Arias, B., Gasto, C., Catalan, R., Gutierrez, B., Pintor, L., & Fananas, L. (2001). The 5-HT(2A) receptor gene 102T/C polymorphism is associated with suicidal behavior in depressed patients. *American Journal of Medical Genetics, 105*(8), 801–804.

Baxter, L. R. J., Schwartz, J. M., Phelps, M. E., Mazziotta, J. C., Guze, B. H., Selin, C. E., et al. (1989). Reduction of prefrontal cortex glucose metabolism common to three types of depression. *Archives of General Psychiatry, 46*(3), 243–250.

Berggard, C., Damberg, M., Longato-Stadler, E., Hallman, J., Oreland, L., & Garpenstrand, H. (2003). The serotonin 2A -1438 G/A receptor polymorphism in a group of Swedish male criminals. *Neuroscience Letter, 347*(3), 196–198.

Bjork, J. M., Moeller, F. G., Dougherty, D. M., Swann, A. C., Machado, M. A., & Hanis, C. L. (2002). Serotonin 2a receptor T102C polymorphism and impaired impulse control. *American Journal of Medical Genetics, 114*(3), 336–339.

Blais, M., Hilsenroth, M., & Castlebury, F. (1997). Content validity of the DSM-IV borderline and narcissistic personality disorder criteria sets. *Comprehensive Psychiatry, 38*(1), 31–37.

Bohman, M., Cloninger, C. R., von Knorring, A., & Sigvardsson, S. (1984). An adoption study of somatoform disorders: III. Cross-fostering analysis and genetic relationship to alcoholism and criminality. *Archives of General Psychiatry, 41*(872–878).

Bohus, M., Schmahl, C., & Lieb, K. (2004). New developments in the neurobiology of borderline personality disorder. *Current Psychiatry Reports, 6*(1), 43–50.

Bondy, B., Kuznik, J., Baghai, T., Schulze, C., Zwanzger, P., Minoz, C., et al. (2000). Lack of association of serotonin-2A receptor gene polymorphism (T102C) with suicidal ideation and suicide. *American Journal of Medical Genetics, 96*(6), 831–835.

Bremner, J. D., Narayan, M., Anderson, E. R., Staib, L. H., Miller, H. L., & Charney, D. S. (2000). Hippocampal volume reduction in major depression. *American Journal of Psychiatry, 157*(1), 115–118.

Bremner, J. D., Randall, P., Vermetten, E., Staib, L., Bronen, R. A., Mazure, C., et al. (1997). Magnetic resonance imaging-based measurement of hippocampal volume in posttraumatic stress disorder related to childhood physical and sexual abuse—a preliminary report. *Biological Psychiatry, 41*(1), 23–32.

Brickner, R. M. (1934). An interpretation of frontal lobe function based upon the study of a case of partial bilateral lobectomy. *Research publications—Association for Research in Nervous and Mental Disease, 13*, 259–351.

Cadoret, R. J., O'Gorman, T. W., Troughton, E., & Heywood, E. (1985). Alcoholism and antisocial personality: Interrelationships, genetic and environmental factors. *Archives of General Psychiatry, 42*(2), 161–167.

Cadoret, R. J., Yates, W. R., Troughton, E., Woodworth, G., & Stewart, M. A. (1995). Genetic-environmental interaction in the genesis of aggressivity and conduct disorders. *Archives of General Psychiatry, 52*(11), 916–924.

Cheung, P., & Schweitzer, I. (1998). Correlates of aggressive behaviour in schizophrenia: An overview. *The Australian and New Zealand Journal of Psychiatry, 32*(3), 400–409.

Coccaro, E. F., Berman, M. E., Kavoussi, R. J., & Hauger, R. L. (1996). Relationship of prolactin response to d-fenfluramine to behavioral and questionnaire assessments of aggression in personality-disordered men. *Biological Psychiatry, 40*(3), 157–164.

Coccaro, E., Bergman, C. S., & McLean, G. E. (1993). Heritability of irritable impulsiveness: A study of twins reared together and apart. *Psychiatry Research, 48*(3), 229–242.

Coccaro, E. F., Kavoussi, R. J., Cooper, T. B., & Hauger, R. L. (1997). Central serotonin activity and aggression: Inverse relationship with prolactin response to d-fenfluramine, but not CSF 5-HIAA concentration, in human subjects. *American Journal of Psychiatry, 154*(10), 1430–1435.

Coccaro, E. F., Kavoussi, R. J., & Hauger, R. L. (1995). Physiological responses to d-fenfluramine and ipsapirone challenge correlate with indices of aggression in males with personality disorder. *International Clinical Psychopharmacology, 10*(3), 177–179.

Coccaro, E. F., Kavoussi, R. J., Trestman, R. L., Gabriel, S. M., Cooper, T. B., & Siever, L. J. (1997). Serotonin function in human subjects: Intercorrelations among central 5-HT indices and aggressiveness. *Psychiatry Research, 73*(1-2), 1–14.

Coccaro, E., F., Siever, L. J., Klar, H. M., Maurer, G., Cochrane, K., Cooper, T. B., et al. (1989). Serotonergic studies in patients with affective and personality disorders. *Archives of General Psychiatry, 46*, 587–599.

Coccaro, E., Silverman, J., Klar, H., Horvath, T., & Siever L. J. (1994). Familial correlates of reduced central serotonergic system function in patients with personality disorders. *Archives of General Psychiatry, 51*(4), 318–324.

Costa, P. T., Jr., & McCrae, R. R. (1997). Stability and change in personality assessment: The revised NEO Personality Inventory in the year 2000. *Journal of Personality Assessment, 68*(1), 86–94.

Crowe, R. R. (1974). An adoption study of antisocial personality. *Archives of General Psychiatry, 31*(6), 785–791.

Damasio, A. R., & Van Hoesen, G. W. (1983). Emotional disturbances associated with focal lesions of the frontal lobe. In K. Heilman & P. Satz (Eds.), *Neuropsychology of human emotion: Recent advances.* New York: Guilford Press.

Damasio, H., Grabowski, T., Frank, R., Galaburda, A. M., & Damasio, A. R. (1994). The return of Phineas Gage: Clues about the brain from the skull of a famous patient. *Science, 264*(5162), 1102–1105.

Davidson, R. J., Putnam, K. M., & Larson, C. L. (2000). Dysfunction in the neural circuitry of emotion regulation—A possible prelude to violence. *Science, 289*(5479), 591–594.

De La Fuente, J. M., Goldman, S., Stanus, E., Vizuete, C., Morlan, I., Bobes, J., et al. (1997). Brain glucose metabolism in borderline personality disorder. *Journal of Psychiatric Research, 31*(5), 531–541.

Devinsky, O., & Bear, D. (1984). Varieties of aggressive behavior in temporal lobe epilepsy. *American Journal of Psychiatry, 141*(5), 651–656.

Dolan, M. C., Deaking, J. F., Roberts, N., & Anderson, I. M. (2002). Quantitative frontal and temporal structural MRI studies in personality-disordered offenders and control subjects. *Psychiatry Research, 116*(3), 133–149.

Donegan, N. H., Sanislow, C. A., Blumberg, H. P., Fulbright, R. K., Lacadie, C., Skudlarski, P., et al. (2003). Amygdala hyperreactivity in borderline personality disorder: Implications for emotional dysregulation. *Biological Psychiatry, 54*(11), 1284–1293.

Dougherty, D., Bjork, J., Huckabee, H., Moeller, F., & Swann, A. (1999). Laboratory measure of aggression and impulsivity in work with borderline personality disorder. *Psychiatry Research, 85*(3), 315–326.

Driessen, M., Herrmann, J., Stahl, K., Zwaan, M., Meier, S., Hill, A., et al. (2000). Magnetic resonance imaging volumes of the hippocampus and the amygdala in women with borderline personality disorder and early traumatization. *Archives of General Psychiatry, 57*(12), 1115–1122.

Ebstein, R. P., Gritsenko, I., Nemanov, L., Frisch, A., Osher, Y., & Belmaker, R. H. (1997). No association between the serotonin transporter gene regulatory region polymorphism and the Tridimensional Personality Questionnaire (TPQ) temperament of harm avoidance. *Molecular Psychiatry, 2*(3), 224–226.

Garza-Trevion, E. S. (1994). Neurobiological factors in aggressive behavior. *Hospital and Community Psychiatry, 45*(7), 690–699.

Gedye, A. (1989). Episodic rage and aggression attributed to frontal lobe seizures. *Journal of Mental Deficiency Research, 33*(Part 5), 369–379.

Gelernter, J., Kranzler, H., & Cubells, J. F. (1997). Serotonin transporter protein (SLC6A4) allele and haplotype frequencies and linkage disequilibria in African- and European-American and Japanese populations and in alcohol-dependent subjects. *Human Genetics, 101*(2), 243–246.

George, M. S., Ketter, T. A., Parekh, P. I., Rosinsky, N., Ring, H. A., Pazzaglia, P. J., et al. (1997). Blunted left cingulate activation in mood disorder subjects during a response interference task (the Stroop). *The Journal of Neuropsychiatry and Clinical Neurosciences, 9*(1), 55–63.

Glatt, C. E., Tampilic, M., Christie, C., DeYoung, J., & Freimer, N. B. (2004). Re-screening serotonin receptors for genetic variants identifies population and molecular genetic complexity. *American Journal of Medical Genetics, 124B*(1), 92–100.

Gorwood, P., Batel, P., Ades, J., & Hamon, M. (2003). Possible association between serotonin transporter promoter region polymorphism and impulsivity in Koreans. *Psychiatry Research, 118*(1), 19–24.

Gorwood, P., Batel, P., Ades, J., Hamon, M., & Boni, C. (2000). Serotonin transporter gene polymorphisms, alcoholism, and suicidal behavior. *Biological Psychiatry, 48*(4), 259–264.

Goyer, P. F., Andreason, P. J., Semple, W. E., Clayton, A. H., King, A. C., Compton-Toth, B. A., et al. (1994). Positron-emission tomography and personality disorders. *Neuropsychopharmacology, 10*(1), 21–28.

Grafman, J., Schwab, K., Warden, D., Pridgen, A., Brown, H. R., & Salazar, A. M. (1996). Frontal lobe injuries, violence, and aggression: A report of the Vietnam Head Injury Study. *Neurology, 46*(5), 1231–1238.

Grafman, J., Vance, S. C., Weingartner, H., Salazar, A. M., & Amin, D. (1986). The effects of lateralized frontal lesions on mood regulation. *Brain, 109*(Part 6), 1127–1148.

Heinz, A., Higley, J. D., Gorey, J. G., Saunders, R. C., Jones, D. W., Hommer, D., et al. (1998). In vivo association between alcohol intoxication, aggression, and serotonin transporter availability in nonhuman primates. *American Journal of Psychiatry, 155*(8), 1023–1028.

Heinz, A., Ragan, P., Jones, D. W., Hommer, D., Williams, W., Knable, M. B., et al. (1998). Reduced central serotonin transporters in alcoholism. *American Journal of Psychiatry, 155*(11), 1544–1549.

Herpertz, S. C., Dietrich, T. M., Wenning, B., Krings, T., Erberich, S. G., Willmes, K., et al. (2001). Evidence of abnormal amygdala functioning in borderline personality disorder: A functional MRI study. *Biological Psychiatry, 50*(4), 292–298.

Herpertz, S., Gretzer, A., Steinmeyer, E., Muelbauer, V., Schuerkens, A., & Sass, H. (1997). Affective instability and impulsivity in personality disorder: Results of an experimental study. *Journal of Affective Disorders, 44*(1), 31–37.

Hichcock, E., & Cairns, V. (1973). Amygdalotomy. *Postgraduate Medical Journal, 49*(578), 894–904.

Hommer, D., Andreasen, P., Rio, D., Williams, W., Ruttimann, U., Momenan, R., et al. (1997). Effects of m-chlorophenylpiperazine on regional brain glucose utilization: A positron emission tomographic comparison of alcoholic and control subjects. *Journal of Neuroscience, 17*(8), 2796–2806.

Hoptman, M. J., Volavka, J., Johnson, G., Weiss, E., Bilder, R. M., & Lim, K. O. (2002). Frontal white matter microstructure, aggression, and impulsivity in men with schizophrenia: A preliminary study. *Biological Psychiatry, 52*(1), 9–14.

Hwu, H. G., & Chen, C. H. (2000). Association of 5HT2A receptor gene polymorphism and alcohol abuse with behavior problems. *American Journal of Medical Genetics, 96*(6), 797–800.

Intrator, J., Hare, R., Stritzke, P., Brichtswein, K., Dorfman, D., Harpur, T., et al. (1997). A brain imaging (single photon emission computerized tomography) study of semantic and affective processing in psychopaths. *Biological Psychiatry, 42*(2), 96–103.

Johnson, D. M., Shea, M. T., Yen, S., Battle, C. L., Zlotnick, C., Sanislow, C. A., et al. (2003). Gender differences in borderline personality disorder: Findings from the Collaborative Longitudinal Personality Disorders Study. *Comprehensive Psychiatry, 44*(4), 282–292.

Juengling, F. D., Schmahl, C., Hesslinger, B., Ebert, D., Bremner, J. D., Gostomzyk, J., et al. (2003). Positron emission tomography in female patients with borderline personality disorder. *Journal of Psychiatric Research, 37*(2), 109–115.

Ketter, T. A., George, M. S., Kimbrell, T. A., Benson, B. E., & Post, R. M. (1996). Functional brain imaging, limbic function, and affective disorders. *The Neuroscientist, 1*(2), 55–65.

Koenigsberg, H. W., Anwunah, I., New, A. S., Mitropoulou, V., Schopick, F., & Siever, L. J. (1999). Relationship between depression and borderline personality disorder. *Depression and Anxiety, 10*(4), 158–167.

Koenigsberg, H., Siever, L., Guo, X., New, A., Goodman, M., & Prohovnik, I. (2004). An fMRI study of emotion processing in borderline personality disorder patients. *Biological Psychiatry, 55*, 89S.

Kusumi, I., Suzuki, K., Sasaki, Y., Kameda, K., Sasaki, T., & Koyama, T. (2002). Serotonin 5-HT(2A) receptor gene polymorphism, 5-HT(2A) receptor function and personality traits in healthy subjects: A negative study. *Journal of Affective Disorders, 68*(2-3), 235–241.

Lane, R. D., Reiman, E. M., Axelrod, B., Yun, L. S., Holmes, A., & Schwartz, G. E. (1998). Neural correlates of levels of emotional awareness: Evidence of an interaction between emotion and attention in the anterior cingulate cortex. *Journal of Cognitive Neuroscience, 10*(4), 525–535.

Lee, G. P., Bechara, A., Adolphs, R., Arena, J., Meador, K. J., Loring, D. W., et al. (1998). Clinical and physiological effects of stereotaxic bilateral amygdalotomy for intractable aggression. *Journal of Neuropsychiatry and Clinical Neuroscience, 10*(4), 413–420.

Lee, R., & Coccaro, E. (2001). The neuropsychopharmacology of criminality and aggression. *Canadian Journal of Psychiatry, 46*(1), 35–44.

Lesch, K., Bengel, D., Heils, A., Sabol, S., Greenberg, B., Petri, S., et al. (1996). Association of anxiety-related traits with a polymorphism in the serotonin transporter gene regulatory region. *Science, 274*, 1527–1531.

Lesch, K., Wolozin, B., Murphy, D., & Reiderer, P. (1993). Primary structure of the human platelet serotonin uptake site: Identity with the brain serotonin transporter. *Journal of Neurochemistry, 60*(6), 2319–2322.

Leyton, M., Okazawa, H., Diksic, M., Paris, J., Rosa, P., Mzengeza, S., et al. (2001). Brain regional alpha-[11C]methyl-L-tryptophan trapping in impulsive subjects with borderline personality disorder. *American Journal of Psychiatry, 158*(5), 775–782.

Linehan, M. M. (1993). *Cognitive-Behavioral Treatment of Borderline Personality Disorder.* New York: Guilford Press.

Lucas, P. B., Gardner, D. L., Cowdry, R. W., & Pickar, D. (1989). Cerebral structure in borderline personality disorder. *Psychiatry Research, 27*(2), 111–115.

Lyoo, I. K., Han, M. H., & Cho, D. Y. (1998). A brain MRI study in subjects with borderline personality disorder. *Journal of Affective Disorders, 50*(2-3), 235–243.

Mann, J. J., Malone, K. M., Diehl, D. J., Perel, J., Cooper, T. B., & Mintun, M. A. (1996). Demonstration in vivo of reduced serotonin responsivity in the brain of untreated depressed patients. *American Journal of Psychiatry, 153*(2), 174–182.

Mann, J. J., Malone, K. M., Diehl, D. J., Perel, J., Nichols, T. E., & Mintun, M. A. (1996). Positron emission tomographic imaging of serotonin activation effects on prefrontal cortex in healthy volunteers. *Journal of Cerebral Blood Flow Metabolism, 16*(3), 418–426.

Manuck, S. B., Flory, J. D., Ferrell, R. E., Dent, K. M., Mann, J. J., & Muldoon, M. F. (1999). Aggression and anger-related traits associated with a polymorphism of the tryptophan hydroxylase gene. *Biological Psychiatry, 45*(5), 603–614.

Mark, V. H., & Ervin, F. R. (1970). *Violence and the Brain.* New York: Harper & Row.

Martinius, J. (1983). Homicide of an aggressive adolescent boy with right temporal lesion: A case report. *Neuroscience and Biobehavioral Reviews, 7*(3), 419–422.

Max, J. E., Smith, W. L., Jr., Lindgren, S. D., Robin, D. A., Mattheis, P., Stierwalt, J., et al. (1995). Case study: Obsessive-compulsive disorder after severe traumatic brain injury in an adolescent. *Journal of the American Academy of Child and Adolescent Psychiatry, 34*(1), 45–49.

Mayberg, H. S., Brannan, S. K., Mahurin, R. K., Jerabek, P. A., Brickman, J. S., Tekell, J. L., et al. (1997). Cingulate function in depression: A potential predictor of treatment response. *Neuroreport, 8*(4), 1057–1061.

Meltzer, H., & Arora, R. (1986). Platelet markers for suicidality. *Annals of the New York Academy of Sciences, 487,* 271–280.

Meyer, J. H., Kapur, S., Wilson, A. A., DaSilva, J. N., Houle, S., & Brown, G. M. (1996). Neuromodulation of frontal and temporal cortex by intravenous d-fenfluramine: An [15O]H2O PET study in humans. *Neuroscience Letter, 207*(1), 25–28.

New, A. S., Gelernter, J., Goodman, M., Mitropoulou, V., Koenigsberg, H., Silverman, J., et al. (2001). Suicide, impulsive aggression, and HTR1B genotype. *Biological Psychiatry, 50*(1), 62–65.

New, A., Gelertner, J., Yovell, Y., Trestman, R., Nielsen, D., Silverman, J., et al. (1998). Increases in irritable aggression associated with "LL" genotype at the tryptophan hydroxylase locus. *American Journal of Medical Genetics, 81*(1), 13–17.

New, A. S., Hazlett, E. A., Buchsbaum, M. S., Goodman, M., Reynolds, D., Mitropoulou, V., et al. (2002). Blunted prefrontal cortical 18fluorodeoxyglucose positron emission tomography response to meta-chlorophenylpiperazine in impulsive aggression. *Archives of General Psychiatry, 59*(7), 621–629.

New, A. S., Trestman, R. L., Mitropoulou, V., Benishay, D. S., Coccaro, E. F., & Siever, L. J. (1997). Serotonergic function and self-injurious behavior in personality disorder patients. *Psychiatry Research, 69,* 17–26.

Nielsen, D. A., Goldman, D., Virkkunen, M., Tokola, R., Rawlings, M. S., & Linnoila, M. (1994). Suicidality and 5-hydroxyindolacetic acid concentration associated with a tryptophan hydroxylase polymorphism. *Archives of General Psychiatry, 51,* 34–38.

Nielsen, D. A., Jenkins, G. L., Stefanisko, K. M., Jefferson, K. K., & Goldman, D. (1997). Sequence, splice site and population frequency distribution analyses of the polymorphic human tryptophan hydroxylase intron 7. *Molecular Brain Research, 45,* 145–148.

Oquendo, M. A., Placidi, G. P., Malone, K. M., Campbell, C., Keilp, J., Brodsky, B., et al. (2003). Positron emission tomography of regional brain metabolic responses to a serotonergic challenge and lethality of suicide attempts in major depression. *Archives of General Psychiatry, 60*(1), 14–22.

Patkar, A. A., Berrettini, W. H., Hoehe, M., Thornton, C. C., Gottheil, E., Hill, K., et al. (2002). Serotonin transporter polymorphisms and measures of impulsivity, aggression, and sensation seeking among African-American cocaine-dependent individuals. *Psychiatry Research, 110*(2), 103–115.

Pfohl, B., Blum, N., & Zimmerman, M. (1997). *Structured Interview for DSM-IV Personality.* Washington, DC: American Psychiatric Publishing, Inc.

Porrino, L. J., & Goldman-Rakic, P. S. (1982). Brainstem innervation of prefrontal and anterior cingulate cortex in the rhesus monkey revealed by retrograde transport of HRP. *Journal of Comparative Neurology, 205*(1), 63–76.

Raine, A., Buchsbaum, M. S., & LaCasse, L. (1997). Brain abnormalities in murderers indicated by positron emission tomography. *Biological Psychiatry, 42*(6), 495–508.

Raine, A., Buchsbaum, M. S., Stanley, J., Lottenberg, S., Abel, L., & Stoddard, J. (1994). Selective reductions in prefrontal glucose metabolism in murderers. *Biological Psychiatry, 36*(6), 365–373.

Raine, A., Meloy, J. R., Bihrle, S., Stoddard, J., LaCasse, L., & Buchsbaum, M. S. (1998). Reduced prefrontal and increased subcortical brain functioning assessed using positron emission tomography in predatory and affective murderers. *Behavioral Sciences and the Law, 16*(3), 319–332.

Raleigh, M. J., & Brammer, G. L. (1993). Individual differences in serotonin 2 receptors and social behavior in monkeys. *Abstracts—Society for Neuroscience, 19,* 592.

Relkin, N., Plum, F., Mattis, S., Eidelberg, D., & Tranel, D. (1996). Impulsive homicide associated with an arachnoid cyst and unilateral frontotemporal cerebral dysfunction. *Seminars in Clinical Neurpsychiatry, 1*(3), 172–183.

Rujescu, D., Giegling, I., Sato, T., & Moller, H. J. (2003). Lack of association between serotonin 5-HT1B receptor gene polymorphism and suicidal behavior. *American Journal of Medical Genetics, 116B*(1), 69–71.

Rusch, N., van Elst, L.T., Ludaescher, P., Wilke, M., Huppertz, H. J., Thiel, T., et al. (2003). A voxel-based morphometric MRI study in female patients with borderline personality disorder. *Neuroimage, 20*(1), 385–392.

Sander, T., Harms, H., Lesch, K. P., Dufeu, P., Kuhn, S., Hoehe, M., et al. (1997). Association analysis of a regulatory variation of the serotonin transporter gene with severe alcohol dependence. *Alcohol, Clinical, and Experimental Research, 21*(8), 1356–1359.

Saudou, F., Amara, D. A., Dierich, A., LeMeur, M., Ramboz, S., Segu, L., et al. (1994). Enhanced aggressive behavior in mice lacking 5-HT1B receptor. *Science, 265*(5180), 1875–1878.

Schmahl, C. G., Vermetten, E., Elzinga, B. M., & Bremmer, J. (2003). Magnetic resonance imaging of hippocampal and amygdala volume in women with childhood abuse and borderline personality disorder. *Psychiatry Research, 122*(3), 193–198.

Schulz, S. C., Koller, M. M., Kishore, P. R., Hamer, R. M., Gehl, J. J., & Friedel, R. O. (1983). Ventricular enlargement in teenage patients with schizophrenia spectrum disorder. *American Journal of Psychiatry, 140*(12), 1592–1595.

Shioe, K., Ichimiya, T., Suhara, T., Takano, A., Sudo, Y., Yasuno, F., et al. (2003). No association between genotype of the promoter region of serotonin transporter gene and serotonin transporter binding in human brain measured by PET. *Synapse, 48*(4), 184–188.

Siever, L. J., Buchsbaum, M. S., New, A. S., Spiegel-Cohen, J., Wei, T., Hazlett, E. A., et al. (1999). d,l-fenfluramine response in impulsive personality disorder assessed with [18F]fluorodeoxyglucose positron emission tomography. *Neuropsychopharmacology, 20*(5), 413–423.

Siever, L. J., & Davis, K. L. (1991). A psychobiological perspective on the personality disorders. *American Journal of Psychiatry, 148*(7), 1647–1658.

Siever, L. J., & Trestman, R. L. (1993). The serotonin system and aggressive personality disorder. *International Clinical Psychopharmacology, 8*(Suppl 2), 33–39.

Snyder, S., Pitts, W. M., Jr., & Grustin, O. (1983). CT scans of patients with borderline personality disorder. *American Journal of Psychiatry, 140*(2), 272.

Soloff, P. H., Meltzer, C. C., Becker, C., Greer, P. J., Kelly, T. M., & Constantine, D. (2003). Impulsivity and prefrontal hypometabolism in borderline personality disorder. *Psychiatry Research, 123*(3), 153–163.

Soloff, P. H., Meltzer, C. C., Greer, P. J., Constantine, D., & Kelly, T. M. (2000). A fenfluramine-activated FDG-PET study of borderline personality disorder. *Biological Psychiatry, 47*(6), 540–547.

Spoont, M. R. (1992). Modulatory role of serotonin in neural information processing: Implications for human psychopathology. *Psychological Bulletin, 112*(2), 330–350.

Staner, L., Uyanik, G., Correa, H., Tremeau, F., Monreal, J., Crocq, M. A., et al. (2002). A dimensional impulsive-aggressive phenotype is associated with the A218C polymorphism of the tryptophan hydroxylase gene: A pilot study in well-characterized impulsive inpatients. *American Journal of Medical Genetics, 114*(5), 553–557.

Tiihonen, J., Kuikka, J. T., Bergstrom, K. A., Karhu, J., Viinamaki, H., Lehtonen, J., et al. (1997). Single-photon emission tomography imaging of monoamine transporters in impulsive violent behaviour. *European Journal of Nuclear Medicine, 24*(10), 1253–1260.

Tonkonogy, J. M. (1991). Violence and temporal lobe lesion: Head CT and MRI data. *The Journal of Neuropsychiatry and Clinical Neurosciences, 3*(2), 189–196.

Tonkonogy, J. M., & Geller, J. L. (1992). Hypothalamic lesions and intermittent explosive disorder. *The Journal of Neuropsychiatry and Clinical Neurosciences, 4*(1), 45–50.

Torgersen, S. (1992). Genetics in borderline conditions. *Acta Psychiatrica Scandinavica., Supplementum* (379), 19–25.

Trull, T., Useda, D., Doan, B., Vieth, A., Burr, R., Hanks, A., et al. (1998). Two year stability of borderline personality measures. *Journal of Personal Disorders, 12*(3), 187–197.

Umekage, T., Tochigi, M., Marui, T., Kato, C., Hibino, H., Otani, T., et al. (2003). Serotonin transporter-linked promoter region polymorphism and personality traits in a Japanese population. *Neuroscience Letter, 337*(1), 13–16.

van Elst, L. T., Hesslinger, B., Thiel, T., Geiger, E., Haegele, K., Lemieux, L., et al. (2003). Frontolimbic brain abnormalities in patients with borderline personality disorder: A volumetric magnetic resonance imaging study. *Biological Psychiatry, 54*(2), 163–171.

van Elst, L. T., Thiel, T., Hesslinger, B., Lieb, K., Bohus, M., Hennig, J., et al. (2001). Subtle prefrontal neuropathology in a pilot magnetic resonance spectroscopy study in patients with borderline personality disorder. *The Journal of Neuropsychiatry and Clinical Neurosciences, 13*(4), 511–514.

Van Woerken, T. C. A. M., Teelken, A. W., & Minderhoud, J. M. (1977). Difference in neurotransmitter metabolism in fronto-temporal-lobe contusion and diffuse cerebral confusion. *Lancet, 1,* 812–813.

Volavka, J., Mohammad, Y., Vitrai, J., Connolly, M., Stefanovic, M., & Ford, M. (1995). Characteristics of state hospital patients arrested for offenses committed during hospitalization. *Psychiatric Services, 46*(8), 796–800.

Volkow, N. D., & Tancredi, L. (1987). Neural substrates of violent behaviour: A preliminary study with positron emission tomography. *British Journal of Psychiatry, 151,* 668–673.

Volkow, N. D., Tancredi, L. D., Grant, C., Gillespie, H., Valentine, A., Mullani, N., et al. (1995). Brain glucose metabolism in violent psychiatric patients: A preliminary study. *Psychiatry Research, 61*(4), 243–253.

Vollm, B., Richardson, P., Stirling, J., Elliott, R., Dolan, M., Chaudhry, I., et al. (2004). Neurobiological substrates of antisocial and borderline personality disorder: Preliminary results of a functional fMRI study. *Criminal Behaviour and Mental Health, 14*(1), 39—54.

Watson, D., & Sinha, B. (1998). Comorbidity of DSM-IV personality disorders in a nonclinical sample. *Journal of Clinical Psychology, 54*(6), 773–780.

Williams, D. (1969). Neural factors related to habitual aggression. *Brain Research, 92*(3), 503–520.

Young, S. N., Leyton, M., & Benkelfat, C. (1999). Pet studies of serotonin synthesis in the human brain. *Advances in Experimental Medicine and Biology, 467,* 11–18.

CHAPTER 4

The Interference of Sustained Adverse Childhood Experiences and the Development of Borderline Personality Disorder: A Neurobiological Perspective

THOMAS RINNE

Key Teaching Points

- Chronic traumatic stress or an accumulation of adverse childhood experiences is associated with the development of severe personality disorders, chronic depression and somatic diseases, and early death.
- About 50 to 60% of patients with a borderline personality disorder (BPD) report a history of sustained childhood abuse.
- Genetic as well as environmental factors are important component causes of BPD.
- Childhood sexual abuse is one of the most important risk factors of suicide attempts.

- Sustained childhood abuse causes a hyporesponsivity of the central serotonergic system in the traumatized borderline patients and nonborderline subject.
- Sustained childhood abuse causes a hyperresponsivity of the hypothalamic pituitary adrenal axis (HPA axis) in the traumatized borderline patient subgroup and nonborderline subject.
- The hyperresponsiveness of the HPA axis renders the victims of childhood abuse susceptible for stress and stress-related disorders.
- Selective serotonin reuptake inhibitor (SSRI) treatment normalizes the trauma-induced hyperresponsiveness of the HPA axis, and chronic SSRI treatment might be, in combination with psychotherapy, aimed at the prevention of depression.
- Chronic traumatic stress during childhood affects the integrative function of the frontolimbic system, (e.g., hippocampus amygdala and prefrontal cortex), which is also found to be compromised in BPD patients.
- The neurobiological alterations related to childhood abuse, post-traumatic stress disorder (PTSD) and BPD are likely to be distinguishable pathophysiological entities.

Introduction

Borderline personality disorder (BPD) is not a singular nosologic entity but a complex syndrome with heterogeneity concerning etiology, neuropathophysiology, symptomatology, and comorbidity. The prevalence in the general population amounts to 1.5 to 2% and BPD is diagnosed 10 to 20% among psychiatric patients (Verheul & van den Brink, 1999). The mortality in this group is high because of a suicide rate of about 10%. This rate is approximately 50 times higher than in a general population. BPD is considerably more often diagnosed in women than in men, with gender differences in the clinical presentation (Johnson et al., 2003; Zlotnick, Rothschild, & Zimmerman, 2002). Chronic traumatic stress or an accumulation of adverse childhood experiences (ACE) is strongly associated with the development of severe personality disorders, chronic depression, and to a lesser extent, post-traumatic stress disorder (PTSD) in adulthood (Felitti et al., 1998). This finding is consistent with the high prevalence of ACE in borderline patients and the high comorbidity of BPD with depression and PTSD (Zanarini et al., 1998; Yen et al., 2002).

Moreover, preclinical stress studies and neurobiological research with humans with chronic childhood abuse experiences provide convincing evidence that chronic (traumatic) stress has a tremendous impact on brain development with a broad variety of persistent functional alterations. This concerns, for example, dysfunction of the central serotonergic system or a hyperreactivity of the hypothalamic pituitary adrenal (HPA) axis. Although not in all, but probably in a major part of the borderline patients, these trauma-related neurobiological alterations due to the exposure to adverse childhood experiences play a crucial role in the development of personality pathology and other severe *psycho*pathology. However, it is still not elucidated whether certain alterations have to be attributed to BPD pathology, or to the consequences of trauma, or to gender differences, and how these factors are interrelated. Up to now, especially neurobiological research on BPD issues is conceptually fragmented, because these various aspects are insufficiently taken into account.

In this chapter, we summarize the literature regarding the relationship between sustained ACE and BPD, and we present an integrated neurobiological perspective on the causal role in the development of BPD of changes in the HPA axis and the serotonergic system due to sustained adverse childhood experiences.

Etiological Aspects

A considerable proportion of BPD patients (25 to 75%) report a history of sustained adverse childhood experiences like emotional neglect, sustained physical and/or sexual abuse, or domestic violence (Herman, Perry, & van der Kolk, 1989; Ogata, Silk, Goodrich, Lohr, Westen, & Hill, 1990; Salzman et al., 1993). In addition, BPD patients report significantly more severe traumas before the age of six than non-BPD patients (53% vs. 13%) (Perry & Herman, 1993). Some authors and many clinicians even consider BPD to be a chronic PTSD (Herman et al., 1989). However, not all BPD patients are victims of sustained childhood abuse, and many chronically abused persons do not develop BPD. Childhood abuse or neglect is neither a necessary nor a sufficient condition for the development of BPD. However, chronic childhood traumatization seems to be an important component cause of BPD.

Genetic vulnerability is another important component cause. Behavioral genetic twin studies clearly show that personality pathology is partially determined by genetic factors (Livesley, Jang, Jackson, & Vernon, 1993; Livesley, Jang, & Vernon, 1998). Torgersen found that 69% of the variance of BPD was explained by heritable factors (Torgersen, Kringlen, & Cramer, 2001). Moreover, behavioral genetics revealed an intensive and mutual interaction between genetic and environmental factors, resulting in a modification of the phenotypic expression of the genetic predisposition. Not one but multiple genes, or so-called additional genetic factors, account for the heritable facets of personality pathology. The interaction between specific genes of the multiple genes set can amplify or mitigate the expression of a specific trait. The interaction of genes with environmental factors can exert the same effect. For example, a specific polymorphism of the gene encoding for the neurotransmitter-metabolizing enzyme monoamine oxidase A (MAO-A), which is related to violent behavior in men, is only switched on in the presence of mal-treatment. An abused boy who is a carrier of this polymorphism has a chance of 85% to develop some form of violent antisocial behavior. In contrast, abused boys who are not carriers as well as not abused boys who are carriers, are at a relatively low risk (20 to 30%) to develop aggressive behavior (Caspi et al., 2002).

Abuse, neglect and environmental instability, parental psychopathology, and lower scores on protective factors are reliable predictors of the development of BPD in persons constitutionally predisposed for the disorder (Helgeland & Torgersen, 2004). This finding points at the more complex interaction between heritable vulnerability factors and untoward environment. Children of parents with psychopathology who also create an insecure environment by their unpredictable behavior are doubly exposed to the pathogenic influence of the genetic factors. This works through the inherited genes and the insecure environment, which is the resultant of the genetic makeup of the parents and their experiences during childhood. These children on their part react in a genetically determined way to this environment, for example, with anxious defensive behavior or impulsive offensive behavior. Both behaviors elicit specific counterreactions. In pathogenic interactions, certain traits will come to an aggravated expression leading to predisposed maladaptive behavior or psychopathology.

It is evident that abused children who are growing up under insecure and unpredictable circumstances suffer from high levels of chronic stress. This exposure to chronic stress during childhood has a strong influence on gene expression and (subsequently) on brain development. Persistent alterations of brain morphology, altered function of neurotransmitter and neuroendocrine systems, and behavior that is related to these alterations, are reported as sequelae of traumatic stress in animal models (Peters, 1986, 1987, 1990; De Kloet, 1995; van Oers, De Kloet, & Levine, 1998; Graham, Heim, Goodman, Miller, & Nemeroff, 1999). Similar effects can be expected from sustained adverse childhood experiences and related chronic stress in genetically vulnerable humans resulting in a serious risk of developing personality pathology including BPD.

ACE, BPD Symptomatology, and Comorbidity

There is an overwhelming epidemiological evidence that sustained ACE and chronic traumatic stress are highly associated with the development of (a) severe personality disorders, (b) other psychiatric disorders such as chronic depression, anxiety disorders, bipolar disorder, and eating disorders, (c) self-destructive behaviors like heavy smoking, alcohol and drug abuse and dependence, and extreme promiscuity, (d) parasuicidal behavior and suicide attempts, and (e) serious somatic diseases (Bohn, 2003; Forman, Berk, Henriques, Brown, & Beck, 2004; Gladstone, Parker, Mitchell, Malhi, Wilhelm, & Austin, 2004; Langeland, Draijer, & van den Brink, 2004; Felitti et al., 1998; Teusch, 2001; Molinari, 2001). Most of these consequences occur independently of the presence of BPD. However, many of the BPD patients with a history of ACE also suffer from other psychiatric disorders, destructive behaviors, and physical ailments. The severity of childhood adverse experiences is strongly associated with the presence of a BPD diagnosis, BPD symptom severity, social dysfunction, and the comorbidity of major psychiatric disorders in BPD patients. Especially, sexual childhood abuse accounts for more severe symptomatology in BPD samples (Bierer et al., 2003; Zanarini et al., 2002).

BPD pathology can be characterized from a more biological point of view, as (a) a disturbance of emotion regulation: dysregulation of the affect with frequent mood shifts to depression, anxiety, dysphoria, and feelings of emptiness, (b) a disturbance of the impulse and aggression regulation with irritability, outward and inward directed aggression, and (c) a disturbance with perceptual impairments during stress. These dysfunctional regulatory mechanisms are affecting general functioning and result in severe psychological, relational, and social impairment and distress. Rapid mood shifts, irritability, impulsive, aggressive, and parasuicidal behavior and suicide attempts are reported to be highly associated with a history of childhood neglect and abuse as an etiologic factor, on the one hand, and a dysfunction of the serotonergic system and frontolimbic network as a neurobiological basis on the other hand (Landecker, 1992; Silk, Lee, Hill, & Lohr, 1995; Coccaro, Siever, Klar, & Maurer, 1989; Landecker, 1992; Asberg, Thoren, Traskman, Bertilsson, & Ringberger, 1975; Hansenne et al., 2002; Forman et al., 2004).

Comorbidity with other major psychiatric disorders constitutes an additional complicating factor in BPD patients because it can interfere with and aggravate BPD core symptomatology. Most BPD patients also suffer from at least one comorbid Axis I disorder. Lifetime prevalences in BPD patients for a mood disorder are about 95% for a depressive episode, about 80% for any anxiety disorder, about 90% for PTSD, 55% for substance abuse, and

50% for eating disorders (Zanarini et al., 1998; Skodol, Gunderson, Pfohl, Widiger, Livesley, & Siever, 2002; Zlotnick, Franklin, & Zimmerman, 2002). These trauma-related comorbid disorders are associated with disturbances of the central serotonergic system and/or HPA axis.

A very interesting, not negligible discovery is the strong and highly significant correlation between the number of adverse childhood experiences and various somatic disorders like morbid obesity, diabetes mellitus, hyperlipidemia, hypertension, coronary heart disease, chronic obstructive pulmonary disease, bone fractures, and sexually transmitted diseases. These somatic diseases in combination with the self-destructive behavior (*vide supra*) make the exposure to adverse childhood experiences a very relevant health risk factor, which contributes to significantly earlier death in the ACE group (Felitti et al., 1998; Hillis, Anda, Felitti, & Marchbanks, 2001; Edwards, Holden, Felitti, & Anda, 2003).

Severe childhood abuse appears to be the most important risk factor for suicide attempts. Female patients with a history of sexual abuse have a four to five times increased risk to become chronically depressed compared to female controls without such experiences. A severely abused woman has a 35 times increased risk to commit a suicide attempt (Dube, Anda, Felitti, Chapman, Williamson, & Giles, 2001). Depressed patients with a childhood abuse history appear to have, besides an increased risk for suicide attempts, a significantly higher level of impulsive aggression. This suggests that childhood abuse may constitute an environmental risk factor for the development of trait impulsivity and aggression, probably superimposed on an inherited predisposition for impulsive and aggressive behavior (Brodsky, Oquendo, Ellis, Haas, Malone, & Mann, 2001). In this context, it is important to mention that the co-occurrence of depression and PTSD also increases the risk of serious suicide attempts and impulsive aggressive behavior (Yehuda, 1999; Oquendo & Mann, 2000). Finally, in borderline patients the prediction of suicidal behavior and suicide attempts (i.e., attempts with the intent to die) should be distinguished (Yen et al., 2004). The BPD criteria *affective instability, identity disturbance,* and *impulsivity* significantly predicted impulsive suicidal behavior. However, suicide attempts were associated only with the BPD criterion affective instability and with childhood sexual abuse. In this study, major depression was not found to predict suicidality. In a study with sexually abused BPD patients, the odds for this group to attempt suicide during adulthood were over 10 times increased compared to the not sexually abused BPD patients (Soloff, Lynch, & Kelly, 2002). Given a history of childhood sexual abuse, the risk of adult suicidal behavior in BPD was increased by antisocial traits, severity of BPD pathology, hopelessness, or comorbid major depressive episode.

In summary, it seems that sustained childhood abuse and accumulating adverse childhood experiences account for a broad range of symptoms, trauma-related disorders, and severe personality disorders. Moreover, many of these disorders are often present in an accumulative way in BPD subjects with a history of chronic and multiple traumatic experiences. We would like to repeat, however, that many patients with BPD do not report a history of childhood abuse, and phenotypically these patients cannot be distinguished from BPD patients with a history of childhood abuse in terms of *Diagnostic and Statistical Manual of Mental Disorders* (DSM-IV) criteria. It therefore seems that different combinations of component causes can lead to BPD or that the diagnostic criteria are too coarse to differentiate between the two groups.

Neurobiology of Stress

Traumatic stress is an etiological risk factor which can exert pathogenic influence on several brain systems depending on the developmental stage of the victim and the exposure to a single traumatic event (Type I trauma) or to chronic traumatic experiences (Type II trauma) and the severity of the traumatic experience (Terr, 1991). Chronic traumatic experiences are likely to have more and a different impact than a single traumatic experience on brain physiology and manifestation of trauma-related disorders. For example, both a single traumatic event and chronic traumatic stress cause PTSD in 10 to 25% of the victims, but early-sustained traumatic stress has more devastating effects on more brain systems with, as a consequence, high rates of depression and maladaptive and self-destructive behavior (Felitti et al., 1998). It is a misconception to think that PTSD is equal to chronic traumatization. The pathophysiological effects related to PTSD and to early and sustained stress can be differentiated. For a better understanding of the trauma-related aspects of BPD symptomatology, the effects of chronic traumatization on frontolimbic stress pathways and on the modulating function of the HPA axis and the central serotonergic system will be discussed in more detail.

The frontolimbic stress pathways include the prefrontal cortex (PFC), hippocampus, amygdala, paraventricular nucleus (PVN) of the hypothalamus, and, in extension, the pituitary and adrenal gland of the HPA axis. The prefrontal cortex is phylogenetically the youngest part of the brain. It is primarily engaged in learning processes concerning complex emotional experiences, which results in the development of cognitive concepts with regard to these emotions. The PFC integrates information of the outer and inner world of the subject. This integrative process is unique in humans and enables them to construct a notion of personal identity and continuity, which, for its part, creates the possibility to make plans for the future in reference to the needs of oneself or others. Moreover, the PFC has an important role in the regulation of stress responses and exerts an inhibitory influence on the amygdala, as mentioned shortly. The limbic system is the center of basal human emotional life. The hippocampus, together with the amygdala, orbitofrontal cortex, and anterior cingulate, plays an important role in information processing and the development of emotional and declarative memories. The hippocampus is crucial in the formation of *declarative memory* which contains conscious representations of facts and experiences and their spatial and temporal context. Hippocampal learning and memory consolidation is mediated by 5-HT1A receptors, glucocorticoid receptors (GR), and mineralocorticoid receptors (MR). The GR and MR also have an important role in the regulation of the HPA axis function with respect to its threshold and excitability. The MR, in close synergism with the GR, exert a tonic inhibitory tone on the hypothalamic PVN. Disturbances of the delicate synergistic equilibrium of these two receptor types affect circadian rhythmicity and the reactivity of the HPA axis to stress stimuli (De Kloet, Vreugdenhil, Oitzl, & Joels, 1998). The amygdala is considered to be the center of the emotional memory and of aggressive and defensive behavior. Many afferent pathways with visual, acoustic, and sensorial information reach the amygdala for an immediate and unconscious screening of emotional relevance of the information.

Hippocampus and amygdala are closely connected with the locus ceruleus (LC), the center of the noradrenergic system in the brainstem. In case of danger, the amygdala can activate the LC for an immediate arousal to get the subject ready to fight or flight. The activation of the noradrenergic system leads to enhanced attention and vegetative signs like increased blood pressure, heart rate, temperature, breathing frequency, and decreased intestinal blood flow. The cognitive processing of the situation by the prefrontal cortex can mitigate the activation of the amygdala. The limbic system in general, and especially the amygdala, are very sensitive to kindling. Kindling is a process of increasing behavioral or convulsive reactions to the repetition of a stimulus over a longer period. On the electrophysiological level, it is a matter of a decreasing excitation threshold. Kindling mechanisms are able to alter neuronal excitability for a long period, or even permanently.

In case of a threatening stressor, acetylcholinergic afferents from the hippocampus, noradrenergic projections from the LC, and serotonergic axonal projection from the brainstem raphe nuclei activate the neuroendocrine stress response in the hypothalamic PVN, and corticotrophin-releasing hormone (CRH) is released. CRH is the main activator of the HPA axis and causes the release of the adrenocorticotropin hormone (ACTH) in the pituitary, which stimulates the exertion of cortisol into the blood. Cortisol is the main stress hormone. It activates energy for the flight or fight reaction by lipolysis, gluconeogenesis, proteolysis, and insulin resistance, and it terminates the stress response when necessary by a negative feedback inhibition on the HPA axis. Cortisol binds to the GR on the pituitary and hypothalamic PVN and breaks the release of ACTH and CRH, respectively.

The central serotonin (5-HT) system is phylogenetically the oldest neurotransmitter system. The cell bodies are located in the raphe nuclei in the brainstem and they have abundant projections to the neocortex, cingulate gyrus, prefrontal cortex, hippocampus, amygdale, hypothalamus, striatum and cerebellum. Serotonin is an important modulator of the stress response, the affect, anxiety, impulsiveness, and aggression, and it plays a crucial role in learning processes. Functional alterations of the central 5-HT system, like blunted responses to neuroendocrine challenge tests, or increased or decreased 5-HT receptor systems, are found in anxiety disorders, depression, suicidality, and impulsive aggression.

Neurobiology of BPD

ACE, HPA Axis, and BPD

In rodents, high circulating corticosterone levels due to chronic unpredictable stress cause a significant reduction of hippocampal 5-HT1A receptors mRNA expression, as well as reduction of their binding capacity (Meijer & De Kloet, 1998). Moreover, related to the alteration of the 5-HT receptors, the very delicate functional equilibrium of the mineralocorticoid receptors (MR) and glucocorticoid receptors (GR) is disturbed (Lopez, Chalmers, Little, & Watson, 1998). This functional equilibrium of the GR and MR is crucial for the downstream regulation of HPA axis functioning. Human suicide victims with a history of depression exhibit similar functional alterations in their hippocampi and a strong induction of arginine vasopressin (AVP) expression in the hypothalamic PVN (van Oers et al., 1998; Hatalski, Guirguis, & Baram, 1998; Sutanto, Rosenfeld, De Kloet, & Levine, 1995; Plotsky & Meaney, 1993; Coplan et al., 1996; De Goeij, Jezova, & Tilders, 1992).

AVP is a very potent coregulator of CRH, which potentiates the effects of CRH on the pituitary ACTH release by a factor of six. Studies of early, chronic stress in animal models also reveal an increased CRH expression and a strongly increased AVP expression in the hypothalamic PVN. The increased CRH release is regarded to be the main pathophysiological cause for the development of major depression (Nemeroff, 1996; Heuser et al., 1998; Raadsheer, Hoogendijk, Stam, Tilders, & Swaab, 1994). This suggests that an increased hypothalamic CRH/AVP drive might be the interface between ACE and depression in genetically vulnerable persons. This view is consistent with finding that depressed boys who still live under adverse circumstances exhibit an increased CRH activity compared to traumatized boys who are recovered from depression after treatment and now live under improved conditions (Kaufman et al., 1997).

Major depressive disorder is a frequently comorbid condition in BPD. It is associated with distinct alterations of the HPA axis, resulting in a hyperfunction characterized by an increased hypothalamic CRH/AVP drive and a decreased negative feedback inhibition of the pituitary GR leading to hypercortisolism and an early escape in the dexamethasone suppression test (DST). In contrast, PTSD is associated with the alterations characterized by markedly low circulating cortisol plasma levels because of an increased cortisol sensitivity of the pituitary GR and therefore also a hypersuppression of cortisol to a low-dose DST.

Net HPA axis (ACTH and cortisol) output is determined by two crucial physiological mechanisms: (1) the hypothalamic CRH/AVP drive as main "accelerator" of the stress response system, and (2) the negative glucocorticoid feedback on the pituitary as the main "break" of the stress response system. In general terms, PTSD is associated with low cortisol levels.

Studies of HPA axis function in chronically traumatized borderline patients therefore have to take into account the complexity of neuroendocrine alterations that may be due to four factors: (1) BPD pathology itself, (2) sustained traumatic stress during childhood, (3) comorbid depression and/or PTSD, and (4) mutual neuroendocrine interactions of these factors.

The study of HPA axis function in BPD patients was started with the DST test in the 1980s. Since those times, about 15 DST studies have been published with rather inconsistent results, probably due to differences in design and various methodological shortcomings. A number of studies report increased cortisol concentrations after DST in BPD patients compared to healthy subjects, but these findings are not controlled for the potential neuroendocrine effects of ACE, depression, or PTSD (Lieb et al., 2004; Krishnan, Davidson, Rayasam, & Shope, 1984; Baxter, Edell, Gerner, Fairbanks, & Gwirtsman, 1984). In some other studies, the DST was used to compare patients with BPD and patients with major depressive disorder. Again the results were very inconsistent. Korzekwa concludes that the DST, because of its low sensitivity and specificity for depression in BPD, is not a useful probe in this population (Korzekwa, Links, & Steiner, 1993;

Baxter et al., 1984; Beeber, Kline, Pies, & Manring, 1984; De la Fuente, Bobes, Vizuete, & Mendlewicz, 2002; Soloff, George, & Nathan, 1982).

Grossman conducted a methodologically sound, low-dose (0.5 mg) DST study in 52 personality disorder patients to detect PTSD-related increased cortisol suppression in this group. He concluded that a high level of cortisol suppression was associated with PTSD in subjects with personality disorder. This finding is similar to published findings for PTSD subjects without a personality disorder. Major depression, gender, age when trauma(s) occurred, and a diagnosis of borderline personality disorder did not have significant main or interaction effects on cortisol suppression (Grossman et al., 2003). Unfortunately, chronic childhood abuse as an independent factor was not included in the analysis of covariance. This omission was resolved in a study by Newport among childhood abused female patients with and without depression. PTSD was *post hoc* taken into account (Newport, Heim, Bonsall, Miller, & Nemeroff, 2004). In the low-dose DST, the abused women who also suffered from PTSD exhibited stronger cortisol suppression than any comparator group, and stronger ACTH suppression than healthy volunteers or nondepressed abuse survivors. Importantly, no differences between nondepressed abused women and healthy volunteers were found. The PTSD analysis produced similar results. Taken together, this means that cortisol super-suppression, due to an increased glucocorticoid inhibition, in victims of childhood abuse is associated with the manifestation of PTSD. Therefore, low cortisol levels are not an invariable consequence of childhood trauma; they are related to a superposed PTSD diagnosis in early traumatized individuals (Newport et al., 2004).

These DST results provide information about GR function on the pituitary level, but given the animal data, sustained childhood abuse is expected also to increase hypothalamic activity, reflected by increased CRH and probably AVP activity. To test this hypothesis, we performed a combined Dexamethasone /Corticotrophin Releasing Hormone test (DEX/CRH) in 25 BPD patients with a history of sustained childhood abuse, 14 not abused BPD patients, and 11 healthy controls. The DEX/CRH test is very sensitive to subtle dysregulations of the HPA axis and also provides information on the activity of the CRH/AVP drive on the hypothalamic level (Heuser, Yassouridis, & Holsboer, 1994; Holsboer & Barden, 1996).

On baseline level and after the application of a high dose (1.5 mg) of dexamethasone (DST), no differences in ACTH and cortisol suppression between the chronically abused, the mildly or not abused BPD subjects, and healthy controls could be detected. However, a significant differential effect occurred between all patients suffering from PTSD with or without an additional comorbid depression. All BPD patients with comorbid PTSD showed maximal suppression of ACTH and cortisol independent of a comorbid depression. The depressed BPD patients without comorbid PTSD exhibited a markedly decreased suppression of these hormones, with significantly higher ACTH and cortisol plasma levels (Rinne, De Kloet, Wouters, Goekoop, DeRijk, & Van den Brink, 2002). This finding is in line with the data of Newport. PTSD in adult childhood-abused subjects appears to have two effects: (1) it accounts fully for the increased negative glucocorticoid feedback inhibition, and (2) it overrides the neuroendocrine effects of a comorbid depression (Yehuda, Southwick, Krystal, Bremner, Charney, & Mason, 1993; Halbreich et al., 1989). After CRH administration (completing the DEX/CRH test), the chronically abused group turned out to be hyperresponsive as reflected by a strong and statistically highly significant increase in ACTH and cortisol plasma levels compared to the mildly or not abused BPD patients and healthy controls (Rinne, DeKloet, Wouters, Goekoop, de Rijk, & van den Brink, 2003). The hyperresponsivity of the HPA axis in the chronically abused borderline patients is due to an enhanced AVP/CRH drive on the hypothalamic level (Holsboer & Barden, 1996).

Analysis of covariance revealed that, in this BPD patient population, sustained childhood abuse was the sole factor that fully accounts for the HPA axis hyperresponsiveness, whereas concurrent depression, PTSD, and BPD pathology are irrelevant. It should be noted, however, that concurrent PTSD mitigates the ACTH and cortisol responses to the DEX/CRH test, due to the increased negative feedback inhibition in the PTSD subjects. Possible effects of comorbid depression could not be detected because of a considerable overlap with concurrent PTSD, which masks the neuroendocrine effects of depression (Rinne et al., 2002). Our findings are in line with the animal models mentioned earlier. Moreover, our results also corroborate the data from a psychological stress challenge study performed by Heim (Heim et al., 2000; Heim, Newport, Bonsall, Miller, & Nemeroff, 2001). She reported severely and significantly increased ACTH and cortisol responses in adult female victims of chronic childhood abuse with and without depression compared to female non-abused patients with depression and healthy controls (Heim et al., 2000; Heim et al., 2001).

These two studies demonstrate that early and sustained adverse experiences modify HPA axis function to a permanent hyperresponsiveness, resulting in a strongly increased hormone output already at small stress stimuli. Moreover, this HPA axis hyperresponsiveness appears to be an independent pathophysiological sequela of childhood abuse experiences, that is, independent of the manifestations of psychiatric syndromes like depression and PTSD (including BPD) (Heim et al., 2002). This implies that HPA axis hyperresponsiveness can be estimated as a biomarker of chronic childhood abuse but not of BPD.

ACE, Serotonin, and BPD

Since the 1980s, the serotonin hypothesis in relation to impulsive aggression and suicidal behavior has become very popular. BPD patients were supposed to have a serotonergic dysfunction because one of the main features of this disorder is impulsivity. The first papers on this issue reported an association between these behaviors and disturbed functions of the central 5-HT system indicated by low 5-hydroxyindoleacetic acid (5-HIAA) levels in the lumbar CSF and blunted neuroendocrine responses to fenfluramine (Traskman, Asberg, Nordstrom, & Stanley, 1989; Asberg & Traskman, 1981; Brown et al., 1982; Coccaro et al., 1989). These observations were done in Caucasian male populations, and the results of serotonergic challenge studies in female samples are very contradictory. Most neuroendocrine challenge studies with female subjects failed to replicate the association between a disturbed serotonergic system and impulsive aggressive behavior with two exceptions. Herpertz reported a blunted prolactin response to a fenfluramine challenge in six female BPD subjects with self-harming behavior, which is supposed to be an expression of impulsive aggressive behavior (Herpertz, Steinmeyer, Marx, Oidtmann, & Sass, 1995). And, very recently, Paris found a blunted prolactin response to a meta-chlorophenylpiperazine (m-CPP) challenge test in subjects with a high score on the Barret Impulsivity Scale (Paris, Zweig-Frank, Kin, Schwartz, Steiger, & Nair, 2004). This study was performed in a sample of 30 female BPD patients and 22 healthy controls. To elucidate gender-specific effects on the relation of serotonergic dysfunction and impulsive aggressive behavior, studies with both genders and sufficient power have to be performed. Soloff recently did this. He studied the relation of serotonergic function with impulsive aggressive behavior in a large BPD sample with 20 male and 44 female patients and 36 male and 21 female healthy controls. Male, but not female, BPD subjects had significantly diminished prolactin responses compared to controls. Impulsivity and aggression were inversely related to delta-prolactin and peak-prolactin responses among male but not female subjects (Soloff, Kelly, Strotmeyer, Malone, & Mann, 2003). A similar gender-specific finding in a study with the serotonergic agonist (m-CPP) in a mixed BPD sample was reported at the annual meeting of the Society of Biological Psychiatry in 2003 (New, Hazlett, Buchsbaum, Goodman, Koenigsberg, & Iskander, 2003).

A more variegated picture on this issue is provided by Leyton. The authors measured brain regional alpha-[11C]methyl-L-tryptophan (alpha-[11C]MTrp), a direct indicator of serotonin synthesis in the brain, with PET in a gender-mixed sample with BPD (N = 13) and a healthy comparison group (N = 11). Impulsiveness was evaluated by a laboratory measure of behavioral disinhibition (go/no-go commission errors) and self-reported impulsivity. In the women with borderline personality disorder, significantly lower alpha-[11C]MTrp trapping was seen and in fewer regions than in men, but in both men and women, negative correlations with impulsivity scores were identified in the medial frontal gyrus, anterior cingulate gyrus, temporal gyrus, and the striatum (Leyton et al., 2001).

The serotonergic function in BPD is not only studied with regard to impulsive aggression and suicidality, but also in relation to chronic childhood abuse. The first study, which demonstrated that sustained childhood abuse leaves persistent alterations of the central serotonergic system, was performed in a sample with seven chronically and five not abused female BPD patients and nine healthy controls also using the m-CPP paradigm. The cortisol and prolactin responses to the m-CPP challenge in BPD patients were significantly lower compared to those in controls. Within the group of patients with BPD, the net prolactin response showed a very high and inverse correlation with the frequency of the physical (r = −0.77) and sexual abuse (r = −0.60), whereas impulsivity and autoaggressive behavior failed to correlate with the blunted prolactin response. A limitation of this study was the lack of an abused non-BPD control group (Rinne, Westenberg, Den Boer, & van den Brink, 2000). These results were replicated in a sample of 35 bulimic and 25 nonbulimic women with and without childhood physical and sexual abuse. Measures of peak change on prolactin levels after m-CPP administration indicated blunted response in abused bulimic women, nonabused bulimic women, and abused women who were normal eaters compared to nonabused women who were normal eaters (Steiger et al., 2001). This study by Steiger extended the finding of the former study because it demonstrated that chronic childhood abuse accounts for severe disturbances of the central 5-HT system also in non-borderline samples, and that it is more likely to be a trauma-related than a BPD-related trait. Moreover, these findings corroborate data obtained from serotonergic studies in animals, which were exposed to chronic stress in early life (Peters, 1987).

The other focus of serotonergic studies is suicidality. Hansenne investigated 5-HT1A receptor function in patients with BPD and depressed patients with the 5-HT1A receptor agonist fesinoxan (Hansenne et al.,

2002). Prolactin response to fesinoxan challenge was blunted in the BPD patients in contrast to the depressed and healthy subjects. Moreover, prolactin response in the BPD patients appeared to be lower in those patients who had a recent suicide attempt. Mann reported a blunted prolactin response in young depressed patients who attempted a suicide compared to older depressed patients and healthy controls. Earlier onset of depression, a greater degree of suicide intention at the recent suicide attempt, a higher degree of hopelessness, and higher rate of BPD diagnosis characterized the young patients. These findings are in line with an article of van Heeringen, who reported a significantly lower 5-HT2A receptor binding potential in the prefrontal cortex of suicide victims, which was correlated with a high level of hopelessness (van Heeringen et al., 2003). Other postmortem studies in suicide victims also indicate an increased 5-HT2A receptor mRNA expression in the prefrontal cortex, whereas the 5-HT binding capacity is likely to be reduced (Pandey et al., 2002). Oquendo elucidated with a PET study that serotonergic hyporesponsiveness to fenfluramine challenge in the ventral, medial, and lateral PFC is correlated with lower lifetime impulsiveness and higher suicidal intent planning (Oquendo et al., 2003).

Taken together, childhood abuse is likely to induce impulsive aggressive behavior and increase the risk for suicide attempts. In addition, it disturbs central serotonergic function. Moreover, serotonergic disturbances are found to be related to impulsive aggressive behavior and suicidality. Gender-specific factors are likely to modify the association between serotonergic disturbances and impulsive aggressive behavior. Future research on these subjects has to address the complex interrelationships of childhood abuse as an etiological risk factor, serotonergic disturbances as probable neurobiological interface, and impulsive, aggressive, and suicidal behavior as the phenomenological expression in gender mix samples.

Neuroanatomical and Functional Imaging Studies

Neuroimaging studies in patients with BPD and victims of childhood abuse are at the very beginning, and the interpretation of results is difficult because of methodological limitations, the use of different techniques, and variables. Structural and functional neuroimaging in BPD patients has revealed disturbances of the frontolimbic network. However, it is not evident whether the findings have to be attributed to BPD pathology, to the effects of childhood trauma, or to comorbid PTSD.

Prefrontal cortex (PFC) functioning was investigated by Soloff in a PET paradigm. He found a hypometabolism, reflected by a decreased glucose uptake, in the medial and orbital prefrontal cortex of BPD patients in relation to healthy controls, and hypothesizes that it might be associated with a diminished regulation of impulsive behavior (Soloff, Meltzer, et al., 2003). New demonstrated that selective serotonin reuptake inhibitor (SSRI) treatment is likely to improve the hypometabolism in the orbitofrontal cortex of male patients with impulsive personality disorders (New et al., 2004). However, childhood abuse is not considered a confounder in either of the studies.

In a PET study, Schmahl revealed that the recall of traumatic memories in BPD patients exposed to childhood abuse is associated with functional disturbance of the dorsolateral and medial PFC (Schmahl, Vermetten, Elzinga, & Bremner, 2004). Driessen performed a comparable study with BPD patients who were exposed to traumatic childhood experiences. He showed that the evocation of traumatic memories lead to an activation of the orbitofrontal cortex in both hemispheres in patients with the BPD without PTSD. In contrast, BPD patients with comorbid PTSD exhibited a clearly distinct lateralized activation in favor of the right hemisphere of the anterior temporal lobes, mesiotemporal areas, amygdala, and posterior cingulate gyrus (Driessen et al., 2004). This finding demonstrates that PTSD as a distinct nosologic entity with specific neurobiological alterations can be segregated from the neurobiological sequelae of chronic childhood abuse.

In a volumetric study with BPD subjects, Tebartz von Eltz found significant reduction of the left orbitofrontal cortex (24%) and a reduction of the right anterior cingulate cortex (26%) in patients with a borderline personality disorder. Left orbitofrontal volumes correlated significantly with decreased amygdala volumes (Tebartz von Eltz et al., 2003). Unfortunately, these results were also not controlled for the effects of childhood abuse and PTSD.

Hippocampus volume reduction in PTSD and depression is extensively discussed in literature (Lloyd, Ferrier, Barber, Gholkar, Young, & O'Brien, 2004; Carroll, 2004; Vythilingam et al., 2002; Bremner, 2002; Vythilingam et al., 2004). Hippocampus atrophy is also observed in BPD subjects (Schmahl, Vermetten, Elzinga, & Douglas, 2003). Moreover, the exposure to chronic childhood abuse appears also to affect the hippocampus volume (Bremner, 2003). Two independent functional nuclear magnetic resonance imaging (fNMRI) studies corroborated the association between childhood trauma and the severity of hippocampal atrophy in BPD patients (Driessen et al., 2000; Brambilla, Soloff, Sala, Nicoletti, Keshaven, & Soares, 2004).

Amygdala volumes in BPD patients were also the subject of magnetic resonance imaging (MRI) investigations. Two studies report smaller amygdala volumes in BPD patients (Schmahl et al., 2003; Driessen et al.,

2000). However, Brambilla did not succeed in replicating this finding (Brambilla et al., 2004).

In BPD patients, two studies revealed enhanced amygdala activation in an fMRI paradigm. Herpertz exposed female BPD patients to negative emotional slides which induced an intense activation pattern of the amygdale on both sides. This hyperresponsiveness is considered to be a neurobiological fear reaction with increased arousal in the subjects with high trait anxiety. Moreover, an additional activation of the medial and inferolateral PFC was observed. These cortical regions are directly connected with the amygdala and thought to modulate or inhibit amygdala-driven emotional responses. This finding emphasizes the sensi-tivity of BPD subjects to emotional aspects of the environment, but proba-bly also to thoughts and memories originating from the hippocampus (Herpertz et al., 2001).

In another study, left amygdala hyperactivity was observed in BPD subjects in reaction to the facial expression of emotions and in particular to neutral faces, which were perceived as frightening and difficult to dissemble (Donegan et al., 2003). Again, a history of childhood abuse was not considered as a confounding factor in either of the two cited studies.

Emotional deprivation, by separating young non-human primates in an early stage of development from their mother, interferes with the develop-ment of the amygdala (Dimond, 1985). The emotion-deprived animals turn out to have smaller amygdalas, exhibited disturbed social behavior, and a stressor provoked exaggerated anxiety and distress in these animals. This raises the question of whether the exposure to sustained ACE might be responsible for the observed smaller volumes and hyperactivity of the amygdale in BPD patients.

Neuroimaging studies revealed functional and anatomical alterations in BPD patients and comparable alterations in BPD and non-BPD patients with a history of sustained ACE. At this point, it is not evident whether the reported alterations are due to the sequelae of sustained ACE or to BPD pathology. In the future, methodologically more sound research needs to elucidate this lack of clarity.

SSRI Treatment of BPD and HPA Axis Hyperresponsiveness

Antidepressants have been shown to normalize HPA axis function in depressed patients (Barden, Reul, & Holsboer, 1995). It was unknown whether SSRI treatment can regulate probable HPA axis alterations in BPD patients. Moreover, the American Psychiatric Association recommends SSRI treatment for BPD patients with affect lability, impulsivity, and aggressiveness. This recommendation is based on at least 10 small open

SSRI studies and 2 double-blind studies with controversial results (Norden, 1989; Cornelius, Soloff, Perel, & Ulrich, 1990; Markovitz, Calabrese, Schulz, & Meltzer, 1991; Salzman et al., 1995; Coccaro, Astill, Herbert, & Schut, 1990; Coccaro & Kavoussi, 1997). Following these recommendations, we investigated the effect of fluvoxamine on borderline symptoms of rapid mood shifts, impulsivity, and anger in a double-blind, placebo-controlled, randomized clinical trial (RCT) with 38 female BPD subjects. To test the effects of fluvoxamine on HPA axis function, the DEX/CRH test was performed before and after the RCT of 6 weeks. PTSD, major depressive disorder (MDD), and sustained childhood abuse were taken into account as covariates.

In contrast to the previous controversial findings, we only found a statistically significant improvement of rapid mood shifts in the fluvoxamine group compared to the placebo group. Impulsivity and anger failed to show a differential effect between either of the two groups (Rinne et al., 2002). The RCT was performed in an exclusively female BPD sample, which may have influenced the negative result with respect to impulsive and aggressive behavior. Moreover, the results turned out to be independent from PTSD, MDD, and sustained childhood abuse. However, the chronically abused subgroup fully accounted for by the significantly reduced ACTH and cortisol response to the DEX/CRH test after SSRI treatment. This finding implicates a suppressive ability of SSRIs on the trauma-related hyperresponsiveness of the HPA axis. The failure to detect a correlation between the improvement of rapid mood shifts and a history of sustained childhood abuse might be due to a large placebo response in the whole BPD sample, and not due to the sufficient statistical power of the subgroups. The regulating effect on HPA axis function persists only during continuation of the SSRI treatment, and HPA axis hyperresponsiveness recovers after termination of the SSRI treatment. This finding emphasizes the conclusion that the exposure to chronic traumatic stress during childhood can change the set point of HPA axis sensitivity to stress for the rest of life (Rinne et al., 2003). Our pharmacological findings are in line with recently published animal data that indicate that antidepressant treatment reduces HPA axis hyperresponsivity in early chronically stressed rats (Stout, Owens, & Nemeroff, 2002).

Discussion

BPD is a complex and heterogeneous diagnostic category, including a number of subtypes related to specific etiological and pathogenic mechanisms. Sustained ACE are reported in a large proportion (25 to 75%) of patients with BPD and in similarly large proportions of patients with disorders frequently co-occurring with BPD, such as major depression, PTSD, and in patients with symptoms such as suicidality, impulsivity, and self-mutilation. In this chapter, we therefore addressed the complexity of BPD pathology from a neurobiological trauma perspective. Accumulation or chronicity of adverse childhood experiences induces chronic stress during the developmental process. Exposure to high and chronic levels of stress results in high levels of cortisol during the critical phases of brain development, which in turn can interfere with the development of the frontolimbic circuit and cause persistent anatomical and functional abnormalities. These abnormalities can compromise the integrative information processing of the frontolimbic circuits with serious long-lasting consequences for the cognitive, emotional, and behavioral development of the traumatized individuals manifested by symptoms such as low self-esteem and negative self-perception, and views about the outside world, unstable mood states, increased anxiety, and maladaptive, self-destructive behaviors.

A central finding in research on the sequelae of sustained ACE is the permanently increased responsivity of the hypothalamic CRH/AVP drive. In other words, chronic ACE permanently decreases the excitation threshold of the HPA axis to stress. Even a small stress stimulus is able to evoke a strong stress response, resulting in frequent exposure of the brain to high levels of CRH and cortisol, and exposure of the body tissues to high levels of cortisol. Cortisol plays a pivotal role in the modification of gene expression. CRH is not only a stress hormone; it also plays an important role as a neurotransmitter in the brain where chronic high levels of CRH produce many pathogenic effects. From animal research, we know that CRH causes behavioral changes similar to depression and anxiety, including increased despair and neophobia (fear of new situations), decreased eating and sexual activity, and reduced slow-wave sleep periods. Moreover, in a positive feedback loop with the locus ceruleus, it increases the central sympathetic outflow and stress-related autonomous functions, resulting in rise of blood pressure and tachycardia. Finally, yet importantly, CRH produces electrographic and behavioral signs of seizure activity resembling amygdala kindling (Holsboer, 1988).

As mentioned previously, the amygdala, in connection with the PFC, is crucial for emotion, aggression, and anxiety regulation, and arousal in case of threat. Activation can be induced by external perceptual stimuli, but also by association with internal unconscious cues and stressful memories. Close interaction of the amygdala with prefrontal cortex areas is essential for processing of emotionally relevant information and the integration with cognition.

Smaller amygdala volumes are found in emotionally deprived non-human primates and in patients with the diagnosis of borderline personality disorder, although ACE was not evaluated in these patients. Moreover, in these patients the amygdala appears to be hyperreactive to aversive stimuli and neutral faces, which were perceived as frightening because of difficulties in encoding the expression (Herpertz et al., 2001; Donegan et al., 2003). Other studies with BPD patients revealed functional disturbances of relevant prefrontal cortex areas. These regions were the anterior cingulate, the orbitofrontal cortex, the dorsolateral PFC, and the ventromedial PFC. Decreased serotonergic function in these regions was found to be associated with impulsiveness in BPD and suicidality in other patient populations. Studies with early and chronically traumatized BPD and non-BPD patients indicate disturbances of almost the same prefrontal brain regions, for example, the anterior cingulate, the orbitofrontal cortex, and medial PFC. Taken together, these functional disturbances of the PFC and amygdala suggest a disturbance of the integration processes. Frequent exposure of the amygdala of chronically traumatized BPD patients to high levels of CRH, which enhances kindling, may play a crucial role in the hyperactivity of this nucleus, resulting in frequent shifts to depressed, irritable, or anxious mood states and impulsive behavior, which is likely insufficiently inhibited by prefrontal processing (Herpertz et al., 2001).

Chronic traumatic stress also can activate or amplify inherited susceptibility for major psychiatric disorders such as depression or aggressive behavior in male victims of childhood abuse, as well as personality disorders (Caspi et al., 2002; Torgersen et al., 2000).

Taken together, it can be hypothesized that the early exposure to sustained ACE can exert its effects in two different ways: (a) by altering the function of pivotal neurobiological systems creating a trait-like vulnerability for stress, and (b) by activating a genetic predisposition. It is not clear yet whether the development of the vulnerability for stress is also dependent on genetic predispositions.

Some studies have shown that the specific state-dependent neurobiological alterations, related to the presence of a psychiatric disorder in patients with sustained ACE, appear to be distinguishable from underlying ACE-related trait-like neurophysiological disturbances. However, state-dependent neurobiological alterations can also modify the expression of trait-like neurobiological alterations (Heim et al., 2000; Driessen et al., 2004). For example, the increased glucocorticoid feedback on the pituitary due to a comorbid PTSD can diminish the effect of the trait-like increase of the AVP/CRH drive in BPD patients with a history of chronic childhood abuse (Rinne et al., 2002). This important finding has methodological as well as conceptual implications.

A well-known strategy to determine whether a certain neurobiological dysfunction in BPD patients is related to early childhood traumatization is the investigation of BPD patients with a comorbid PTSD diagnosis. This approach, however, is inadequate and the results are spurious because many chronically traumatized BPD patients do not suffer from PTSD and BPD patients without a history of childhood abuse can suffer from PTSD due to traumatic experiences during adult life. Moreover, early-traumatized BPD patients without PTSD show impressive neurobiological alterations which are missed when PTSD is chosen as the trauma selection criterion. Therefore, research aimed at the identification of the neurobiological endophenotypes of BPD pathology and symptomatology has to control for a broad spectrum of potential confounders, such as gender, ACE, PTSD, and depression.

The same holds when suicidality and impulsiveness are taken as the starting point for research into the etiology and pathogenesis of borderline pathology and symptomatology. A history of accumulating ACE and especially sustained childhood sexual abuse is a major risk factor for suicide attempts. The combination of ACE with the manifestations of depression and/or PTSD strongly potentiates the risk of suicide attempts (Yehuda, 1999; Dube et al., 2001). In personality disorder research, suicidal behavior and impulsive aggressive behavior often are considered as an expression of the same trait, and the role of ACE in this context is underestimated. However, recent data on impulsive, suicidal behavior in BPD patients provide a more differentiated view. In females, impulsiveness is associated with higher rates of suicide attempts but lower suicide fatality rates because impulsive attempts are mostly meant as a "time out," or escape from the hard reality, and the suicide intent in these cases is lower then in planned attempts (Yen et al., 2004). In contrast, in male subjects with impulsive aggressive personality disorders, impulsive suicides are reported to be aggressive, often fatal, and associated with central serotonergic dysfunctions (Coccaro et al., 1989; Linnoila & Virkkunen, 1992). However, the effect of ACE in these impulsive aggressive males is unknown yet. Furthermore, the question of whether ACE also contributes to the serotonergic dysfunction in impulsive aggressive male subjects, as it does in females, is not answered, yet. Moreover, childhood abuse is likely to affect the same prefrontal areas, hippocampus, and the serotonergic receptor subtypes that are found to be dysfunctional in suicidal patients, for example, the orbitofrontal cortex and ventral and medial PFC. The relationships of ACE with seritonergic dysfunctions and impulsive aggressive and suicidal behavior have to be subjected to further investigations.

A last aspect concerns the trauma-related somatic disorders. Cortisol is the main stress hormone. It serves as a catabolic hormone, that is, as a provider of energy for the behavioral stress response. Cortisol activates lipolyse, proteolysis, gluconeogenese, and insulin resistance. HPA axis hyperresponsiveness as a consequence of chronic ACE leads to frequent exposure of the body tissues to high levels of cortisol, which is likely to deregulate immune responses and metabolic functions, resulting in the development of a metabolic syndrome similar to chronic depression. The metabolic syndrome is characterized by obesity, insulin resistance comparable with diabetes II, cardiovascular disorders, and early cardiac arrest (Dong et al., 2004; Williamson, Thompson, Anda, Dietz, & Felitti, 2002; Heuser, 2002). ACE constitutes a considerable and seriously underestimated health risk.

This attempt to explain borderline symptomatology from a neuro-biological trauma perspective provides a model only for the BPD subgroup with chronic childhood abuse and/or neglect, and needs more empirical underpinnings. It does not explain why not traumatized BPD patients who have normal neuroendocrine responses are phenomenologically not distinguishable from chronically traumatized BPD subjects in terms of DSM criteria.

Conclusions

Up to now, the attempts to identify biological markers based on which distinct subgroups of BPD patients could be formed were unsuccessful. However, a growing number of independent studies successfully isolated a distinct and large subgroup of BPD patients of the otherwise very heterogeneous population of BPD patients based on a probably important risk factor, that is, sustained childhood abuse and neurobiological alterations related to it. This distinct subgroup is, because of the changed neuroendocrine function, very sensitive to stress and at high risk to develop stress-related disorders like depression, somatic diseases, and even premature death. Moreover, psychiatrists and psychotherapists have to be aware of the high risk of the comorbid depression and PTSD in this subgroup, which increases the probability of suicide attempts considerably. In this context, the finding that SSRIs are capable of regulating the pathophysiological source of the vulnerability might be important, as it probably opens a new perspective in the treatment of childhood-abused BPD patients aimed at the prevention of stress-related pathology like depression and suicidality.

Given the fact that borderline personality patients have, inherent to their psychopathology, a stress-generating lifestyle, it is important to address this problem in psychotherapeutic interventions. Therefore, stress management should to be a relevant and integrated part of psychotherapy and other treatment programs for borderline patients. The combination of chronic SSRI treatment with stress management and other psychotherapeutic strategies could be a new treatment strategy to prevent stress-related psychopathology and possibly also somatic disorders. Obviously, this provocative hypothesis has to be tested in future studies.

Taken together, maltreatment and abuse of children or other chronic traumatic experiences leave neurobiological scars in their brains. These scars are still detectable during adult life and they render the victims vulnerable to stress-related disorders. The neurobiological sequelae of chronic traumatic childhood experiences and the state-dependent neurobiological alterations of current psychiatric disorders have to be taken into account as important confounders in neurobiological research on BPD pathology. In addition, more research with more refined diagnostic systems than DSM criteria has to be conducted in order to better characterize the not or mildly abused BPD patients.

The identification of a circumscribed subgroup challenges the broad and heterogeneous DSM-IV BPD concept. A trauma-related multidimensional BPD subcategory is preferable as it takes into account the ACE-related neurobiological alterations in trauma-related disorders. Such a subcategory can contribute to a better understanding and treatment of the complex pathology of the BPD, and it can support the development of more specific treatment strategies.

Last but not least, programs addressing early detection of childhood abuse and prevention of the sequelae of childhood abuse are badly needed in order to protect the victims from a lifelong suffering from emotional distress and psychiatric disorders, and to save the community the high costs of medical service consumption.

Acknowledgment

The author expresses his gratitude to Wim van den Brink for his critical remarks and valuable comments on the manuscript of this book chapter.

References

Asberg, M., Thoren, P., Traskman, L., Bertilsson, L., & Ringberger, V. (1975). Serotonin depression —A biochemical subgroup within the affective disorders? *Science, 191,* 478–480.

Asberg, M., & Traskman, L. (1981). Studies of CSF 5-HIAA in depression and suicidal behaviour. *Advances in Experimental Medicine and Biology, 133,* 739–752.

Barden, N., Reul, J. M., & Holsboer, F. (1995). Do antidepressants stabilize mood through actions on the hypothalamic-pituitary-adrenocortical system? *Trends in Neurosciences, 18,* 6–11.

Baxter, L., Edell, W., Gerner, R., Fairbanks, L., & Gwirtsman, H. (1984). Dexamethasone suppression test and Axis I diagnoses of inpatients with DSM-III borderline personality disorder. *Journal of Clinical Psychiatry, 45,* 150–153.

Beeber, A. R., Kline, M. D., Pies, R. W., & Manring, J. M. (1984). Dexamethasone suppression test in hospitalized depressed patients with borderline personality disorder. *The Journal of Nervous and Mental Disease, 172,* 301–303.

Bierer, L. M., Yehuda, R., Schmeidler, J., Mitropoulou, V., New, A. S., Silverman, J. M., et al. (2003). Abuse and neglect in childhood: Relationship to personality disorder diagnoses. *CNS Spectrum, 8,* 737–754.

Bohn, D. K. (2003). Lifetime physical and sexual abuse, substance abuse, depression, and suicide attempts among Native American women. *Issues of Mental Health Nursing, 24,* 333–352.

Brambilla, P., Soloff, P. H., Sala, M., Nicoletti, M. A., Keshavan, M. S., & Soares, J. C. (2004). Anatomical MRI study of borderline personality disorder patients. *Psychiatry Research, 131,* 125–133.

Bremner, J. D. (2002). Structural changes in the brain in depression and relationship to symptom recurrence. *CNS Spectrum, 7,* 129–130.

Bremner, J. D. (2003). Long-term effects of childhood abuse on brain and neurobiology. *Child Adolescent Psychiatric Clinical N.Am, 12,* 271–292.

Brodsky, B. S., Oquendo, M., Ellis, S. P., Haas, G. L., Malone, K. M., & Mann, J. J. (2001). The relationship of childhood abuse to impulsivity and suicidal behavior in adults with major depression. *American Journal of Psychiatry, 158,* 1871–1877.

Brown, G. L., Ebert, M. H., Goyer, P. F., Jimerson, D. C., Klein, W. J., Bunney, W. E., et al. (1982). Aggression, suicide, and serotonin: Relationships to CSF amine metabolites. *American Journal of Psychiatry, 139,* 741–746.

Carroll, B. J. (2004). Untreated depression and hippocampal volume loss. *American Journal of Psychiatry, 161,* 1309–1310.

Caspi, A., McClay, J., Moffitt, T. E., Mill, J., Martin, J., Craig, I. W., et al. (2002). Role of genotype in the cycle of violence in maltreated children. *Science, 297,* 851–854.

Coccaro, E. F., Astill, J. L., Herbert, J. L., & Schut, A. (1990). Fluoxetine treatment of impulsive aggressionin DSM-III-R personality disorder patients. *Journal of Clinical Psychopharmacology, 10,* 373–375.

Coccaro, E. F., & Kavoussi, R. J. (1997). Fluoxetine and impulsive aggressive behavior in personality-disordered subjects. *Archives of General Psychiatry, 54,* 1081–1088.

Coccaro, E. F., Siever, L., Klar, H. M., & Maurer, G. (1989). Serotonergic studies in patients with affective and personality disorders. *Archives of General Psychiatry, 46,* 587–599.

Coplan, J. D., Andrews, M. W., Rosenblum, L. A., Owens, M. J., Friedman, S., Gorman, J. M., et al. (1996). Persistent elevations of cerebrospinal fluid concentrations of corticotropin-releasing factor in adult nonhuman primates exposed to early-life stressors: Implications for the pathophysiology of mood and anxiety disorders. *Proceedings of the National Acadamy of Science, U.S.A, 93,* 1619–1623.

Cornelius, J., Soloff, P. H., Perel, J., & Ulrich, R. F. (1990). Fluoxetine trial in borderline personality disorder. *Psychopharmacology Bulletin, 26,* 151–154.

De Goeij, D. C. E., Jezova, D., & Tilders, F. J. H. (1992). Repeated stress enhances vasopressin synthesis in corticotropin releasing factor neurons in the paraventricular nucleus. *Brain Research, 577,* 165–168.

De Kloet, E. R. (1995). Stress hormone and brain development. *Medical Pharmacology,* 7–22.

De Kloet, E. R., Vreugdenhil, E., Oitzl, M. S., & Joels, M. (1998). Brain corticosteroid receptor balance in health and disease. *Endocrinology Review, 19,* 269–301.

De la Fuente, J. M., Bobes, J., Vizuete, C., & Mendlewicz, J. (2002). Biological nature of depressive symptoms in borderline personality disorder: Endocrine comparison to recurrent brief and major depression. *Journal of Psychiatric Research, 36,* 137–145.

Donegan, N. H., Sanislow, C. A., Blumberg, H. P., Fulbright, R. K., Lacadie, C., Skudlarski, P., et al. (2003). Amygdala hyperreactivity in borderline personality disorder: Implications for emotional dysregulation. *Biological Psychiatry, 54,* 1284–1293.

Dong, M., Giles, W. H., Felitti, V. J., Dube, S. R., Williams, J. E., Chapman, D. P., et al. (2004). Insights into causal pathways for ischemic heart disease: Adverse childhood experiences study. *Circulation, 110,* 1761–1766.

Driessen, M., Beblo, T., Mertens, M., Piefke, M., Rullkoetter, N., Silva-Saavedra, A., et al. (2004). Posttraumatic stress disorder and fMRI activation patterns of traumatic memory in patients with borderline personality disorder. *Biological Psychiatry, 55,* 603–611.

Driessen, M., Herrmann, J., Stahl, K., Zwaan, M., Meier, S., Hill, A., et al. (2000). Magnetic resonance imaging volumes of the hippocampus and the amygdala in women with borderline personality disorder and early traumatization. *Archives of General Psychiatry, 57,* 1115–1122.

Dube, S. R., Anda, R. F., Felitti, V. J., Chapman, D. P., Williamson, D. F., & Giles, W. H. (2001). Childhood abuse, household dysfunction, and the risk of attempted suicide throughout the life span: Findings from the Adverse Childhood Experiences Study. *Journal of the American Medical Association, 286,* 3089–3096.

Edwards, V. J., Holden, G. W., Felitti, V. J., & Anda, R. F. (2003). Relationship between multiple forms of childhood maltreatment and adult mental health in community respondents: Results from the adverse childhood experiences study. *American Journal of Psychiatry, 160,* 1453–1460.

Felitti, V. J., Anda, R. F., Nordenberg, D., Williamson, D. F., Spitz, A. M., Edwards, V., et al. (1998). Relationship of childhood abuse and household dysfunction to many of the leading causes of death in adults. The Adverse Childhood Experiences (ACE) Study. *American Journal of Preventive Medicine, 14,* 245–258.

Forman, E. M., Berk, M. S., Henriques, G. R., Brown, G. K., & Beck, A. T. (2004). History of multiple suicide attempts as a behavioral marker of severe psychopathology. *American Journal of Psychiatry, 161,* 437–443.

Gladstone, G. L., Parker, G. B., Mitchell, P. B., Malhi, G. S., Wilhelm, K., & Austin, M. P. (2004). Implications of childhood trauma for depressed women: An analysis of pathways from childhood sexual abuse to deliberate self-harm and revictimization. *American Journal of Psychiatry, 161,* 1417–1425.

Graham, Y. P., Heim, C., Goodman, S. H., Miller, A. H., & Nemeroff, C. B. (1999). The effects of neonatal stress on brain development: Implications for psychopathology. *Developments in Psychopathology, 11,* 545–565.

Grossman, R., Yehuda, R., New, A., Schmeidler, J., Silverman, J., Mitropoulou, V., et al. (2003). Dexamethasone suppression test findings in subjects with personality disorders: Associations with posttraumatic stress disorder and major depression. *American Journal of Psychiatry, 160,* 1291–1298.

Halbreich, U., Olympia, J., Carson, S., Glogowski, J., Yen, C.-H., Axelrod, S., et al. (1989). Hypothalamo-pituitary-adrenal activity in endogenously depressed post-traumatic stress disorder patients. *Psychoneuroendocrinology, 14*(5), 365–370.

Hansenne, M., Pitchot, W., Pinto, E., Reggers, J., Scantamburlo, G., Fuchs, S., et al. (2002). 5-HT1A dysfunction in borderline personality disorder. *Psychological Medicine, 32,* 935–941.

Hatalski, C. G., Guirguis, C., & Baram, T. Z. (1998). Corticotropin releasing factor mRNA expression in the hypothalamic paraventricular nucleus and the central nucleus of the amygdala is modulated by repeated acute stress in the immature rat. *Journal of Neuroendocrinology, 10,* 663–669.

Heim, C., Newport, D. J., Bonsall, R., Miller, A. H., & Nemeroff, C. B. (2001). Altered pituitary-adrenal axis responses to provocative challenge tests in adult survivors of childhood abuse. *American Journal of Psychiatry, 158,* 575–581.

Heim, C., Newport, D. J., Heit, S., Graham, Y. P., Wilcox, M., Bonsall, R., et al. (2000). Pituitary-adrenal and autonomic responses to stress in women after sexual and physical abuse in childhood. *Journal of the American Medical Association, 284,* 592–597.

Heim, C., Newport, D. J., Wagner, D., Wilcox, M. M., Miller, A. H., & Nemeroff, C. B. (2002). The role of early adverse experience and adulthood stress in the prediction of neuroendocrine stress reactivity in women: A multiple regression analysis. *Depression and Anxiety, 15,* 117–125.

Helgeland, M. I., & Torgersen, S. (2004). Developmental antecedents of borderline personality disorder. *Comprehensive Psychiatry, 45,* 138–147.

Herman, J. L., Perry, J. C., & van der Kolk, B. A. (1989). Childhood trauma in borderline personality disorder. *American Journal of Psychiatry, 146,* 490–495.

Herpertz, S. C., Dietrich, T. M., Wenning, B., Krings, T., Erberich, S. G., Willmes, K., et al. (2001). Evidence of abnormal amygdala functioning in borderline personality disorder: A functional MRI study. *Biological Psychiatry, 50*, 292–298.

Herpertz, S. C., Steinmeyer, S. M., Marx, D., Oidtmann, A., & Sass, H. (1995). The significance of aggression and impulsivity for self-mutilative behavior. *Pharmacopsychiatry, 28*, 64–72.

Heuser, I. (2002). Depression, endocrinologically a syndrome of premature aging? *Maturitas, 41*, Supplement 1, S19–S23.

Heuser, I., Bissette, G., Dettling, M., Schweiger, U., Gotthardt, U., Schmider, J., et al. (1998). Cerebrospinal fluid concentrations of corticotropin-releasing hormone, vasopressin, and somatostatin in depressed patients and healthy controls: Response to amitriptyline treatment. *Depression and Anxiety, 8*, 71–79.

Heuser, I. J. E., Yassouridis, A., & Holsboer, F. (1994). The combined dexamethasone/CRH test: A refined laboratory test for psychiatric disorders. *Journal of Psychiatric Research, 28*, 341–356.

Hillis, S. D., Anda, R. F., Felitti, V. J., & Marchbanks, P. A. (2001). Adverse childhood experiences and sexual risk behaviors in women: A retrospective cohort study. *Family Planning Perspectives, 33*, 206–211.

Holsboer, F. (1988). Implications of altered limbic-hypothalamic-pituitary-adrenocotrical (LHPA)-function for neurobiology of depression. *Acta Psychiatrica Scandinavica, 77*, 72–111.

Holsboer, F., & Barden, N. (1996). Antidepressants and hypothalamic-pituitary-adrenocortical regulation. *Endocrinology Review, 17*, 187–205.

Johnson, D. M., Shea, M. T., Yen, S., Battle, C. L., Zlotnick, C., Sanislow, C. A., et al. (2003). Gender differences in borderline personality disorder: Findings from the Collaborative Longitudinal Personality Disorders Study. *Comprehensive Psychiatry, 44*, 284–292.

Kaufman, J., Birmaher, B., Perel, J., Dahl, R. E., Moreci, P., Nelson, B., et al. (1997). The corticotropin-releasing hormone challenge in depressed abused, depressed nonabused, and normal control children. *Biological Psychiatry, 42*, 669–679.

Korzekwa, M., Links, P., & Steiner, M. (1993). Biological markers in borderline personality disorder: New perspectives. *Canadian Journal of Psychiatry, 38* Supplement 1, S11–S15.

Krishnan, K. R. R., Davidson, J. R., Rayasam, K., & Shope, F. (1984). The dexamethasone suppression test in borderline personality disorder. *Biological Psychiatry, 19*, 1149–1153.

Landecker, H. (1992). The role of childhood sexual trauma in the etiologiy of borderline personality disorder: Considerations for diagnosis and treatment. *Psychotherapy, 29*, 234–242.

Langeland, W., Draijer, N., & van den Brink, W. (2004). Psychiatric comorbidity in treatment-seeking alcoholics: The role of childhood trauma and perceived parental dysfunction. *Alcoholism: Clinical & Experimental Research, 28*, 441–447.

Leyton, M., Okazawa, H., Diksic, M., Paris, J., Rosa, P., Mzengeza, S., et al. (2001). Brain regional alpha-[11C]methyl-L-tryptophan trapping in impulsive subjects with borderline personality disorder. *American Journal of Psychiatry, 158*, 775–782.

Lieb, K., Rexhausen, J. E., Kahl, K. G., Schweiger, U., Philipsen, A., Hellhammer, D. H., et al. (2004). Increased diurnal salivary cortisol in women with borderline personality disorder. *Journal of Psychiatric Research, 38*, 559–565.

Linnoila, M., & Virkkunen, M. (1992). Aggression, suicidality, and serotonin. *Journal of Clinical Psychiatry, 53*, 46–51.

Livesley, W. J., Jang, K. L., Jackson, D. N., & Vernon, P. A. (1993). Genetic and environmental contributions to dimensions of personality disorder. *American Journal of Psychiatry, 150*(12), 1826–1831.

Livesley, W. J., Jang, K. L., & Vernon, P. A. (1998). Phenotypic and genetic structure of traits delineating personality disorder. *Archives of General Psychiatry, 55*, 941–948.

Lloyd, A. J., Ferrier, I. N., Barber, R., Gholkar, A., Young, A. H., & O'Brien, J. T. (2004). Hippocampal volume change in depression: Late- and early-onset illness compared. *British Journal of Psychiatry, 184*, 488–495.

Lopez, J. F., Chalmers, D. T., Little, K. Y., & Watson, S. J. (1998). A.E. Bennett Research Award. Regulation of serotonin1A, glucocorticoid, and mineralocorticoid receptor in rat and human hippocampus: Implications for the neurobiology of depression. *Biological Psychiatry, 43*, 547–573.

Markovitz, P. J., Calabrese, J. R., Schulz, S. C., & Meltzer, H. Y. (1991). Fluoxetine in the treatment of borderline and schizotypal personality disorders. *American Journal of Psychiatry, 148,* 1064–1067.

Meijer, O. C., & De Kloet, E. R. (1998). Corticosterone and serotonergic neurotransmission in the hippocampus: Functional implications of central corticosteroid receptor diversity. *Critical Review of Neurobiology, 12,* 1–20.

Molinari, E. (2001). Eating disorders and sexual abuse. *Eating and Weight Disorders, 6,* 68–80.

Nemeroff, C. B. (1996). The corticotropin-releasing factor (CRF) hypothesis of depression: New findings and new directions. *Molecular Psychiatry, 1,* 336–342.

New, A. S., Buchsbaum, M. S., Hazlett, E. A., Goodman, M., Koenigsberg, H. W., Lo, J., et al. (2004). Fluoxetine increases relative metabolic rate in prefrontal cortex in impulsive aggression. *Psychopharmacology, 145 (Berlin).*

New, A. S., Hazlett, E. A., Buchsbaum, M. S., Goodman, M., Koenigsberg, H. W., & Iskander, L. (2003). M-CPP PET and impulsive aggression in borderline personality disorder. *Biological Psychiatry, 53,* 104S.

Newport, D. J., Heim, C., Bonsall, R., Miller, A. H., & Nemeroff, C. B. (2004). Pituitary-adrenal responses to standard and low-dose dexamethasone suppression tests in adult survivors of child abuse. *Biological Psychiatry, 55,* 10–20.

Norden, M. (1989). Fluoxetine in borderline personality disorder. *Progress in Neuro-Psychopharmacology and Biological Psychiatry, 13,* 885–893.

Ogata, S. N., Silk, K. R., Goodrich, S., Lohr, N., Westen, D., & Hill, E. M. (1990). Childhood sexual and physical abuse in adult patients with borderline personality disorder. *American Journal of Psychiatry, 147,* 1008–1013.

Oquendo, M. A., & Mann, J. J. (2000). The biology of impulsivity and suicidality. *Psychiatric Clinics of North America, 23,* 11–25.

Oquendo, M. A., Placidi, G. P., Malone, K. M., Campbell, C., Keilp, J., Brodsky, B., et al. (2003). Positron emission tomography of regional brain metabolic responses to a serotonergic challenge and lethality of suicide attempts in major depression. *Archives of General Psychiatry, 60,* 14–22.

Pandey, G. N., Dwivedi, Y., Rizavi, H. S., Ren, X., Pandey, S. C., Pesold, C., et al. (2002). Higher expression of serotonin 5-HT(2A) receptors in the postmortem brains of teenage suicide victims. *American Journal of Psychiatry, 159,* 419–429.

Paris, J., Zweig-Frank, H., Kin, N. M., Schwartz, G., Steiger, H., & Nair, N. P. (2004). Neurobiological correlates of diagnosis and underlying traits in patients with borderline personality disorder compared with normal controls. *Psychiatry Research, 121,* 239–252.

Perry, J. C., & Herman, J. L. (1993). Trauma and defense in the etiology of borderline personality disorder. In J. Paris (Ed.), *Borderline Personality Disorder* (1st ed., pp. 123–140). Washington, DC: American Psychiatric Publishing, Inc.

Peters, D. A. V. (1986). Prenatal stress: Effects on development of rat brain serotonergic neurons. *Pharmacology Biochemistry & Behavior, 24,* 1377–1382.

Peters, D. A. V. (1987). Both prenatal and postnatal factors contribute to the effects of maternal stress on offspring behavior and central 5-hydroxyptanine receptors in the rat. *Pharmacology Biochemistry & Behavior, 30,* 669–673.

Peters, D. A. V. (1990). Maternal stress increases fetal brain and neonatal cerebral cortex 5-hydroxytrypamine synthesis in rats: A possible mechanism by which stress influences brain development. *Pharmacology Biochemistry & Behavior, 35,* 943–947.

Plotsky, P. M., & Meaney, M. J. (1993). Early postnatal experience alters hypothalamic corticotropin-releasing factor (CRF) mRNA, median eminence CRF content and stress-induced release in adult rats. *Molecular Brain Research, 18,* 195–200.

Raadsheer, F. C., Hoogendijk, W. J., Stam, F. C., Tilders, F. J., & Swaab, D. F. (1994). Increased numbers of corticotropin-releasing hormone expressing neurons in the hypothalamic paraventricular nucleus of depressed patients. *Neuroendocrinology, 60,* 436–444.

Rinne, T., De Kloet, E. R., Wouters, L., Goekoop, J. G., DeRijk, R. H., & van den Brink, W. (2002). Hyperresponsiveness of hypothalamic-pituitary-adrenal axis to combined dexamethasone/corticotropin-releasing hormone challenge in female borderline personality disorder subjects with a history of sustained childhood abuse. *Biological Psychiatry, 52,* 1102–1112.

Rinne, T., De Kloet, E. R., Wouters, L., Goekoop, J. G., de Rijk, R. H., & van den Brink, W. (2003). Fluvoxamine reduces responsiveness of HPA axis in adult female BPD patients with a history of sustained childhood abuse. *Neuropsychopharmacology* (New York), 28, 126–132.

Rinne, T., Westenberg, H. G. M., Den Boer, J. A., & van den Brink, W. (2000). Serotonergic blunting to meta-chlorophenylpiperazine (m-CPP) highly correlates with sustained childhood abuse in impulsive and autoaggressive female borderline patients. *Biological Psychiatry, 47,* 548–556.

Salzman, C., Wolfson, A. N., Schatzberg, A., Looper, J., Henke, R., Albanese, M., et al. (1995). Effect of fluoxetine on anger in symptomatic volunteers with borderline personality disorder. *Journal of Clinical Psychopharmacology, 15,* 23–29.

Salzman, J. P., Salzman, C., Wolfson, A. N., Albanese, A., Looper, J., Ostacher, M., et al. (1993). Association between borderline personality structure and history of childhood abuse in adult volunteers. *Comprehensive Psychiatry, 34,* 254–257.

Schmahl, C. G., Vermetten, E., Elzinga, B. M., & Bremner, J. D. (2004). A positron emission tomography study of memories of childhood abuse in borderline personality disorder. *Biological Psychiatry, 55,* 759–765.

Schmahl, C. G., Vermetten, E., Elzinga, B. M., & Douglas, B. J. (2003). Magnetic resonance imaging of hippocampal and amygdala volume in women with childhood abuse and borderline personality disorder. *Psychiatry Research, 122,* 193–198.

Silk, K. R., Lee, S., Hill, E. M., & Lohr, N. (1995). Borderline personality disorder symptoms and severity of sexual abuse. *American Journal of Psychiatry, 152,* 1059–1064.

Skodol, A. E., Gunderson, J. G., Pfohl, B., Widiger, T. A., Livesley, W. J., & Siever, L. J. (2002). The borderline diagnosis I: Psychopathology, comorbidity, and personality structure. *Biological Psychiatry, 51,* 936–950.

Soloff, P. H., George, A., & Nathan, R. S. (1982). The dexamethasone suppression test in patients with borderline personality disorders. *American Journal of Psychiatry, 139,* 1621–1623.

Soloff, P. H., Kelly, T. M., Strotmeyer, S. J., Malone, K. M., & Mann, J. J. (2003). Impulsivity, gender, and response to fenfluramine challenge in borderline personality disorder. *Psychiatry Research, 119,* 11–24.

Soloff, P. H., Lynch, K. G., & Kelly, T. M. (2002). Childhood abuse as a risk factor for suicidal behavior in borderline personality disorder. *Journal of Personality Disorders, 16,* 201–214.

Soloff, P. H., Meltzer, C. C., Becker, C., Greer, P. J., Kelly, T. M., & Constantine, D. (2003). Impulsivity and prefrontal hypometabolism in borderline personality disorder. *Psychiatry Research, 123,* 153–163.

Steiger, H., Gauvin, L., Israel, M., Koerner, N., Ng Ying Kin, N. M., Paris, J., et al. (2001). Association of serotonin and cortisol indices with childhood abuse in bulimia nervosa. *Archives of General Psychiatry, 58,* 837–843.

Stout, S. C., Owens, M. J., & Nemeroff, C. B. (2002). Regulation of corticotropin-releasing factor neuronal systems and hypothalamic-pituitary-adrenal axis activity by stress and chronic antidepressant treatment. *Journal of Pharmacologic ExperimentalTherapy, 300,* 1085–1092.

Sutanto, W., Rosenfeld, P., De Kloet, E. R., & Levine, S. (1995). Long-term effects of neonatal maternal deprivation and ACTH on hippocampal mineralocorticoid and glucocorticoid receptors. *Developmental Brain Research, 92,* 156–163.

Tebartz von Eltz, E., Hesslinger, B., Thiel, T., Geiger, E., Haegele, K., Lemieux, L., et al. (2003). Frontolimbic brain abnormalities in patients with borderline personality disorder: A volumetric magnetic resonance imaging study. *Biological Psychiatry, 54,* 163–171.

Terr, L. C. (1991). Childhood traumas: An outline and overview. *American Journal of Psychiatry, 148,* 10–20.

Teusch, R. (2001). Substance abuse as a symptom of childhood sexual abuse. *Psychiatric Services, 52,* 1530–1532.

Torgersen, S., Kringlen, E., & Cramer, V. (2001). The prevalence of personality disorders in a community sample. *Archives of General Psychiatry, 58,* 590–596.

Torgersen, S., Lygren, S., Oien, P. A., Skre, I., Onstad, S., Edvardsen, J., et al. (2000). A twin study of personality disorders. *Comprehensive Psychiatry, 41,* 416–425.

Traskman, L., Asberg, M., Nordstrom, P., & Stanley, M. J. (1989). Biochemical aspects of suicidal behavior. *Progress in Neuro-Psychopharmacology and Biological Psychiatry, 13,* S35–S44.

van Heeringen, C., Audenaert, K., van Laere, K., Dumont, F., Slegers, G., Mertens, J., et al. (2003). Prefrontal 5-HT2a receptor binding index, Hopelessness and personality characteristics in attempted suicide. *Journal of Affective Disorders, 74*, 149–158.

van Oers, H. J., De Kloet, E. R., & Levine, S. (1998). Early vs. late maternal deprivation differentially alters the endocrine and hypothalamic responses to stress. *Developmental Brain Research, 111*, 245–252.

Verheul, R., & van den Brink, W. (1999). Persoonlijkheidsstoornissen. In A. de Jong, W. van den Brink, J. Ormel, & D. Wiersma (Eds.), *Handboek psychiatrische epidemiologie* (pp. 347–378). Maarsden, The Netherlands: Elsevier/de Tijdstroom.

Vythilingam, M., Heim, C., Newport, J., Miller, A. H., Anderson, E., Bronen, R., et al. (2002). Childhood trauma associated with smaller hippocampal volume in women with major depression. *American Journal of Psychiatry, 159*, 2072–2080.

Vythilingam, M., Vermetten, E., Anderson, G. M., Luckenbaugh, D., Anderson, E. R., Snow, J., et al. (2004). Hippocampal volume, memory, and cortisol status in major depressive disorder: Effects of treatment. *Biological Psychiatry, 56*, 101–112.

Williamson, D. F., Thompson, T. J., Anda, R. F., Dietz, W. H., & Felitti, V. (2002). Body weight and obesity in adults and self-reported abuse in childhood. *International Journal of Obesity and Related Metabolic Disorders, 26*, 1075–1082.

Yehuda, R. (1999). Managing anger and aggression in patients with posttraumatic stress disorder. *Journal of Clinical Psychiatry, 60 Supplement 15*, 33–37.

Yehuda, R., Southwick, S., Krystal, J. H., Bremner, J. D., Charney, D. S., & Mason, J. W. (1993). Enhanced suppression of cortisol following dexamethasone administration in posttraumatic stress disorder. *American Journal of Psychiatry, 150*, 83–86.

Yen, S., Shea, M. T., Battle, C. L., Johnson, D. M., Zlotnick, C., Dolan-Sewell, R., et al. (2002). Traumatic exposure and posttraumatic stress disorder in borderline, schizotypal, avoidant, and obsessive-compulsive personality disorders: Findings from the collaborative longitudinal personality disorders study. *Journal of Nervous and Mental Disorders, 190*, 510–518.

Yen, S., Shea, M. T., Sanislow, C. A., Grilo, C. M., Skodol, A. E., Gunderson, J. G., et al. (2004). Borderline personality disorder criteria associated with prospectively observed suicidal behavior. *American Journal of Psychiatry, 161*, 1296–1298.

Zanarini, M. C., Frankenburg, F. R., Dubo, E. D., Sickel, A. E., Trikha, A., Levin, A., et al. (1998). Axis I comorbidity of borderline personality disorder. *American Journal of Psychiatry, 155*, 1733–1739.

Zanarini, M. C., Yong, L., Frankenburg, F. R., Hennen, J., Reich, D. B., Marino, M. F., et al. (2002). Severity of reported childhood sexual abuse and its relationship to severity of borderline psychopathology and psychosocial impairment among borderline inpatients. *Journal of Nervous and Mental Disorders, 190*, 381–387.

Zlotnick, C., Franklin, C. L., & Zimmerman, M. (2002). Is comorbidity of posttraumatic stress disorder and borderline personality disorder related to greater pathology and impairment? *American Journal of Psychiatry, 159*, 1940–1943.

Zlotnick, C., Rothschild, L., & Zimmerman, M. (2002). The role of gender in the clinical presentation of patients with borderline personality disorder. *Journal of Personality Disorders, 16*, 277–282.

CHAPTER 5

Personality Disorders and the Course and Outcome of Substance Abuse: A Selective Review of the 1984 to 2004 Literature

PER VAGLUM

Key Teaching Points

- Large proportions of alcohol abusers and substance abusers have at least one personality disorder. The most prevalent may be antisocial, obsessive compulsive, and paranoid personality disorders.
- Overall evidence shows worse outcome of alcohol abuse in those with personality disorders.
- Overall findings of substance abusers indicate a poorer outcome for those with personality disorders.
- Although antisocial and borderline personality disorders may be predictors of poor outcome, the presence or absence of any personality disorder may be more important.
- Personality disorders are associated with poorer treatment compliance.

- Pure antisocial personality disorder is associated with a worse outcome than when antisocial is combined with depression.
- Personality disorders are often associated with poor outcome in legal, medical, social, and psychiatric problems.
- Each treatment program needs competence in identifying personality disorders and in devising approaches to them relevant to their particular circumstances.

Introduction

It is well established that a high proportion of help-seeking substance users have at least one personality disorder (PD) (Verheul, 2001). In a recent national survey on alcohol use and related conditions in the general population in the United States (Grant, Stinson, Dawson, Chou, Ruan, & Pickering, 2004), among individuals with a current alcohol use disorder, 28.6% had at least one *Diagnostic and Statistical Manual of Mental Disorders* (4th ed.) (DSM-IV) PD. Among those with a current drug use disorder, this was the case in 47.7%. Antisocial (ASPD), obsessive-compulsive, and paranoid PDs were the most prevalent in both subgroups. Both alcohol- and drug-use disorders were most strongly related to antisocial, histrionic, and dependent PD in the general population. In a U.S. sample of patients referred for treatment of PDs, 60% of the patients with substance-use disorders (SUD) had a PD, with borderline PD (BPD) and ASPD being most strongly associated with the use of nonalcoholic, noncannabinoid drugs (Skodol, Oldham, & Gallaher, 1999). In a Dutch sample of 370 treated substance users, Verheul, Kranzler, Poling, Tennen, Ball, and Rounsaville (2000) found that 57% had at least one DSM-III PD, with the paranoid subtype the most prevalent among cluster A disorders, BPD among cluster B, and avoidant among cluster C disorders. The strongest associations between PD and Axis I disorders were between social phobia and avoidant and schizotypal PD, and between major depression and BPD. In a Norwegian consecutive sample of treated substance users from two catchment areas (Landheim, Bakken, & Vaglum, 2003), 72% had one or more PD, with the incidence reaching 79% among polysubstance users and 66% among pure alcoholics. Polysubstance users significantly more often had cluster B disorders (58% vs. 27%), and pure alcoholics more often had cluster A disorders (44% vs. 31%) and cluster C disorders (28% vs. 11%).

Relations Between PDs/SUDs

The high co-occurrence of PD and SUD has made it important to clarify the nature of this comorbidity. The co-occurrence of PDs (Axis I) and symptom disorders (Axis II) in the same person does not necessarily imply that they are related. First, the co-occurrence may be due to a chance overlap in the population, or to a selection bias of people with both disorders fronting to treatment ("Bergson's fallacy"). However, these possibilities can be ruled out because the prevalence of several PDs is much higher among SUD patients than in the general population, but only slightly higher among treatment-seeking SUD people compared with SUD people in the general population.

Having excluded these two possibilities, five possible relations between PD and SUD remain: (1) the presence of one or more PD may predispose a person to develop a secondary SUD; (2) PD and SUD could be the same disorder due to overlapping criteria (for example, antisocial and borderline PD share some criteria with the SUD diagnosis); (3) PD and SUD may be spuriously linked together through a third factor that is correlated to both (for example, genetic, common environment, emotional dyshabituation, etc.); (4) the use of substances increases certain personality disorder traits such as poor impulse control, unstable affectivity, or increased risk of being traumatized, with resulting secondary development of a PD; and (5) the existence of one or more PDs may negatively (or positively) influence the treatment response and/or ensuing course of the substance use.

An examination of the first four possibilities is not the purpose of this chapter. The purpose of this chapter is to review the research literature that has explored the empirical evidence for the fifth possibility: the existence of one or more PDs may negatively (or positively) influence the treatment response and/or ensuing course of the substance use. It is important to identify such a possible negative relation between PD and SUD because if such a reasonably strong relation exists, it would provide strong arguments for including the treatment of PDs in all SUD treatment programs. However, it is not easy to identify this relation, because the influence of PD on SUD can be both directly from PD to SUD, and indirectly through mediating variables. PDs may, for example, indirectly influence the course of the substance use by influencing the treatment response (such as level of involvement in treatment, working alliance, compliance with or completion of treatment), which again influences the outcome. This means that the treatment response may mediate (or moderate) the effect of PD on the substance-use outcome measured after the treatment is finished. It is also possible that the influence of the treatment response on the course of the substance use is further mediated (or moderated) by a change in, for example, posttreatment social functioning, which makes it even more difficult to identify the nature of a possible connection between PD and substance use. To identify such mediating (or moderating) variables, we ideally need studies with longitudinal designs that measure outcome both at the end of treatment and several times thereafter.

On this background, this literature review examines articles concerning treatment response separately from articles exploring posttreatment outcome. Studies on compliance with methadone maintenance treatment are reviewed, together with treatment response studies. A growing literature has shown that SUD patients, who are only abusing alcohol ("pure alcoholics") differ according to psychopathological comorbidity and clinical course from SUD patients using one or more illegal drugs (opiate users, cocaine users, amphetamine users, etc.); most patient samples consist of polysubstance users. Therefore, the articles on alcoholics and illegal drug users (included polysubstance users) are reviewed separately.

Identification of Papers

Included in this review are articles reporting prospective follow-up studies of treated SUD patients in which the DSM-III, DSM-III-R, or DSM-IV diagnostic systems have been used to diagnose PDs. This implies that articles using instruments that measure normal personality traits, for example, NEO-PI (Neuroticism, Extraversion/Introversion, Openness to Experience Personality Inventory) and MMPI (Minnesota Multiphasic Personality Inventory), are not included. The main (dependent) outcome variables are either treatment response or substance use. Findings that indicate a relation between PD and outcome variables other than substance use (like arrests, psychiatric disorder, and somatic health) are briefly mentioned. Studies comparing the effect of different types of treatment programs are not reviewed (see Gold and Brady, 2003).

The papers have been identified through Medline and the reference lists of the identified papers, as well as one recent extensive review of all predictors of substance use (mentioning 10 relevant studies) (Cirolau, Piechniczek-Buczek, & Iscan, 2003).

In all, this chapter reviews 36 studies that were published in the past 20 years (1984 to 2004). Of these studies, 12 examined alcoholics, with 24 studies concerned with illegal substance users. All PDs were diagnosed in 27 papers, most often using the structured clinical interview for the DSM (SCID), although a few used dimensional scores from MCMI (Millon Clinical Multiaxial Inventory) or SCID. One study only diagnosed BPD (using Diagnostic Interview for Borderline PD) (Nace, Saxon, & Shore, 1986). Eight studies only diagnosed antisocial PD (ASPD), all but one of them using the structured interview DIS (Diagnostic Interview Schedule), which only explores ASPD. A couple of studies (Cacciola, Alterman, Rutherford, & Snider, 1995; Cecero, Ball, Tennen, Kranzler, & Rounsaville, 1999) followed separate groups of alcoholics and illegal substance users. They have been classified based on the most important subgroup.

Alcoholics

Alcoholics and Treatment Completion

Only two studies that examined the association between PD and treatment completion among alcoholics were identified. Poldugro and Forti (1988) explored compliance among 404 male alcoholics who completed their detoxification program followed by outpatient group therapy. Patients with ASPD had the poorest compliance, and those with dependent PD had the best. Verheul, van den Brink, and Hartgers (1998) conducted a very important study to attempt to identify a possible PD effect on treatment response and relapse among alcoholics. They followed 105 outpatients and 82 inpatients for 12 to 24 months after admission. Motivation for change and time in the program did not *mediate* the effect of PD on relapse within 3 months; neither did working alliance for the inpatient sample. However, these variables *modified* the negative effect of PD on relapse rate for those who were less motivated or were in the program for less than 4 months. Inpatients with a PD showed poorer working alliance than the no-PD patients.

Alcoholics and Outcome

Of the 11 studies concerning alcoholics, seven found a negative relation between PD and outcome (see Table 5.1). Studies by Schuckit (1985); Rounsaville, Dolinsky, Babor, and Meyer (1987); Kranzler, Del Boca, and Rounsaville (1996); and Wølwer, Burtscheidt, Redner, Schwarz, and Gaebel (2001) found that ASPD is related to poor outcome 1 to 3 years later in samples of both men and women. One study of inpatients found that patients with BPD used more drugs after 1 year, but not more alcohol than the non-BPD group (Nace et al., 1986). In one study of female alcoholics in an outpatient program (nearly none with ASPD), schizoid PD was related to a poor drinking outcome 2 years posttreatment (Haver, 2003). In addition, the study by Verheul et al. (1998) found that the presence of any PD is associated with time to relapse within the first 3 months of inpatient/outpatient treatment. One study found a positive relation between PD and SUD outcome. Moggi, Brodbeck, Koltzsch, Hirsbrunner, and Bachmann (2002) found that, among their dual-diagnosis inpatients, the 1-year outcome was *better* among PD patients than among patients with depressive or schizophrenic comorbidity.

Table 5.1 Outcome Studies on Alcoholism

Authors	N	Sex	Treatment	Follow-up	Outcome
Schuckit (1985)	577	M	VA Hospital	12 months	Primary ASPD: poor outcome, more criminal and social problems
Nace et al. (1986)*	74	M/F	Private hospital	12 months	BPD more drug use
Rounsaville (1987)	266	M/F	Mixture	12 months	ASPD and other PD poorer outcome
Powell et al. (1992)	360	M	Inpatient, 28 days	12 months	ASPD more unemployment
Cacciola et al. (1995)	224	M	Psychotherapy, 28 inpatient days	7 months	No PD–SUD relation
Kranzler et al. (1996)	225	M/F	Mixture	3 years	ASPD poorer outcome
Tómasson & Vaglum (1997)	351	M/F	Detoxification inpatient	15 months	No ASPD–SUD relation
Tómasson & Vaglum (1998)	351	M/F	Detoxification inpatients	28 months	No ASPD–SUD relation ASPD more arrests
Wolwer (2001)	120	M/F	6 months outpatient treatment	24 months	ASPD, BPD more often relapse
Moggi et al. (2002)	118	M/F	4 months inpatients	12 months	PD better improvement of drinking
Haver (2003)	120	F	In- and outpatient	24 months	Schizoid poorer outcome

The three studies that found no relation between a PD and outcome were a study of 360 veterans by Powell et al. (1992), a study of 224 men in a psychotherapeutic day program by Cacciola et al. (1995), and a study of an Icelandic nationwide sample of 351 treated male and female alcoholics who were followed up after 15 months and then after 28 months (Tomasson & Vaglum, 1997; 1998). In the two last studies, only ASPD was measured.

In the two other studies, a negative association between PD and outcome variables other than substance use was identified. In the nationwide sample of Icelandic alcoholics, ASPD was predictive of more frequent arrests during the 28 months observation time (Tomasson & Vaglum, 1998). In a study of male Veterans Administration (VA) inpatients, Powell et al. (1992) found that they were more often unemployed 1 year later.

Illegal Substance Users

Illegal Substance Users and Treatment Completion and Compliance

Of the 10 studies identified under this heading, 7 reported a relation between PD and compliance (see Table 5.2). Ravndal and Vaglum (1991a, 1991b) found that therapeutic community (TC)-treated addicts (n = 144) who scored high for ASPD on the MCMI, both at admittance and after 1 year in the Phoenix house inpatient program, had more often dropped out of the ensuing outpatient phase. During the 1-year inpatient phase, patients who scored high for schizotypal PD or low for histrionic PD also had a significantly increased dropout rate. A combination of treatment programs for both genders in Greece showed that the presence of a PD predicted dropout among 226 men and women (Kokkevi, Stefanis, Anastasopoulou, & Kostogianni, 1998). King, Kidorf, Stoller, Carter, and Brooner, (2001) found no relation between PD and dropout or retention after 12 months among 513 men and women admitted to a methadone program, but the ASPD patients showed better compliance after 25 days in the program. Cacciola, Rutherford, Alterman, McKay, and Snider (1996) found the presence of a PD among 197 men was a predictor of dropout from a methadone program. However, ASPD had the same effect as other PDs. In a study of the first 50 methadone clients in Norway, patients scoring high for borderline and passive-aggressive PD on the MCMI and low for compulsive PD after 4 months of treatment (but not at admittance!) had a significantly higher dropout rate during the following 20 months (Ravndal & Vaglum, 1999a). The dropout rate among patients with ASPD was not increased. Ouimette, Gima, Moos, and Finney (1999) followed 3,008 VA patients with all types of SUD over 1 year using an intake form and a follow-up form. The patients with a PD had a longer inpatient stay than the psychotic ones, the anxiety/depression and the SUD only subgroups, as well as the PD group and the SUD-only group, attended more inpatient 12-step meetings during the stay. However, after discharge, the PD group attended fewer mental health outpatient meetings than the other subgroups. Ross, Dermatis, Levounis, and Galanter (2003) examined 100 consecutive inpatients admitted to a

Table 5.2 Illegal Drugs: Personality Disorder and Compliance, Dropout, and Retention

Authors	N	Sex	Treatment	Follow-up	Outcome
Craig (1984)	100	M	Detoxification	30 days	No relation
Stark & Campbell (1988)	100	M/F	Outpatient	60 days	No
Ravndal & Vaglum (1991a)	144	M/F	TC	18 months	High schizotypal and ASPD: Dropout low histrionic: dropout
Ravndal & Vaglum (1991b)	36	M/F	TC	18 months	Antisocial aggression high at admittance and discharge: More dropout
Alterman et al. (1996)	184	M	Methadone	7 months	No
Cacciola et al. (1996)	197	M	Methadone	7 months	PD more dropout. ASPD = other PD
Kokkevi et al. (1998)	226	M/F	Mixture	3 to 6 weeks	PD (= ASPD) more dropout
Ouimette et al. (1999)	3008	M	Mixture	12 months	PD longer stay, more dropout from outpatient treatment
Ravndal & Vaglum (1999a)	50	M/F	Methadone	24 months	High BPD, passive–aggressive: Dropout low on compulsive: dropout ASPD: No difference
King et al. (2001)	513	M/F	Methadone	12 months	No
Ross et al. (2003)	100	M/F	Dual diagnosis program	One week post discharge	No difference as inpatient. PD dropout as outpatient

dual-diagnosis inpatient unit. Outcome was measured during hospitalization (dropout, etc.), and after discharge, outcome was assessed as compliance, via a follow-up appointment. PD and no-PD patients had the same course during the inpatient stay, but the PD patients were again less likely to be compliant with the initial aftercare appointment. This difference between inpatient and outpatient compliance concurs with the study by Ravndal and Vaglum (1991b).

Three studies found no relation between PD and compliance. Craig (1984) studied the dropout rate among 100 men in an inpatient detoxification program, and Stark and Campbell (1988) among 100 men and women in a community outpatient center, using MCMI for the PD measurement. PD was not associated with a dropout within 30 or 60 days, respectively, in these studies. Alterman, Tutherford, Cacciola, McKay, and Woody (1996) found no relation between PD and 7-month compliance among 184 men admitted to a methadone program.

Illegal Substance Use and Outcome

Of the 16 studies identified under this heading, 10 found a relation between PD and substance use outcome (see Table 5.3). Woody, McLellan, Luborsky, and O'Brien (1985) followed-up on 110 methadone maintenance patients in a psychotherapy outcome study and found that ASPD was a negative predictor of the 7-month outcome. Nace and Davis (1993) followed, over 12 months, a mixed group of alcoholics and substance users from an intensive inpatient psychotherapy-oriented treatment program. At treatment completion, PD and no-PD patients had the same level of drug use, and the PD group used significantly more alcohol. Cacciola et al. (1996) examined the 7-month treatment outcome in 197 men admitted to methadone maintenance. PD subjects entered treatment with more severe self-reported drug, alcohol, psychiatric, and legal problems, and remained more problematic in these areas relative to no-PD patients. In addition, BPD predicted medical, alcohol, family/social, and psychiatric problems at follow-up. ASPD also predicted more criminal problems. Marlowe, Kirby, Festinger, Husband, and Platt (1997) followed over 33 weeks a sample of 137 male and female urban, impoverished cocaine users in a behaviorally oriented outpatient or day treatment. No significant differences in outcome were found between categorically diagnosed PD patients and no-PD patients. However, dimensional analyses of personality symptoms generated from SCID II accounted for substantial proportions of variance in outcome. BPD symptoms were fairly consistently associated with negative outcomes, whereas ASPD, paranoid, and compulsive PD were associated with some parts of negative outcome. Dependent PD was associated with a positive outcome. Ravndal and Vaglum (1998) also studied the relation between MCMI dimensions and 5-year outcome among 200 polysubstance users who were consecutively admitted to a therapeutic community. PD dimensions were not directly related to substance use 5 years later, but were associated indirectly, through social functioning after discharge. However, a high score on narcissistic (and antisocial) dimension predicted death during the 5-year follow-up (OR = 4.98). Thomas, Melchert, and

Table 5.3 Illegal Drugs: Personality Disorder and Outcome

Authors	N	Sex	Treatment	Follow-up	Outcome
Woody et al. (1985)	110	M	Methadone + psychotherapy	7 months	ASPD poorer outcome
Kosten et al. (1989)	150	M/F	Mixture	2, 5 years	ASPD more legal BPD more depression Narcissistic more medical
Gill et al. (1992)	55	M/F	Methadone	12 months	No
Nace & Davis (1993)	100	M/F	Mixture	12 months	PD used more alcohol
Cacciola et al. (1996)	197	M	Methadone	7 months	No
Marlowe et al. (1997)	137	M/F	Outpatient	33 weeks	Dimensional BPD, ASPD, Compulsive: Negative outcome Dependent: Positive outcome
Ravndal & Vaglum (1998)	200	M/F	TC	5 years	Dimensional antisocial, Narcissistic: Increased rate of death (OR = 4.8)
Cecero et al. (1999)	370	M/F	Mixture	12 months	No
Messina et al. (1999, 2002)	275	M/F	TC	12 months	No
Ouimette et al. (1999)	3008	M	Mixture	12 months	No. Axis I more important
Thomas et al. (1999)	104	M/F	Inpatient	12 months	PD relapse more often
Galen et al. (2000)	235	M/F	Outpatient	6 months	PD worse outcome
McKay et al. (2000)	127	M	Mixture	12 months	No
Compton et al. (2003)	401	M/F	Mixture	12 months	ASPD men poorer outcome

(*Continued*)

Table 5.3 Illegal Drugs: Personality Disorder and Outcome (continued)

Authors	N	Sex	Treatment	Follow-up	Outcome
Grella et al. (2003)	707	M/F	Mixture	5 years	Male ASPD poor outcome substances Female ASPD more psychiatric problems
Haro et al. (2004)	74	M/F	Detoxification	6 months	ASPD poorer outcome

Banken (1999) conducted a 1-year follow-up of 104 polysubstance users of both genders. Patients with one or more PD relapsed more often during the 1st year. Galen, Brower, Gillespie, and Zucker (2000) followed 235 treatment center outpatients for 6 months. ASPD was related to poorer substance-related outcomes, but not to psychiatric outcomes. Compton, Cottler, Jacobs, Ben Abdallah, and Spitznagel (2003) followed 401 male and female drug-dependent subjects admitted to a mixture of treatment programs over 1 year. Men with ASPD had poorer outcome. Grella, Joshi, and Hser (2003) examined long-term outcomes following drug treatment in male (n = 453) and female (n = 254) cocaine users with and without ASPD. At the 5-year follow-up, men with ASPD had an increased likelihood of heavy alcohol use and additional substance use treatment, whereas women with ASPD were more likely to report psychological problems and to receive mental health services. Haro, Mateu, Martinez-Raga, Valderrama, Castellano, and Cervera (2004) followed up over 6 months a sample of 74 opiate users admitted for detoxification. ASPD was the only PD that influenced the substance use negatively.

Seven studies found no relation between PD and substance use outcome. However, in their study of 150 opiate addicts from a mixture of treatments, Kosten, Kosten, and Rounsaville (1989) found that ASPD patients more often had legal problems, narcissistic PD patients had more medical problems, and BPD patients had more depressive and alcohol-related problems at two-and-a-half-year follow-up. In the study of VA inpatients by Ouimette et al. (1999), the PD group did not have a significantly lower percentage of abstinent people, substance use problems, or arrests at 1-year follow-up. Instead, the psychotic or anxiety/depressive subgroups had significantly higher level of nervous distress and psychiatric symptoms, and were less likely to be employed at 1-year follow-up (35.9%) than the PD subgroup, a finding that has been replicated by Moggi et al. (2002). In the studies by Gill, Nolimal, and Crowley (1992), Cecero et al. (1999), Messina, Wish, and Nemes (1999), Messina, Wish, Hoffman, and Nemes (2002), and McKay, Alterman, Cacciola,

Mulvaney, and O'Brien (2000), which examined patients from different treatment modalities, there was no relationship between PD and the course of substance use.

Subgroups of ASPD

Several studies have tried to identify subtypes of ASPD patients with different prognoses. Cecero et al. (1999) compared different subtypes of ASPD from a mixture of treatment modalities, but found no difference in outcome. They found, however, that ASPD patients with a history of lifetime depression had a greater reduction in psychiatric severity during the 1-year follow-up. This was a replication of the findings from the study by Woody et al. (1985) of psychotherapy patients with ASPD, and the study by Alterman et al. (1996) of a sample from a methadone program. It was later replicated by Tomasson and Vaglum (2000) in a nationwide sample of treated Icelandic alcoholics. King et al. (2001) also examined the effect of comorbidity of other Axis I or II diagnoses on the relationship between ASPD and substance use outcome after 1 year. ASPD-only patients exhibited higher rates of cocaine and heroin use than ASPD-mixed patients (with other psychiatric disorders), who had more psychiatric problems and used more benzodiazepines at follow-up.

Discussion

Methodological Considerations, Research Implications

The reviewed studies were mostly done with a "before and after" follow-up design, and only five studies did more than one follow-up examination (Tomasson & Vaglum, 1996, 1997; Ravndal & Vaglum, 1998; Verheul et al., 1998; Kranzler et al., 1996; Grella et al., 2003). The last four found a relationship between PD and SUD outcome.

The methods for PD diagnosis were primarily the structured diagnostic interviews SCID II and DIS. They have a high-potential reliability, but only few studies have published interrater reliability tests. A few studies used the self-report instrument MCMI (Craig, 1984; Stark & Campbell, 1988; Ravndal & Vaglum, 1991a, b, 1998, 1999a, b; Messina et al., 2002), which may have a tendency to overdiagnose PDs if one uses the data categorically. One study used SCID II criteria dimensionally (Marlowe et al., 1997). In the last study, there was no PD-SUD outcome relationship when one used categorical PD diagnoses, but a clear correlation emerged when one used SCID dimensionally. The findings from Ravndal and Vaglum (1991a, b, 1998), who revealed that dimensionally measured PDs affected treatment response and death at 5-year follow-up, also indicate a possible advantage of using dimensional instruments. With more use of dimensional measurements, a more differentiated picture of the influence of PDs may have emerged. It is also possible that, using dimensional personality instruments measuring normal traits (like NEO-PI), one may glean important additional information regarding the influence of personality on course and outcome.

In the eight studies that measured ASPD only, one may have missed the effect of other PDs, and thereby underestimated the importance of PDs in general. However, several studies found that the effect on outcome of ASPD was not very specific among the different PDs. Because the prevalence of most of the PDs was relatively low in each sample, most of the authors collapsed all PDs and only analyzed the differences between PD and no-PD, as well as ASPD and no-ASPD. In some samples, the prevalence of ASPD was very low (Nace & Davis, 1993; Haver, 2003), and the importance of ASPD may be greater than that identified in the total sample of studies. A few studies, mostly using dimensional scores, identified a relationship between outcome and narcissistic, histrionic, borderline, schizoid, compulsive, and dependent PDs. One may think that the patients' relationship to the therapists would be less difficult and provoking in the methadone maintenance programs compared with the psychosocial/TC/psychotherapy programs, and the importance of PD therefore should be greater in the psychosocial programs. This difference was not found, and therefore warrants more focused research. There is also a clear need for studies that focus on PDs other than ASPD and BPD, even if these two PDs are the most prevalent in the majority of samples. In all, it seems that the most important difference that has been identified in the literature to date is the importance of the presence or absence of one or more PDs.

The diagnosis of treatment completion or compliance has face validity, whereas the measurement of SUD outcome may be less reliable and valid. The source of information on substance use outcome varies significantly, and most studies had an attrition rate that was not described in relation to PD. Consequently, the unexplained attrition may have resulted in an underestimation of the importance of PD for the outcome. If, for example, the PD diagnosis of the deceased people had not been known and included in the analyses, the study by Ravndal and Vaglum (1998) would have missed the result that a high score on the MCMI narcissistic (and antisocial) dimension was highly predictive of death during 5-year follow-up. The conclusion based upon the interviewed sample would therefore have been that there was no connection between PD and SUD outcome.

The samples usually included both genders, but only one study (Grella et al., 2003) found a difference in outcome between the genders. The most common treatment modalities, and the most frequent types of substances among treated substance users, were represented in the studies. The samples were also sufficiently large to be clinical samples, but the representativity of nearly all of the samples was, as always in clinical research, somewhat unclear. There is therefore a need for more studies from different drug scenes, countries, and treatment modalities to separate general trends from the local influence of PDs. Five studies (none of which were European) concerned relatively large samples from a mixture of treatment modalities (Rounsaville et al., 1987; Kosten et al., 1989; Nace & Davis, 1993; Kranzler et al., 1996; Ouimette et al., 1999; Compton et al., 2003), and should therefore be able to detect a possible connection between PD and SUD across treatment modalities. All these studies found a negative influence of PD on treatment response or outcome, a strong indication that the variation in results among the studies of single programs may be due to special, but undefined, characteristics of the samples, or differences in the quality of the treatment delivered.

Compliance with Treatment

Among the 12 studies of treatment completion or dropout, in only four studies was PD unrelated to poor compliance or completion; these were from two methadone maintenance programs, one detoxification program, and one outpatient program. This finding is very important, because it shows that most treatment programs have comparatively lower success in establishing a working relationship with PD patients compared with non-PD patients. This is not surprising, because a main characteristic of people with cluster B and A type PDs is that they have great problems both establishing and maintaining close relationships, including therapeutic relationships. In addition, they have poor impulse control, affective instability and often, a narcissistic disturbance of the self, all personality disturbances that make establishing contact especially difficult and demanding on clinical competence.

Most of the research on compliance and completion has been based on the notion that completion of treatment is strongly related to outcome. There is some evidence for this (De Leon & Ziegenfuss, 1986); however, some of the studies in this review showed that completion of an inpatient program is not necessarily followed by compliance with the ensuing outpatient program (Ravndal & Vaglum, 1999b; Ouimette et al., 1999; Ross et al., 2003). This means that a program may overvalue the effects of inpatient treatment on PD patients if one does not include in the evaluation the compliance with the outpatient regime.

Relation between Personality Disorder and Substance Use at Follow-Up

Among the 12 outcome studies of alcoholics, 7 found a relation between PD and SUD outcome. In addition, one study found that ASPD is related to unemployment, and another demonstrated that ASPD is related to the number of criminal arrests. One study (Moggi et al., 2002) even found that PD is a positive predictor of the results of inpatient treatment; however, an evaluation after the outpatient period is required to ascertain the true importance of this finding. Among the 16 studies of illegal drug users, 10 found a relationship between PD and SUD outcome. In addition, one study found that PDs are related to legal, psychiatric, or medical outcome (Kosten et al., 1989). In all, this means that, from 28 studies, 17 (60%) revealed that the index treatment (or unknown additional help or treatment during follow-up) does not completely reduce the importance of PD for the further course and outcome. A discussion of how and why PDs continue to be related to the course of substance use is outside the scope of this review. There may be different mechanisms driving a possible etiological influence of PDs on the development of substance use, and behind the influence of PDs on the course of an already-established substance use. The mechanisms of the last type of influence (biological, psychological, social) are still poorly studied, although there are studies of the possible mechanisms determining the general PD-SUD association (see, for example, Mueser, Drake, & Wallach, 1998; Mulder, 2002; Sher & Trull, 2002).

The characteristics of the studies concerning gender, type of substance, PD diagnostic method, type of treatment modality, and length of follow-up have been thoroughly scrutinized to find any systematic difference between those studies that identified a relationship between PD and SUD outcome and those that did not. It is not possible to identify any systematic differences between studies. This indicates that the differences may be due to other factors, like the degree of dependence, the local level of employment, or possibly the quality of the local treatment and helping system in general. There is still a need for qualitative and quantitative research that attempts to identify the qualities of the treatment programs within a certain treatment modality (methadone maintenance, TC, psychotherapy programs, etc.) in which the influence of PD on course and outcome is nullified.

Some studies have tried to identify subgroups of ASPD patients who were more available for therapy or had a better prognosis. The clearest finding is that pure ASPD patients (who may be the most psychopathic) have a poorer course than ASPD patients who also report that they have been depressed. In short, this finding shows that the importance of ASPD diagnosis for course and outcome may be highly dependent on the type of comorbidity, and ASPD should by itself not be an exclusion criterion for any treatment program.

In several studies, PDs also have been found to be related to the course of legal, medical, social, and psychiatric problems such as suicidal behavior, anxiety, and depression. This is not systematically reviewed here. Nevertheless, the relation between different PDs and the course of psychiatric, legal, medical, and social functioning is in itself an indication of the importance of addressing PD problems in the patient population of the SUD treatment systems. Together with the findings that PDs also are directly related to compliance and completion of treatment, and to the ongoing course of the use, this may imply that focusing more on PDs may facilitate greater treatment gains. However, the magnitude of this is difficult to predict, as the reliability of the outcome measure concerning substance use is unclear, and the correlation between PD and SUD outcome may have been underestimated. It must also be underlined that there is a great need for studies that focus on the effect of different programs that explicitly try to change severe PDs among the patients (van den Bosch, Verheul, Schippers, & van den Brink, 2002).

Clinical Implications

This review shows that a proportion of treatment programs do not manage to reduce the effect of PDs, neither regarding treatment compliance and completion nor the ensuing posttreatment course of substance use. However, it is not possible to identify variables that characterize the successful programs, and this implies that each program must do its own evaluation to identify whether patients with PD experience a poorer outcome in the particular program. For such a systematic evaluation, the instruments used in the reviewed studies may give reliable and valid information. Based on which types of PD are found to be related to poor compliance or outcome in a particular program, the program should develop a strategy for how to develop a better working relationship with the PD patients, and how to dissociate their main personality problems from the need for substances. It is important to note that one cannot know whether a treatment program manages to involve and treat PD and no-PD patients equally without following up one's own sample.

Gold and Brady (2003) recently summarized our knowledge concerning evidence-based treatment for substance users. They highlighted the need for more research, and underlined that the choice of therapy or therapies should be based on the needs of the individual patient (see also McLellan, Grissom, Zanis, Randall, Brill, & O'Brien [1997] on "matching"). For people with chronic severe addictions, which was the case for most of the samples in this review, they advocated a comprehensive approach with a continuing treatment format and participation in community support groups. The findings in this review concerning the importance of PD for outcome strongly support these conclusions. For increasing the effect of treatment of PD patients, it is also important to recognize that, in all types of treatment programs, there is a need for the therapists to have the necessary competence in diagnosing PDs, and in establishing and continuing a relationship with patients with severe PDs like ASPD, BPD, and narcissistic PD. There is a growing literature on the application of psychotherapy methods among substance users. For example, Woody, McLellan, Luborsky, and O'Brien (1995) described the use of psychotherapy in community methadone programs. Ball (1998) described dual schema-focused therapy for substance users with PD. Crits-Christoph and Siqueland (1996) reviewed the psychosocial treatments for drug use, and Crits-Christoph et al. (1999) identified a successful program with a combination of individual and group drug counseling for cocaine use. Van den Bosch et al. (2002) found that dialectical behavior therapy could be effectively applied to substance users with BPD, but it did not have a better effect on the substance using problems than treatment as usual. It should also be mentioned that the 12-step programs are designed in a way that may fit very well in a relationship with substance users with narcissistic personality problems (Vaglum, 1999).

In conclusion, this literature review has shown that PDs often are related to treatment compliance and completion and to the posttreatment course of substance use. In addition, PDs may be related to the outcome of legal, psychiatric, medical, and social problems. In spite of several methodological limitations and flaws connected to the studies so far, it is reasonable to conclude that, independent of the type of treatment program, therapists should be able to diagnose PDs and to establish a working relationship with people with severe PDs. There is a need for further research on the effect of changing PD traits in substance use treatments.

Summary

This review of the literature from the years 1984 to 2004 shows that both the treatment response and the posttreatment course and outcome of substance abuse very often are directly negatively related to the presence of one or more personality disorders. In all types of treatment modalities, several programs were not able to neutralize this relationship. In addition, studies indicate that PDs also are related to the course of other types of psychopathology and disturbed behavior than substance abuse. It is important that each treatment program has focus on the PDs that are most important in the particular patient population, and develop a strategy for increased involvement of patients with PDs in working relationships. Therapists in the substance abuse field highly need competence in diagnosing and treating personality disorders, regardless of type of treatment modality. Further research, especially concerning psychotherapeutic treatment of PDs among substance abusers, is necessary.

References

Alterman, A. I., Rutherford, M. J., Cacciola, J. S., McKay, J. R., & Woody, G. E. (1996). Response to methadone maintenance and counseling in antisocial patients with and without major depression. *Journal of Nervous and Mental Disease, 184,* 695–702.

Ball, S. A. (1998). Manualized treatment for substance abusers with personality disorders: Dual focus schema therapy. *Addictive Behaviors, 23,* 883–891.

Cacciola, J. S., Alterman, A. I., Rutherford, M. J., & Snider, E. C. (1995). Treatment response of antisocial substance abusers. *Journal of Nervous and Mental Disease, 183,* 166–171.

Cacciola, J. S., Rutherford, M. J., Alterman, A. I., McKay, J. R., & Snider, E. C. (1996). Personality disorders and treatment outcome in methadone maintenance patients. *Journal of Nervous and Mental Disease, 184,* 234–239.

Cecero, J. J., Ball, S. A., Tennen, H., Kranzler, H. R., & Rounsaville, B. J. (1999). Concurrent and predictive validity of antisocial personality disorder subtyping among substance abusers. *Journal of Nervous and Mental Disease, 187,* 478–486.

Ciraulo, D. A., Piechniczek-Buczek, J., & Iscan, E. N. (2003). Outcome predictors in substance use disorders. *Psychiatric Clinics of North America, 26,* 381–409.

Compton, W. M., III, Cottler, L. B., Jacobs, J. L., Ben Abdallah, A., & Spitznagel, E. L. (2003). The role of psychiatric disorders in predicting drug dependence treatment outcomes. *American Journal of Psychiatry, 160,* 890–895.

Craig, R. J. (1984). Can personality tests predict treatment dropouts? *The International Journal of the Addictions, 19,* 665–674.

Crits-Christoph, P., & Siqueland, L. (1996). Psychosocial treatment for drug abuse. Selected review and recommendations for national health care. *Archives of General Psychiatry, 53,* 749–756.

Crits-Christoph, P., Siqueland, L., Blaine, J., Frank, A., Luborsky, L., Onken, L. S., et al. (1999). Psychosocial treatments for cocaine dependence: National Institute on Drug Abuse Collaborative Cocaine Treatment Study. *Archives of General Psychiatry, 56,* 493–502.

De Leon, G., & Ziegenfuss, J. T. (1986). *Therapeutic communities for addictions.* Springfield, IL: Charles C. Thomas.

Galen, L. W., Brower, K. J., Gillespie, B. W., & Zucker, R. A. (2000). Sociopathy, gender, and treatment outcome among outpatient substance abusers. *Drug and Alcohol Dependence, 61,* 23–33.

Gill, K., Nolimal, D., & Crowley, T. J. (1992). Antisocial personality disorder, HIV risk behavior and retention in methadone maintenance therapy. *Drug and Alcohol Dependence, 30,* 247–252.

Gold, P. B., & Brady, K. T. (2003). Evidence-based treatments for substance use disorders. *FOCUS The Journal of Lifelong Learning in Psychiatry, 1,* 115–122.

Grant, B. F., Stinson, F. S., Dawson, D. A., Chou, S. P., Ruan, W. J., & Pickering, R. P. (2004). Co-occurrence of 12-month alcohol and drug use disorders and personality disorders in the United States: Results from the National Epidemiologic Survey on Alcohol and Related Conditions. *Archives of General Psychiatry, 61,* 361–368.

Grella, C. E., Joshi, V., & Hser, Y. I. (2003). Followup of cocaine-dependent men and women with antisocial personality disorder. *Journal of Substance Abuse Treatment, 25,* 155–164.

Haro, G., Mateu, C., Martinez-Raga, J., Valderrama, J. C., Castellano, M., & Cervera, G. (2004). The role of personality disorders on drug dependence treatment outcomes following inpatient detoxification. *European Psychiatry, 19,* 187–192.

Haver, B. (2003). Comorbid psychiatric disorders predict and influence treatment outcome in female alcoholics. *European Addiction Research, 9,* 39–44.

King, V. L., Kidorf, M. S., Stoller, K. B., Carter, J. A., & Brooner, R. K. (2001). Influence of antisocial personality subtypes on drug abuse treatment response. *Journal of Nervous and Mental Disease, 189,* 593–601.

Kokkevi, A., Stefanis, N., Anastasopoulou, E., & Kostogianni, C. (1998). Personality disorders in drug abusers: Prevalence and their association with AXIS I disorders as predictors of treatment retention. *Addictive Behaviors, 23,* 841–853.

Kosten, T. A., Kosten, T. R., & Rounsaville, B. J. (1989). Personality disorders in opiate addicts show prognostic specificity. *Journal of Substance Abuse Treatment, 6,* 163–168.

Kranzler, H. R., Del Boca, F. K., & Rounsaville, B. J. (1996). Comorbid psychiatric diagnosis predicts three-year outcomes in alcoholics: A posttreatment natural history study. *Journal of Studies on Alcohol, 57,* 619–626.

Landheim, A. S., Bakken, K., & Vaglum, P. (2003). Gender differences in the prevalence of symptom disorders and personality disorders among poly-substance abusers and pure alcoholics. Substance abusers treated in two counties in Norway. *European Addiction Research, 9,* 8–17.

Marlowe, D. B., Kirby, K. C., Festinger, D. S., Husband, S. D., & Platt, J. J. (1997). Impact of comorbid personality disorders and personality disorder symptoms on outcomes of behavioral treatment for cocaine dependence. *Journal of Nervous and Mental Disease, 185,* 483–490.

McKay, J. R., Alterman, A. I., Cacciola, J. S., Mulvaney, F. D., & O'Brien, C. P. (2000). Prognostic significance of antisocial personality disorder in cocaine-dependent patients entering continuing care. *Journal of Nervous and Mental Disease, 188,* 287–296.

McLellan, A. T., Grissom, G. R., Zanis, D., Randall, M., Brill, P., & O'Brien, C. P. (1997). Problem-service 'matching' in addiction treatment. A prospective study in 4 programs. *Archives of General Psychiatry, 54,* 730–735.

Messina, N. P., Wish, E. D., Hoffman, J. A., & Nemes, S. (2002). Antisocial personality disorder and TC treatment outcomes. *American Journal of Drug and Alcohol Abuse, 28,* 197–212.

Messina, N. P., Wish, E. D., & Nemes, S. (1999). Therapeutic community treatment for substance abusers with antisocial personality disorder. *Journal of Substance Abuse Treatment, 17,* 121–128.

Moggi, F., Brodbeck, J., Koltzsch, K., Hirsbrunner, H. P., & Bachmann, K. M. (2002). One-year follow-up of dual diagnosis patients attending a 4-month integrated inpatient treatment. *European Addiction Research, 8,* 30–37.

Mueser, K. T., Drake, R. E., & Wallach, M. A. (1998). Dual diagnosis: A review of etiological theories. *Addictive Behaviors, 23,* 717–734.

Mulder, R. T. (2002). Alcoholism and personality. *Australian and New Zealand Journal of Psychiatry, 36,* 44–52.

Nace, E. P., & Davis, C. W. (1993). Treatment outcome in substance-abusing patients with a personality disorder. *The American Journal on Addictions, 2,* 26–33.

Nace, E. P., Saxon, J. J., Jr., & Shore, N. (1986). Borderline personality disorder and alcoholism treatment: A one-year follow-up study. *Journal of Studies on Alcohol, 47,* 196–200.

Ouimette, P. C., Gima, K., Moos, R. H., & Finney, J. W. (1999). A comparative evaluation of substance abuse treatment IV. The effect of comorbid psychiatric diagnoses on amount of treatment, continuing care, and 1-year outcomes. *Alcoholism: Clinical and Experimental Research, 23,* 552–557.

Poldrugo, F., & Forti, B. (1988). Personality disorders and alcoholism treatment outcome. *Drug and Alcohol Dependence, 21,* 171–176.

Powell, B. J., Penick, E. C., Nickel, E. J., Liskow, B. I., Riesenmy, K. D., Campion, S. L., et al. (1992). Outcomes of co morbid alcoholic men: a 1-year follow-up. *Alcoholism: Clinical and Experimental Research, 16,* 131–138.

Ravndal, E., & Vaglum, P. (1991a). Psychopathology and substance abuse as predictors of program completion in a therapeutic community for drug abusers: A prospective study. *Acta Psychiatrica Scandinavica, 83,* 217–222.

Ravndal, E., & Vaglum, P. (1991b). Changes in antisocial aggressiveness during treatment in a hierarchical therapeutic community. A prospective study of personality changes. *Acta Psychiatrica Scandinavica, 84,* 524–530.

Ravndal, E., & Vaglum, P. (1998). Psychopathology, treatment completion and 5 years outcome. A prospective study of drug abusers. *Journal of Substance Abuse Treatment, 15,* 135–142.

Ravndal, E., & Vaglum, P. (1999a). Retention in a methadone programme: The importance of psychopathology. A prospective study. *Journal of Substance Use, 4,* 16–23.

Ravndal, E., & Vaglum, P. (1999b). Overdoses and suicide attempts: Different relations to psychopathology and substance abuse? A 5-year prospective study of drug abusers. *European Addiction Research, 5,* 63–70.

Ross, S., Dermatis, H., Levounis, P., & Galanter, M. (2003). A comparison between dually diagnosed inpatients with and without Axis II comorbidity and the relationship to treatment outcome. *American Journal of Drug and Alcohol Abuse, 29,* 263–279.

Rounsaville, B. J., Dolinsky, Z. S., Babor, T. F., & Meyer, R. E. (1987). Psychopathology as a predictor of treatment outcome in alcoholics. *Archives of General Psychiatry, 44,* 505–513.

Schuckit, M. A. (1985). The clinical implications of primary diagnostic groups among alcoholics. *Archives of General Psychiatry, 42,* 1043–1049.

Sher, K. J., & Trull, T. J. (2002). Substance use disorder and personality disorder. *Current Psychiatry Reports, 4,* 25–29.

Skodol, A. E., Oldham, J. M., & Gallaher, P. E. (1999). Axis II comorbidity of substance use disorders among patients referred for treatment of personality disorders. *American Journal of Psychiatry, 156,* 733–738.

Stark, M. J., & Campbell, B. K. (1988). Personality, drug use, and early attrition from substance abuse treatment. *American Journal of Drug and Alcohol Abuse, 14,* 475–485.

Thomas, V. H., Melchert, T. P., & Banken, J. A. (1999). Substance dependence and personality disorders: Comorbidity and treatment outcome in an inpatient treatment population. *Journal of Studies on Alcohol, 60,* 271–277.

Tómasson, K., & Vaglum, P. (1996). Psychopathology and alcohol consumption among treatment-seeking alcoholics: A prospective study. *Addiction, 91,* 1019–1030.

Tómasson, K., & Vaglum, P. (1997). The 2-year outcome of substance abuse and psychiatric distress: the influence of psychiatric comorbidity. *Eur Arch Psychiatry Clin Neuroscience, 247,* 320–327.

Tómasson, K., & Vaglum, P. (1998). Social consequences of substance abuse: The impact of comorbid psychiatric disorders. A prospective study of a nation-wide sample of treatment-seeking patients. *Scandinavian Journal of Social Medicine, 26,* 63–70.

Tómasson, K., & Vaglum, P. (2000). Antisocial addicts: The importance of additional axis I disorders for the 28-month outcome. *European Psychiatry, 15,* 443–449.

Vaglum, P. (1999). The narcissistic personality disorder and addiction. In J. Derksen, C. Maffei, & H. Groen (Eds.), *Treatment of personality disorders* (pp. 241–253). New York: Kluwer Academic/Plenum Publishers.

van den Bosch, L. M., Verheul, R., Schippers, G. M., & van den Brink, W. (2002). Dialectical Behavior Therapy of borderline patients with and without substance use problems. Implementation and long-term effects. *Addictive Behaviors, 27,* 911–923.

Verheul, R. (2001). Co-morbidity of personality disorders in individuals with substance use disorders. *European Psychiatry: The Journal of the Association of European Psychiatrists, 16,* 274–282.

Verheul, R., Kranzler, H. R., Poling, J., Tennen, H., Ball, S., & Rounsaville, B. J. (2000). Co-occurrence of Axis I and Axis II disorders in substance abusers. *Acta Psychiatrica Scandinavica, 101,* 110–118.

Verheul, R., van den Brink, W., & Hartgers, C. (1998). Personality disorders predict relapse in alcoholic patients. *Addictive Behaviors, 23,* 869–882.

Wolwer, W., Burtscheidt, W., Redner, C., Schwarz, R., & Gaebel, W. (2001). Out-patient behaviour therapy in alcoholism: Impact of personality disorders and cognitive impairments. *Acta Psychiatrica Scandinavica, 103,* 30–37.

Woody, G. E., McLellan, A. T., Luborsky, L., & O'Brien, C. P. (1985). Sociopathy and psychotherapy outcome. *Archives of General Psychiatry, 42,* 1081–1086.

Woody, G. E., McLellan, A. T., Luborsky, L., & O'Brien, C. P. (1995). Psychotherapy in community methadone programs: A validation study. *American Journal of Psychiatry, 152,* 1302–1308.

PART II
Treatment

CHAPTER **6**

Drug Treatment of Personality Disorder Traits

JAMES REICH

Key Teaching Points

- We do not have drug cures for specific personality disorders, but can sometimes reduce dysfunctional personality traits.
- It is best to try to minimize the total number of drugs and, as much as possible, to use the same drugs to treat both the patient's Axis I and Axis II disorders.
- Due to the intermittent and fluctuating nature of personality symptoms, trials can take somewhat longer than in Axis I disorders.
- Traditional neuroleptics are probably best used only in acute crisis situations.
- Tricyclic antidepressants are relatively contraindicated. If used for some other condition, it is best to use the desmethylated versions (e.g., nortriptaline, etc.).

- Monoamine oxidase inhibitors (MAOI) have been shown to be useful in rejection sensitivity, but interactions with other drugs and drug reactions (beer, wine, cheese) are a strong relative contraindication.
- SSRIs have been shown to be useful in a number of dysfunctional personality traits. If in doubt, not a bad place to start.
- Lithium has been shown to be helpful in certain impulsive disorders, although toxicity and drug interactions limit its use.
- Some evidence is present that carbamezepine is useful in behavioral dyscontrol. It is hard to use due to drug interactions. There is no evidence on more easy-to-use variants of the drug.
- Some evidence is present that divalproex sodium may be useful in the treatment of aggressive behavior, especially in personality cluster B (borderline cluster) patients.
- Short-acting benzodiazepines are strongly relatively contraindicated in treatment of personality traits. Long-acting benzodiazepines should be used only with great caution (if at all) in patients with disinhibiting personality traits.
- There is a small amount of information that naltrexone may be useful in borderline personality traits involving self-injurious behavior.
- An important principle of personality trait treatment is to minimize or eliminate alcohol and illegal substance use.
- Best results will be found if the patient is concurrently in therapy of some sort in addition to drug treatment.

Introduction

Personality disorders have a long history of being difficult to treat. Not many years ago it was felt that they could only be treated by skilled experts in intensive long-term psychotherapy. As our understanding of these disorders has improved with empirical research, so has our vision of what treatments can and should be. This includes our concept of psychopharmacologic treatment. At one time it was thought counterproductive to use drugs in the treatment of personality disordered patients at all as it would interfere with psychotherapy. Of course, as with any difficult patient group, clinicians will try whatever might work. This led to the realization that in at least some circumstances in some patients, drug treatment could be beneficial. We have found, however, that we do not have specific drug treatments for categorical personality disorders such as we have, for instance, for major depression or panic disorder. What we have is an array of drugs that help to some extent with certain symptoms traits commonly found in personality disorders.

We should approach drug treatment of personality disorder traits with caution and humility. Even when there is success in treatment, there are many possible pathways that might effect the change and we do not know which ones are responsible. For example, there could, of course, be a direct effect on the personality symptoms. There might also be an effect on comorbid Axis I disorders and these might indirectly affect the personality symptoms. There might also be a direct effect on the neuroendocrine system of the HPA axis which could indirectly affect both Axis I and Axis II symptoms. In addition, these systems (HPA axis, Axis I and axis II) interact with each other.

This chapter will update my previous review in this area (Reich, 2002). It will first examine some of the drugs that have been used and examine some of the evidence for their effectiveness. It will then take the mind-set of a clinician and look at how some symptoms clusters might be approached (see Table 6.1).

Evidence for Treatment of Personality Traits for Different Drugs

Traditional Neuroleptics

Because they are established as effective in the treatment of psychotic symptoms, traditional neuroleptics have been used extensively to treat paranoia, dissociation, ideas of reference, and illusions in personality disordered patients.

In a double-blind placebo-controlled study comparing low-dose haloperidol, tricyclic antidepressant, and placebo, Soloff, George, Nathan, Schulz, Ulrich, and Perel (1986) found that patients on haloperidol experienced gains in a number of areas. Improvements were reported in depression, anxiety, anger, hostility, impulsiveness, and paranoia. The superiority of haloperidol was not replicated in a subsequent study which compared it to phenelzine (an MAOI) and placebo (Soloff, Cornelius, George, Nathan, Perel, & Ulrich 1993). In this latter study, phenelzine produced superior results in the areas of depression, anxiety, anger, hostility, and other measures. Soloff hypothesized that haloperidol might be more effective in more impaired individuals. This was consistent with the conclusions of Goldberg, Schulz, Resnick, Hamer, and Friedel (1986) who used thiothixene in a double-blind placebo-controlled study, and found some usefulness in psychotic symptoms only, for severe borderline and schizotypal patients.

Cornelius, Soloff, Perel, and Ulrick (1993) performed a double-blind placebo-controlled continuation study comparing haloperidol (neuroleptic), phenelzine (MAOI), and placebo in borderline patients. The purpose

TABLE 6.1 Drug Classes Used in Treatment of Personality Traits

Drug Class	Indications	Contraindications and Comments
Traditional Neuroleptics	Acute exacerbation of personality symptoms for rapid control.	Efficacy is less impressive long term. This combined with high dropout rate and risk of tardive dyskinesia limits situations where it is used.
Atypical antipsychotics	These appear to be of use on a number of symptoms of borderline personality disorder, psychotic symptoms, and perhaps self-injury.	Side effects vary by the agent used. Best studied is cloazaril which is probably a good choice in treatment-resistant cases.
Tricyclic antidepressants	Some evidence in borderline personality patients.	Little used due to instances of paradoxical rage reactions, weight gain, orthostatic hypotension, and lethality in overdose. Almost entirely replaced by SSRIs. If used, desmethylated forms (i.e., nortiptaline) should be used.
Monoamine oxidase inhibitors	Good evidence helpful in some personality traits especially rejection sensitivity.	Seldom used due to drug interactions, "beer, wine and cheese reaction," and lethality in overdose.
Selective seritonergic response inhibitors (SSRIs)	First-line drug for personality symptoms involving mood shifts, irritability, and aggression.	Very well studied with 11 double-blind studies. Relatively few side effects.
Mood stabilizers	Many mood stabilizers appear to have positive effects with depakote currently being the first line for bipolar disorders with cluster B personality traits.	Good evidence for depakote and cluster B traits. Good evidence for lithium and impulsive and aggressive symptoms, but limited by toxicity. Lesser information on other compounds.

(Continued)

TABLE 6.1 Drug Classes Used in Treatment of Personality Traits (continued)

Drug Class	Indications	Contraindications and Comments
Benzodiazepines	Used for acute control of symptoms and possibly cluster C pathology. Strongly contraindicated in cluster B and where there is impulsive behavior.	Can worsen impulsive behavior. Relative contraindication in substance abuse. If used drugs with longer half-life are preferred.
Naltrexone	Possible use in self-injury and dissociative symptoms.	Little data, but may help treat important personality symptoms.

of the study was to determine whether patients could receive benefit from drug treatment past the initial crisis stage. Haloperidol lacked strong efficacy, but did reduce irritability beyond the acute treatment phase. When dropout rates are examined, haloperidol was again unimpressive. Mean survival time was 8.4 weeks compared to 13.4 weeks for phenelzine and 17.8 weeks for placebo.

Cowdry and Gardner (1988) did a double-blind study on 16 women with borderline personality comparing alprazolam (benzodiazepine), carbemazepine (mood stabilizer), tranylcypromine (MAOI), trifluperazine (neuroleptic), and placebo. This was a crossover design where all patients received all five conditions. Although there was some reported gain with trifluperazine in anxiety reduction, suicidality, depression, and sensitivity rejection, 50% discontinued this trial arm due to side effects or exacerbation of symptoms.

In sum, although some gains have been reported using traditional neuroleptics, the results are not impressive after the initial crisis, and the dropout rate is high. The literature indicates they should be used in low doses and, even so, there is a high dropout rate. The risk of tardive dyskinesia should always be kept in mind. They seem to be of most use in the most severely ill patients.

Atypical Antipsychotics

Clozapine. The literature on the atypical neuroleptics is nowhere near as extensive as the traditional neuroleptics. There are several trials with clozapine. An open label report by Frankenburg and Zanarini (1993) on 15 severe patients with borderline personality disorder showed some improvement of psychotic symptoms. The doses were relatively high and there were many side effects. Another study of 12 borderline patients using lower doses of clozapine also found reduced psychotic symptoms and increase in global functioning. There were fewer side effects in this study, most likely due to the lower dose (Benedetti, Sforzini, Colombo, Maffei, & Smeraldi, 1998). A report on seven severe borderline patients treated with clozapine indicated a significant reduction in self-mutilation (Chengappa, Ebeling, Kang, Levine, & Parepally, 1999). A single case report also indicated clozapine reduced self-mutilation (Ferrerri, Loze, Roullon, & Limosin, 2004). Clozapine is probably a good choice for a trial with highly treatment-resistant cases.

Risperidone. Risperidone was shown to reduce psychotic symptoms in seven borderline patients (Verhoven et al., 1999). In a larger open trial of borderline patients without other currently active Axis I disorders, risperidone (mean dose of 3.27 mg) significantly reduced aggression (Rocca, Marchiaro, Cocuzza, & Bogetto, 2002). Although there were only 15 patients and an open trial, the results are promising.

There is a study of patients with schizotypal personality disorder (Koenigsberg et al., 2003). This was a double-blind placebo-controlled study of 25 patients over 9 weeks. Significant reductions in the Positive and Negative Syndrome Scale (PANSS) were found. There are two case reports of decreased self-mutilation (Szigethy & Schulz, 1997; Khouzam & Donnelly, 1997).

Olanzapine. There are a few reports on olanzapine. One studied 11 borderline patients on olanzapine monotherapy and reported significant reductions in five global ratings (Schulz, Camlin, Berry, & Jesberger, 1999). A case report indicates decreased self-mutilation behavior (Hough, 2001). A chart review study of 10 patients on from 2.5 to 20 mg indicated a significant reduction of symptoms (Zullino, Quinche, Hafliger, & Stigler, 2002).

There are two reports in this area from Zanarini et al. The first was a preliminary report of 45 borderline women, randomized to either fluoxetine, olanzapine, or a combination of the two drugs (Zanarini, Frankenberg, & Parachini, 2004). Treatment outcomes were depression and impulsivity. They concluded that olanzapine alone or in combination produced clinical benefits. The second report compared olanzapine to placebo in 27 borderline females (Zanarini & Frankenberg 2001). Six months of treatment resulted in improvement in anxiety, paranoia, anger/hostility, and interpersonal sensitivity.

Perhaps the best study so far is by Bogenschutz and Nurnberg (2004). Here 40 borderline patients (both males and females) without other current Axis I disorder were randomized to either placebo or olanzapine (2.5 to 20 mg a day). Outcome was like rt scales of borderline criteria. Significant improvement within personality symptoms was found.

Quetiapine. There are two reports on quetiapine. The first is two case reports on female borderlines with severe cutting behavior (Hilger, Barnas, & Kasper, 2003). This indicates that quetiapine in doses between 200 and 800 mg a day might be useful in stopping self-injurious behavior. The second (Walker, Thomas, & Allen, 2003) indicated that in four antisocial personality disorder patients, quetiapine in doses from 600 to 800 mg a day reduced impulsivity, hostility, aggressiveness, and rage reactions.

Tricyclic Antidepressants

The use of tricyclic antidepressants has been fairly well investigated in borderline personality disorder. Early open label trials showed some benefit (Fink, Pollack, & Klein, 1964; Klein, 1968). Later double-blind trials found a modest improvement in some patients treated with amytriptaline; however, there was a paradoxical effect in some patients with an increase in hostility and affective instability (Soloff, George, Nathan, Schulz, & Peel, 1986a; Soloff, George, Nathan, Schulz, Ulrich, & Perel, 1986b). The paradoxical effects, low efficacy, and side effects (lethality in overdose, weight gain, sedation, and dry mouth) are strong relative contraindications to its use, at least in borderline patients.

Monoamine Oxidase Inhibitors (MAOI)

MAOIs have been of interest for personality features before the borderline personality diagnosis was widespread. It was hypothesized that MOAI treatment would be useful for an atypical type of depression with extreme rejection sensitivity called hysteroid dyshporia. Liebowitz et al. (1988) examined the effects of phenelzine (MAOI), imipramine (TCA), and placebo in this population. Phenelzine was superior to imipramine and placebo. Parsons et al. (1989) examined a subsample from the study of patients who had maintained mood reactivity while depressed. Among these patients, there was a response rate of 92% on phenelzine, 35% for imipramine, and 25% for placebo.

In a double-blind placebo study of borderline personality, Soloff et al. (1993) found that phenelzine produced superior results compared to a TCA and placebo. This superiority included the areas of depression, anxiety, and hostility. Cowdry and Gardner (1988) in their crossover study found significant improvement for tranylcypromine in the areas of depression, anger, loneliness, and rejection sensitivity. (These were patients who had comorbid borderline personality and hysteroid dsyphoria and who, therefore, had extreme rejection sensitivity.)

From the information we have, MAOIs represent a possible treatment of borderline personality traits of affective lability, hostility, and rejection sensitivity. Their use is limited by their lethality in overdose and drug interactions (beer, wine, and cheese reaction) in a group of patients who at times tend to react suddenly and impulsively.

Selective Seritonergic Response Inhibitors (SSRIs)

There are now 11 double-blind studies on the effect of SSRIs on personality traits. Cocarro and Kavoussi (1997) examined a population of personality-disordered patients without concurrent affective disorder, schizophrenia, or substance abuse. Treatment with fluoxetine resulted in sustained reduction of irritability and aggression scores.

A study of a normal population treated with paroxetine demonstrated a reduction in hostility and negative affect (Knutson et al., 1998). One study has examined the additive effects of fluoxetine when compared to dialectic behavior therapy (DBT) (Simpson et al., 2004). Although the sample size was relatively small (20 patients) the results are intriguing. They report that fluoxetine had no advantage when added to a group that successfully completed a 12-week DBT program.

Rinne, van den Brink, Wouters, and van Dyck (2002) performed a double-blind study of the use of fluvoxamine in female borderline patients. They reported a significant decrease in rapid mood shifts with active treatment. They did not find any improvement in impulsivity and aggression, as previously reported in other studies. They hypothesized that this may have been due to their female sample.

There are a number of studies of the treatment of personality traits in patients with depressive illness. Fava, Bouffides, Pava, McCarthy, Steingard, and Rosenbaum (1994) found a general reduction in personality disorder traits treated with paroxetine. Salzman et al. (1995) studied an outpatient borderline population with anxiety and depressive symptoms, but not major depression. Treatment with fluoxetine resulted in a significant decrease in anger. A treatment study of major depression with sertraline or paroxetine over 24 weeks demonstrated reductions in all three DSM personality clusters (Aberg-Wistedt, Agren, Ekselius, Bengtson, & Akerblad, 2000). Zanarini et al. (2004) reported fluoxetine improved depression and impulsivity in a population of depressed female borderline patients. They concluded that it was less effective than olanzapine or olanzapine and fluoxetine in combination.

Ekselius and von Knorring (1998) examined the effect of treatment of sertraline and citalopram on the personality status of depressed patients in primary care. Both active treatments reduced the frequency of measured paranoid, avoidant, and dependent personality disorder diagnoses. Reductions of dimensional personality traits were found in most categories. Importantly, the effect of state changes on the outcome was examined. Although the change in state depression did effect the reduction in personality traits, the R squared never exceeded 0.24 (this was in the cluster C personality disorders).

Another report examining the use of paroxetine, fluvoxetine, and fluoxetine indicated a general reduction in personality pathology (Black & Sheline, 1997). A large double-blind study of sertraline on dysthymic patients showed a significant reduction in harm avoidance (Hellerstein, Kocsis, Chapman, Stewart, & Harrison, 2000). One report examined the effect of paroxetine on chronically suicidal patients who did not have major depression (Verkes, Vander Mast, Hengeveld, Tuyl, Zwinderman, & Van Kempen 1998). A significant reduction in both personality traits and suicidal behavior was found.

The overall findings indicate that SSRIs can be of significant help in the reduction of personality pathology. Most positive findings are in the area of irritability and aggression and mood shifts, but may affect much broader areas of personality functioning. The onset can be relatively rapid (1 to 2 weeks). Dosage ranges are from those used to treat depression up to the dosages used to treat obsessive compulsive disorder. It is possible it may turn out that the symptoms treated may be different in males and females with mood shifts more treated in female borderline patients. Further studies are required. Further work will have to be done on how these treatments interact with psychosocial treatments.

Mood Stabilizers

Lithium. There have been a number of studies of lithium for mood lability in the personality disorders. Early work using the diagnosis emotionally unstable character disorder demonstrated some evidence against mood lability in adolescent girls (Rifkin, Levitan, Galewski, & Klein, 1972). Lithium was also reported to have efficacy against impulsive aggression in adult criminal subjects (Tupin, Smith, Clanon, Kim, Nugent, & Groupe 1973; Sheard, Marini, Bridges, & Wagner, 1976) and in delinquent adolescents (Shader, Jackson, & Dodes, 1974). There is a report of treatment of borderline patients with some positive effects (Goldberg, 1989).

There has been only one double-blind placebo-controlled study. Links, Steiner, Boiago, & Irwin (1990) compared lithium to desipramine in a double-blind crossover study. Therapists rated their patients as more improved on lithium on measures of irritability, anger, and suicidal symptoms.

Overall, it appears that lithium may be of use in some patients for impulsive aggressive symptoms. This should be balanced against its toxicity in overdose and side effects.

Carbamezepine (CPZ). There are two double-blind studies of CPZ. There is a 1986 study of 16 borderline personality disorder patients (all female) with a history of behavioral dyscontrol (Gardner & Cowdry, 1986). The study lasted 33 days, and CBZ significantly reduced the severity of the dyscontrol. The same authors later did a four-drug placebo-controlled crossover study described earlier (Cowdry & Gardner, 1988). This study showed significantly less behavioral dyscontrol on CBZ at an average dose of 820 mg. Unexpectedly, three subjects developed melancholic depression, which improved when the medication was discontinued.

CPZ appears to have potential use in some patients with episodic dyscontrol. It is a bit more complicated to use in patients on multiple medication due to its tendency to autoinduce its own metabolism and change blood levels of various medications. There is no evidence on the easier-to-use related compounds.

Divalproex Sodium. Divalproex sodium is another mood stabilizer that has received attention as a possible treatment. There are two double-blind placebo-controlled studies that I am aware of. In the first, Hollander et al. performed a 10-week trial in borderline patients (Hollander et al., 2001). There was a significant improvement in global measures in the actively treated group, but a high dropout rate precluded finding significant differences between active treatment and placebo.

The second double-blind study was also by Hollander et al. (2003). This was a study to treat impulsive aggression. Ninety-six patients in the study met the criteria for a cluster B personality disorder, 116 intermittent explosive disorder, and 34 for post-traumatic stress disorder. Treatment was with divalproex with a recommended serum level of 80 to 120. The only group to respond to treatment was the cluster B personality disorder group, which showed reductions in aggression, irritability, and severity of illness. The specificity of response of cluster B personality disorder makes this an important study.

Frankenburg and Zanarini (2002) reported a much smaller (n = 30) double-blind study of divalproex for the treatment of women with comorbid borderline personality disorder and bipolar disorder type two. Divalproex appeared useful in this population.

There are some open label studies. Stein, Simeon, Frenkel, Islam, and Hollander (1995) performed an 8-week treatment trial in borderline patients without comorbid depression or history of bipolar disorder. Only four of eight patients completing the trial reported significant improvement in mood and impulse symptoms. Wilcox studied a severe borderline population without comorbid disorders (Wilcox, 1995). When divalproex was added to ongoing medications, patients improved globally, especially in anxiety and tension.

Kavoussi and Coccaro (1998) reported a study showing divalproex to be useful across multiple personality diagnoses against irritability and impulsive aggressive behavior in patients who had failed treatment with an SSRI antidepressant. Townsend, Cambre, and Barbee (2001) used divalproex in a small population selected to meet the DSM borderline criteria for mood instability. Their preliminary findings were positive.

There is now some good evidence that divalproex may be of use for the treatment of impulsive and aggressive symptoms in cluster B personality disorders. The best estimate for effective blood levels at this time would be between 50 and 120 micrograms per ml. There is the likelihood that divalproex may be a good choice in patients with cluster B disorders combined with a bipolar disorder. There is preliminary evidence that divalproex might be useful for the symptom of mood instability.

Lamotrigine. There is one chart review report on lamotrigine in borderline personality disorder (Pinto & Akiskal, 1998). Eight patients were identified who had failed numerous prior trials of antidepressants and mood stabilizers. One developed rash, one was noncompliant, and three failed the trial. The other three showed significant response on doses of 75 to 300 mg a day.

A second report (Preston, Marchant, Reimherr, Strong, & Hedges, 2004) started with the observation that borderline personality is frequently comorbid in bipolar patients. They did a retrospective review of borderline symptoms in patients being treated for bipolar disorder. Borderline symptoms seemed to decrease in parallel with bipolar symptoms. It generally took a second medication in addition to lamotrigine to treat these patients.

Benzodiazepines

Benzodiazepines have a long history of effectiveness for anxiety. Their tendency to reduce anxiety and promote disinhibition makes them potentially useful in personality disorders characterized by anxiety and inhibition (i.e., avoidant personality disorder). However, disinhibition and anxiety reduction can be a problem in personality disorders characterized by impulsive behavior, hostile behavior, or behavior that is already disinhibited or self-destructive.

There is only one double-blind study of a benzodiazepine in a borderline population. This is the Cowdry and Gardner (1988) crossover study. Here alprazolam (a short half-life benzodiazepine) increased suicide and episodes of behavioral dyscontrol. Four of the 16 patients had to be removed from the alprazolam arm prior to completion. Of the remaining 12, 7 experienced heightened aggression. There was a paradoxical effect in some patients where they had improved mood while they had increased behavioral dyscontrol. (They "felt good about themselves" while they did bad things.) On the basis of this study short-acting benzodiazepines appear to be somewhat strongly contraindicated in maintenance treatment of borderline patients.

Benzodiazepines are often used during acute episodes of dyscontrol instead of traditional neuroleptics. Clonazepam, which has been associated with an increase in serotonin levels and which has a long half-life, is sometimes used to treat anxiety symptoms in personality disorders that are impulsive or irritable.

The bottom line is that benzodiazepines are useful for acute crisis situations and personality disorders involving inhibition. A history of either substance abuse or impulsive behavior is a strong relative contraindication to their use. Although the data are sparse, it would appear that if it was absolutely necessary to use in patients with a history of impulsive behavior over a longer term, clonazepam or a longer-acting benzodiazepine should be used—not short-acting benzodiazepines.

Naltrexone

There are only two open label and one case report on the use of naltrexone for personality disorder traits. Although preliminary, the results are intriguing. One report on 13 patients attempted to reduce dissociative episodes with naltrexone and reported a significant reduction in the duration and intensity of dissociative phenomena (Bohus, Landwehrmeyer, Stiglmays, Limberger, Bohme, & Schmahl, 1999). Another trial of seven patients examined self-injurious behavior (cutting) (Roth, Ostroff, & Hoffman, 1996). In six of seven patients there was significant improvement on naltrexone. A case report of one patient also indicated an improvement of self-injurious behavior on naltrexone (McGee, 1997).

Although not a strong data base, these preliminary findings are of interest. They indicate that, in some patients, naltrexone at doses from 50 to

400 mg a day may be useful in the treatment of dissociative behavior and/or self-injury.

Other

There are two reports on the use of venlafaxine. Both are open label. One studied 12 social phobic patients (Altamura, Pioli, Vitto, & Mannu, 1999) It indicates that treatment reduced avoidant personality traits. This is not a tremendously surprising finding as it is becoming more recognized that avoidant personality disorder is only quantitatively different from social phobia (Reich, 2000). It is likely that drugs that treat social phobia will also have a helpful effect on avoidant personality traits.

The second report treated a group of 39 borderline patients with up to 200 mg a day of venlafaxine (Markovitz & Wagner, 1995). The findings are made more interesting in that many of these patients had had a previous trial with an SSRI. The report indicates a reduction in overall symptom severity, somatic complaints, and the number of patients who were engaging in self-injurious behavior.

Drug-and Alcohol-Abusing Patients

Good drug treatment should concern itself not only with drugs to add to a regimen, but also with drugs to remove. Many of our personality trait patients are comorbid for substance and alcohol abuse. For our patients with problems with acting out on impulse, disinhibiting drugs can of course be a major problem. Even those with the problem of inhibition, such as our personality cluster C patients (i.e., avoidant traits, etc.), the use of these substances places them at risk for addiction. There is as always something of a clinical art here. Many of us have treated functioning patients who use drugs or alcohol to their detriment and who are resistant to specific substance or alcohol treatment. Some of these will move toward reduced use in the course of treatment. On the other hand there are patients whose use is causing significant current decline in function or medical or legal problems. Here, of course, there is no substitute for more rapid intervention. In general our goal should be to reduce or eliminate alcohol and illegal drug use in personality trait patients. I believe this will result in an increase in personality functioning and do a service to our patients.

General Rules for Treatment

As with the possible exception of avoidant personality disorder we have no specific drugs for specific disorders, we are then treating comorbid disorders and personality disorder traits. In this effort we are trying to find the fewest medications that can appropriately treat the individual array of symptoms that a patient presents with. I call this search for the proper combination the search for elegance in psychopharmacologic treatment.

Although comoribidity of both Axis I and Axis II disorders is common in personality disorders, it is less of a problem when traits are being treated rather than specific categorical Axis II diagnoses. Again the goal is to find the smallest combination of drugs that treats both the categorical Axis I disorders and the Axis II traits.

Models of Treatment

The challenge involved in treating personality traits is to keep firmly in mind a model of treatment to guide oneself. Without a model, it is more likely that treatment goals become confused. This is made more difficult because there is not a single treatment model that has preeminence over the others.

There are five common models of treatment: (1) the belief that what we are calling Axis II disorders are actually Axis I disorders (this position is best exemplified by Akiskal who argues that borderline personality is an Axis I affective disorder (Akiskal, Judd, Gillin, & Lemmi, 1997)); (2) the concept that Axis II symptoms are merely *formes frustes* (attenuated versions) of Axis I disorders; (3) the concept that we are treating an underlying temperament(this means that we are treating dispositions to behaviors such as impulsiveness); (4) the focus of treatment is clusters of Axis II symptoms that tend to occur together(it should be noted here that not all authors use exactly the same symptoms in their clusters); (5) the state personality disorder model (Reich, 1999; Reich & Hofmann, 2002; and also the related chapter in this book). (This concept is that some disorders that appear to be personality disorders are reflections of a patient with varying severity of personality pathology that may remit rapidly.)

It may be that one treatment model may seem more useful for one given patient, and another model more useful for another. Often the clinical choices are the same under different models. The important thing may not be which model is used, but deciding a model to follow for any given patient.

Treatment by Cluster

As mentioned above, different authors define different clusters differently, and the search for drug treatment elegance can take many paths. I will, however, give a starting place for the treatment of several clusters of personality traits.

Treatment of the Paranoid, Mild Thought Disorder and Dissociation Cluster. Except for acute crisis episodes, I would tend to avoid the traditional neuroleptics. Their efficacy after initial crisis is not impressive, the dropout rate is high, and there is a risk of tardive dyskinesia. My preference instead is to start with an atypical antipsychotic at one quarter to one half the ordinary top-range maintenance dose for psychosis. If there is no response, I would go by steps up to the top maintenance dose. If there is no response, a trial of a different atypical is a reasonable option. Clozapine should be considered in refractory patients. If there is a partial response, a trial of divalproex as an adjunctive agent might be considered. If dissociative symptoms are prominent, a trial of naltrexone might be considered.

The Depressed, Angry, Labile Mood Cluster. I would start with an SSRI antidepressant at antidepressant doses. This should be titrated to dosages used for obsessive compulsive disorder as indicated. If one SSRI fails, a trial of another is a reasonable step. Perhaps an equally good approach, and preferred in bipolar disorder, would be the use of depakote. If there is a partial response to either approach, an adjunctive atypical neuroleptic or a mood stabilizer could be added. For patients who have good compliance and rejection sensitivity who have failed these trials, a trial of an MAOI might be considered if all other approaches have failed. An adjunctive trial of naltrexone for self-harming behavior could be considered if necessary.

The Anxious, Inhibited Behavior Cluster
For Patients without Impulsive Behavior I would start with a trial of an SSRI. If this trial fails, a trial of a second SSRI should be undertaken. A long-acting benzodiazepine may also be added for partial response or tried as a sole agent if there are multiple SSRI failures. If these approaches fail, a trial of beta blockers or atypical antipsychotics might be indicated.

For Patients with Impulsive, Dangerous Behavior or a History of Substance Abuse For these patients, I would again start with trials of SSRIs. If SSRIs fail, atypical antipsychotics and beta blockers would be the mainstay of antianxiety treatment.

Length of Treatment and Adjunctive Psychotherapy. Treatment trials, barring side effects that require termination, should go for at least 4 to 6 weeks. Symptoms of personality disorders often fluctuate. It can take a longer trial period before it is evident whether a given intervention is successful or not. Although no patient should be on a medication for longer than necessary, it should be remembered that personality problems are often long term. If a drug or combination of drugs improves symptoms or function and has an acceptable low level of side effects, long-term treatment can be justified.

Comment on Psychotherapy

Although, as I have described above, drug treatment can help some symptoms of personality disorder dysfunction, no one represents it as a cure, and no one would suggest that psychopharmacology should be done in the absence of a psychotherapy treatment program. Discussion of specific psychotherapy treatments is beyond the scope of this chapter and is discussed in another chapter in this book.

Summary

Gradually, empirical evidence has been accumulating that now gives us some guidance for drug treatments for dysfunctional personality traits. Unlike many Axis I disorders, such as depression, there is not treatment available for entire personality syndromes. For example, there is no specific drug for borderline personality disorder. However, we can often reduce some personality traits that exist within a larger personality dysfunction. Although not complete cures, the reduction of morbidity can be quite significant for many patients.

The mechanism by which our drug treatments work is not completely understood. Most likely it is some combination of direct effect on personality traits, direct effects on the neuroendocrine HPA axis, the effect of reduction of the aggravating effects of axis I symptoms, and interactions of all of the causes listed above. Most likely because our understanding of mechanisms is incomplete, there are many different models of treatment to guide us. I do not recommend one more than others, but suggest that a specific model be kept clearly in mind for each patient's treatment.

As delineated above, many different drugs may have a part in treatment of personality traits. These include the traditional neuroleptics, the atypical antipsychotics, MAOIs, SSRIs, various mood stabilizers, natrexone, and others. I recommend, to reduce overall patient drug load and to minimize drug interactions, that attempts be made to choose the fewest number of drugs that might be expected to treat both Axis I and Axis II disorders.

Drug treatment of personality traits ideally should be part of an overall approach that includes some form of appropriate psychotherapy and keeps in mind problems that may be caused by drugs and alcohol.

References

Aberg-Wistedt, A., Agren, H., Ekselius, L., Bengtson, F., & Akerblad, A. C. (2000). Sertraline versus paroxetine in major depression: Clinical outcome after six months of continuous therapy. *Journal of Clinical Psychopharacology, 20*, 645–652.

Akiskal, H. S., Judd, L. L., Gillin, J. C., & Lemmi, H. (1997). Subthreshold depressions: Clinical and polysomnographic validation of dysthymic, residual and masked forms. *Journal of Affective Disorders, 45*, 53–63.

Altamura, A. C., Pioli, R., Vitto, M., & Mannu, P. (1999). Venlafaxine in social phobia: A study in selective serotonin reuptake inhibitor non-responders. *International Clinics of Psychopharmacology, 14*, 239–245.

Benedetti, F., Sforzini, L., Colombo, C., Maffei, C., & Smeraldi, E. (1998). Low-dose clozapine in acute and continuation treatment of severe borderline personality disorder. *Journal of Clinical Psychiatry, 59*, 103–107.

Black, K. J., & Sheline, Y. I. (1997). Personality disorder scores improve with effective pharmacotherapy of depression. *Journal of Affective Disorders, 43*, 11–18.

Bogenschutz, M. P., & Nurnberg, H. G. (2004). Olanzapine versus placebo in the treatment of Borderline personality disorder. *Journal of Clinical Psychiatry, 65*, 104–109.

Bohus, M. J., Landwehrmeyer, G. B., Stiglmayr, C. E., Limberger, M. F, Bohme, R., & Schmahl, C. G. (1999). Naltrexone in the treatment of dissociative symptoms in patients with borderline personality disorder: An open-label trial. *Journal of Clinical Psychiatry, 60*, 598–603.

Chengappa, K. N. R., Ebeling, T., Kang, J. S., Levine, J., & Parepally, H. (1999). Clozapine reduces severe self-mutilation and aggression in psychotic patients with borderline personality disorder. *Journal of Clinical Psychiatry, 60*, 477–484.

Coccaro, E. F., & Kavoussi, R. J. (1997). Fluoxetine and impulsive aggressive behavior in personality-disordered subjects. *Archives of General Psychiatry, 54*, 1081–1088.

Cornelius, J. R., Soloff, P. H., Perel, J. M., & Ulrick, R. F. (1993). Continuation pharmacotherapy of borderline personality disorder with haloperidol and phenelzine. *American Journal of Psychiatry, 150*, 1843–1848.

Cowdry, R. W., & Gardner, D. L. (1988). Pharmacotherapy of borderline personality disorder: Alprazolam, carbamazepine, trifluoperazine, and tranylcypromine. *Archives of General Psychiatry, 45*, 111–119.

Ekselius, L., & von Knorring, L. (1998). Personality disorder comorbidity with major depression and response to treatment with sertraline or citalopram. *International Clinics of Psychopharmacology, 13*, 205–211.

Fava, M., Bouffides, E., Pava, J. A., McCarthy, M. K., Steingard, R. J., & Rosenbaum, J. F. (1994). Personality disorder comorbidity with major depression and response to fluoxetine treatment. *Psychotherapeutics and Psychosomatics, 62*, 160–167.

Ferrerri, M. M., Loze, J., Roullon, F., & Limosin, F. (2004). Clozapine treatment of a borderline personality disorder with severe self-mutilating behaviors. *European Psychiatry, 19*, 177–178.

Fink, M., Pollack, M., & Klein, D. F. (1964). Comparative studies of chlorpromazine and imipramine: I. Drug discriminating patterns. *Neuropsychopharmacology, 3*, 370–372.

Frankenburg, F. R., & Zanarini, M. C. (1993). Clozapine treatment of borderline patients: A preliminary study. *Comprehensive Psychiatry, 34*, 402–405.

Frankenburg, F. R., & Zanarini, M. C. (2002). Divalproex sodium treatment of women with borderline personality disorder and bipolar II disorder: A double blind placebo controlled pilot study. *Journal of Clinical Psychiatry, 65*, 442–446.

Gardner, D. L., & Cowdry, R. W. (1986). Positive effects of carbamazepine on behavioral dyscontrol in borderline personality disorder. *American Journal of Psychiatry, 143*, 519–522.

Goldberg. S. C. (1989). Lithium in the treatment of borderline personality disorder. *Psychopharmacological Bulletin, 25*, 550–555.

Goldberg, S. C., Schulz, C., Schulz, P. M., Resnick, R. J., Hamer, R. M., & Friedel, R. O. (1986). Borderline and schizotypal personality disorders treated with low-dose thiothixene vs. placebo. *Archives of General Psychiatry, 43*, 680–686.

Hellerstein, D. J., Kocsis, J. H., Chapman, D., Stewart, J. W., & Harrison, W. (2000). Double-blind comparison of sertraline, imipramine, and placebo in the treatment of dysthymia: Effects on personality. *American Journal of Psychiatry, 157*, 1436–1444.

Hilger, E., Barnas, C., & Kasper, S. (2003). Quetiapine in the treatment of Borderline personality disorder. *World Journal of Biological Psychiatry, 4*, 42–44.

Hollander, E., Allen, A., Lopez, R. P., Bienstock, C. A., Grossman, R., Siever, L. J., et al. (2001). A preliminary double-blind, placebo-controlled trial of divalproex sodium in borderline personality disorder. *Journal of Clinical Psychiatry, 62*, 199–203.

Hollander, E., Tracy, K. A., Swann, A. C., Coccaro, E. F., McElroy, S. L., Wozniak, P., et al. (2003). Divalproex in the treatment of impulsive aggression: Efficacy in cluster B personality disorders. *Neuropsychopharmacology, 28*, 1186–1197.

Hough, D. W. (2001). Low-dose olanzapine for self-mutilation behavior in patients with borderline personality disorder. *Journal of Clinical Psychiatry, Special Issue 62*, 296–297.

Kavoussi, R. J., & Coccaro, E. F. (1998). Divalproex sodium for impulsive aggressive behavior in patients with personality disorder. *Journal of Clinical Psychiatry, 59*, 676–680.

Khouzam, H. R., & Donnelly, N. J. (1997). Remission of self-mutilation in a patient with borderline personality during risperidone therapy. *Journal of Nervous & Mental Disease, 185*, 348–349.

Klein, D. F. (1968). Psychiatric diagnosis and a typology of clinical drug effects. *Psychopharmacologia, 13*, 359–386.

Knutson, B., Wilkowitz, O. M., Cole, S. W., Chan, T., Moore, E. A., Johnson, R. C., et al. (1998). Selective alteration of personality and social behavior by serotonergic intervention. *American Journal of Psychiatry, 155*, 373–379.

Koenigsberg, H. W., Reynolds, D., Goodman, M., New, A. S., Mitropoulou, V., Trestman, R. L., et al. (2003). Risperdone in the treatment of schizotypal personality disorder. *Journal of Clinical Psychiatry, 64*, 628–634.

Liebowitz, M. R., Quitkin, F. M., Stewart, J. W., McGrath, P. J., Harrison, W. M., Markowitz, J. G., et al. (1988). Antidepressant specificity in atypical depression. *Archives of General Psychiatry, 45*, 129–137.

Links, P. S., Steiner, M., Boiago, I., & Irwin, D. (1990). Lithium therapy for borderline patients: Preliminary findings. *Journal of Personality Disorders, 4*, 173–181.

Markovitz, P. J., & Wagner, S. C. (1995). Venlafaxine in the treatment of borderline personality disorder. *Psychopharmacological Bulletin, 31*, 773–777.

McGee, M. D. (1997). Cessation of self-mutilation in a patient with borderline personality disorder treated with naltrexone. *Journal of Clinical Psychiatry, 58*, 32–33.

Parsons, B., Quitkin, F. M., McGrath, P. J., Stewart, P. J., Trilam, O. E., Ocepek-Welikson, K., et al. (1989). Phenelzine, imipramine, and placebo in borderline patients meeting criteria for atypical depression. *Psychopharmacological Bulletin, 25*, 524–534.

Pinto, O. C., & Akiskal, H. S. (1998). Lamotrigine as a promising approach to borderline personality: An open case series without concurrent DSM-IV major mood disorder. *Journal of Affective Disorders, 51*, 333–343.

Preston, G. A., Marchant, B. K., Reimherr, F. W., Strong, R. E., & Hedges, D. W. (2004). Borderline personality disorder in patients with bipolar disorder and response to lamotrigine. *Journal of Affective Disorders, 79*, 297–303.

Reich, J. (1999). An Empirical examination of the concept of "stress induced" personality disorders. *Psychiatric Annals, 29*, 701–706.

Reich, J. (2000). The relationship of social phobia to the personality disorders. *European Psychiatry, 15*, 151–159.

Reich, J. (2002). Drug treatment of personality disorder traits. *Psychiatric Annals, 32*, 590–596.

Reich, J., & Hofmann, S. (2002). State personality disorder in social phobia. *Annals of Clinical Psychiatry, 16*, 130–144.

Rifkin, A., Levitan, S. J., Galewski, J., & Klein, D. F. (1972). Emotionally unstable character disorder: A follow-up study. *Biological Psychiatry, 4*, 65–79.

Rinne, T., van den Brink, W., Wouters, L., & van Dyck, R. (2002). SSRI treatment of borderline personality disorder: a randomized, placebo-controlled clinical trial for female patients with borderline personality disorder. *American Journal of Psychiatry, 159*, 2048–2054.

Rocca, P., Marchiaro, L., Cocuzza, E., & Bogetto, F. (2002). Treatment of borderline personality disorder with risperidone. *Journal of Clinical Psychiatry, 63*, 241–244.

Roth, A. S., Ostroff, R. B., & Hoffman, R. E. (1996). Naltrexone as a treatment for repetitive self-injurious behavior: An open-label trial. *Journal of Clinical Psychiatry, 57*, 233–237.

Salzman, C., Wolfson, A. N., Schatzberg, A., Looper, J., Henke, R., Albanese, M., et al. (1995). Effect of fluoxetine on anger in symptomatic volunteers with borderline personality disorder. *Journal of Clinical Psychopharmacology, 15,* 23–29.

Schulz, S. C., Camlin, K. L., Berry, S. A., & Jesberger, J. A. (1999). Olanzapine safety and efficacy in patients with borderline personality disorder and comorbid dysthymia. *Biological Psychiatry, 46,* 1429–1435.

Shader, R. I., Jackson, A. H., & Dodes, L. M. (1974). The anti-aggressive effects of lithium in man. *Psychopharmacologia (Berlin), 40,* 17–24.

Sheard, M. H., Marini, J. L., Bridges, C. L., & Wagner, E. (1976). The effect of lithium on impulsive aggressive behavior in man. *American Journal of Psychiatry, 133,* 1409–1413.

Simpson, E. B., Yen, S., Costello, E., Rosen, K., Begin, A., Pistorello, J., et al. (2004). Combined dialectical behavior therapy and fluoxetine in the treatment of borderline personality disorder. *Journal of Clinical Psychiatry, 65,* 379–385.

Soloff, P. H., Cornelius, J., George, A., Nathan, S., Perel, J. M., & Ulrich, R. F. (1993). Efficacy of phenelzine and haloperidol in borderline personality disorder. *Archives of General Psychiatry, 50,* 377–385.

Soloff, P. H., George, A., Nathan, R. S., Schulz, P. M., & Peel, J. M. (1986a). Paradoxical effects of amitriptyline on borderline patients. *American Journal of Psychiatry, 143,* 1603–1605.

Soloff, P. H., George, A., Nathan, R. S., Schulz, P. M., Ulrich, R. F., & Perel, J. (1986b). Progress in pharmacotherapy of borderline disorders. *Archives of General Psychiatry, 43,* 691–697.

Soloff, P. H., George, A., Nathan, R. S., Schulz, P. M., Ulrich, R. F., & Perel, J. M. (1986). Progress in pharmacotherapy of borderline disorders. *Archives of General Psychiatry, 43,* 691–697.

Stein, D. J., Simeon, D., Frenkel, M., Islam, M. N., & Hollander E. (1995). An open trial of valproate in borderline personality disorder. *Journal of Clinical Psychiatry, 56,* 506–510.

Szigethy, E. M., & Schulz, S. C. (1997). Risperidone in comorbid borderline personality disorder and dysthymia. *Journal of Clinical Psychopharmocology, 17,* 326–327.

Townsend, M. H., Cambre, K. M., & Barbee, J. G. (2001). Treatment of borderline personality disorder with mood instability with divalproex sodium: Series of ten cases. *Journal of Clinical Psychopharacology, 21,* 249–251.

Tupin, J. P., Smith, D. B., Clanon, T. L., Kim, L. I., Nugent, A., & Groupe, A. (1973). Long-term use of lithium in aggressive disorders. *Comprehensive Psychiatry, 14,* 311–317.

Verhoeven, W. M. A., Marijnissen, G., Van Ooy, J. M., Tuinier, S., Van Den Berg, Y. W. M. M., Pepplinkhuizen, L., et al. (1999). Dysperceptions and serotonergic parameters in borderline personality disorders: Effects of treatment with risperidone. *New Trends in Experimental and Clinical Psychiatry, 15,* 9–16.

Verkes, R. J., Van der Mast, R. C., Hengeveld, M. W., Tuyl, J. P., Zwinderman, A. H., & Van Kempen, G. M. J. (1998). Reduction by paroxetine of suicidal behavior in patients with repeated suicide attempts but not major depression. *American Journal of Psychiatry, 155,* 543–547.

Walker, C., Thomas, J., & Allen, T. S. (2003). Treating impulsivity, irritability, and aggression of antisocial personality disorder with quetiapine. *International Journal of Offender Therapy and Comparative Criminology, 47,* 556–567.

Wilcox, J. A. (1995). Divalproex sodium as a treatment for borderline personality disorder. *Annals of Clinical Psychiatry, 7,* 33–37.

Zanarini, M. C., & Frankenburg, F. R. (2001). Olanzapine treatment of female borderline personality disorder patients: A double-blind, placebo controlled pilot study. *Journal of Clinical Psychiatry, 62,* 849–854.

Zanarini, M. C., Frankenburg, F. R., & Parachini, B. A. (2004). A preliminary randomized trial of fluoxetine, olanzapine and the olanzapine-Fluoxetine combination in women with borderline personality disorder. *Journal of Clinical Psychiatry, 65,* 903–907.

Zullino, D. F., Quinche, P., Hafliger, T., & Stigler, M. (2002). Olanzapine improves social dysfunction in cluster B personality disorder. *Human Psychopharmacology, 17,* 247–251.

CHAPTER 7

Cognitive Therapy for Clients with Personality Disorders and Comorbid Axis I Psychopathology

DAVID P. BERNSTEIN

Key Teaching Points

- Personality disorders appear to render Axis I treatments less effective, at least for some clients, particularly if premature dropout and treatment noncompliance are considered forms of poor outcome.
- *Early maladaptive schemas* (EMSs) are long-standing, repetitive, self-defeating themes or patterns that originate in the interplay between early adverse life experiences and early temperament. Young has identified 18 specific EMSs.
- The three *maladaptive coping responses* identified by Young are *schema avoidance, schema surrender,* and *schema overcompensation.*
- *Schema modes* are transient, state-related manifestations of EMSs. They combine aspects of EMSs and coping responses, and are usually associated with intense, disruptive effects.

- In the *schema therapy* assessment phase, the aim is to familiarize the client with the schema therapy conceptual model; assess the client's EMSs, coping responses, and schema modes; and share this information with the client.
- *Empathic confrontation* refers to the need to confront the client about his or her self-defeating EMSs, coping responses, and schema modes in a manner that is both firm and direct, but also empathic.
- *Limited reparenting* refers to the basic therapeutic stance in schema therapy, which is one of warmth, genuineness, acceptance, and guidance. The schema therapist adjusts his or her therapeutic stance to meet the individual needs of the client.
- In the schema therapy treatment phase, cognitive restructuring enables the client to achieve some healthy intellectual distance toward his or her EMSs. Schema flash cards help the client counteract the effects of schema activation in situations where EMSs are being triggered. Role playing and guided imagery exercises release painful emotions and help clients work through their schemas emotionally. Behavioral interventions help clients to enact behavioral changes.

Introduction

There is accumulating evidence that clients with personality disorders show poorer treatment outcomes for Axis I disorders, including anxiety, mood, and substance use disorders (Reich, 2003; Vaglum & Ravndal, 2003). In a recent review of the research literature on this topic, Reich (2003, 400) concluded, "Pathological personality traits are a negative predictor of the outcome of treatment for anxiety and depressive disorders — a conclusion that is not confined to one set of personality disorder traits or one cluster of traits." Possible explanations for the negative treatment effects cited by Reich (p. 390) include greater likelihood of personality disorder clients dropping out of treatment, poorer treatment compliance, interpersonal difficulties with treating clinicians, and clients reporting more side effects from psychotropic medications.

It should be noted, however, that there is not unanimity of opinion regarding this issue (Dreessen & Arntz, 1998; Muller, 2002). For example, Dreessen and Arntz have argued that apparent differences in treatment outcome may be explained by the fact that personality disorder clients show more symptomatic severity at the beginning of treatment. Thus, they may respond equally well to standard Axis I treatments, but still show more severe symptoms than nonpersonality disorder clients when treatment ends. Moreover, some studies have shown little or no difference in the treatment response of clients with and without personality disorders to Axis I treatments (Dreessen & Arntz, 1998; Muller, 2002). On the other hand, Reich (2003) has argued that some studies failed to find differences in treatment outcome because they did not take differential dropout rates into account. Had they counted dropouts as treatment failures, rather than excluding them from analyses of outcome, they would have demonstrated negative treatment effects for personality disorders. To make matters even more complicated, reviewers (Dreessen & Arntz, 1998; Reich, 2003) have disagreed about the methodological soundness of various treatment studies, leading them to reach different conclusions about the effect of personality disorders on Axis I treatments.

Despite these controversies, there does appear to be sufficient evidence that personality disorders render treatments for Axis I disorders less effective for some clients, particularly if dropping out of treatment or treatment noncompliance is considered a form of poor outcome. For example, in a recent large multicenter study in Norway, drug-addicted clients with personality disorders were twice as likely to prematurely drop out of treatment, compared to clients without personality disorders (dropout rate = 66% vs. 32% for drug-addicted clients with and without personality disorders, respectively)(Vaglum & Ravndal, 2003). Similarly, in another recent study (Ross, Dermatis, Levounis, & Galanter, 2003), substance-abusing clients with and without personality disorders were equally likely to improve during an inpatient hospitalization; however, the clients with personality disorders were less compliant with outpatient treatment recommendations following discharge from the inpatient unit. Thus, although the relationship between personality disorders and treatment outcome may be complex, personality disorders do appear to be an impediment to successful Axis I treatment in some or perhaps many cases.

In this chapter, I will consider the question of why some clients with personality disorders respond poorly to standard cognitive and behavioral interventions for Axis I disorders. I will then describe an integrative form of cognitive therapy, *schema therapy* (Young, Klosko, & Weishaar, 2003), which was developed for difficult-to-treat clients, such as clients with personality disorders and comorbid mood and anxiety disorders, that may be resistant to more standard cognitive and behavioral approaches. After describing the schema therapy conceptual model and treatment methods, I will illustrate the schema therapy approach with a case example of a client with a personality disorder and comorbid major depressive disorder (MDD).

In a 3-year randomized clinical trial of borderline personality disorder that was recently conducted in the Netherlands by Arntz and colleagues (Giesen-Bloo, Arntz, van Dyck, Spinhoven, & van Tilburg, 2004), schema therapy was found to be highly effective. Clients assigned to the schema therapy treatment condition were less than twice as likely to drop out of treatment compared to clients given transference-focused psychotherapy, a form of psychoanalytic psychotherapy (Yoemans, Clarkin, & Kernberg, 2002). Moreover, clients who received schema therapy showed substantial improvements from baseline in every domain that was measured, including borderline personality disorder symptoms, other psychopathological symptoms, and quality of life. These improvements were significantly greater than for the clients given transference-focused psychotherapy. Although these findings need to be replicated, they suggest that schema therapy reduces both core personality pathology and comorbid Axis I psychopathology, even in difficult-to-treat cases, such as clients with borderline personality disorder.

Why Do Some Clients with Personality Disorders Respond Poorly to Standard Cognitive and Behavioral Interventions?

Cognitive and behavioral treatments are usually predicated on the ability of therapist and client to form a productive collaborative relationship. However, clients with personality disorders often have difficulty forming such relationships, because interpersonal mistrust, fear of rejection, avoidance of emotion, or other interpersonal difficulties get in the way (Taft, Murphy, Musser, & Remington, 2004). Particularly in the case of more severe personality disorders, such as borderline, narcissistic, antisocial, and paranoid personality disorders, these interpersonal issues may negatively color the client's experience of the therapist. Therapists who are usually seen by their clients as caring, compassionate people may be viewed by personality disorder clients as emotionally withholding, critical, demeaning, or even abusive. Personality disorders can also provoke significant countertransference reactions in therapists. Personality disorder clients are often difficult to work with, which can interfere with the therapist's empathy toward them. As a result, personality disorders can undermine the working alliance between client and therapist (Taft et al., 2004).

Standard cognitive and behavioral interventions, such as asking clients to recognize and modify typical cognitive biases (e.g., "all or nothing thinking"), may feel abstract and irrelevant to clients whose deeper issues concern their feelings about themselves and their relationships with other people. Personality disorders can also interfere with the client's ability or willingness to carry out homework assignments (Persons, Burns, & Perloff, 1988), such as self-monitoring exercises, which are frequently used by cognitive-behavioral therapists. For example, personality disorder clients may fail to complete homework assignments because of their perfectionism, fear of failure or ridicule, feelings of resentment and subjugation, avoidant tendencies, or disorganization.

Fundamentally, personality disorders involve lifelong, repetitive, self-defeating patterns of behavior that significantly interfere with the individual's well-being (Young et al., 2003). These patterns are often "ego-syntonic," that is, personality disorder clients are often unaware of these patterns, or see no need to change them. They may "externalize" the problem (e.g., "My standards aren't too high. It's just that I haven't met the right woman yet."), and see little reason to examine or modify their behavior. Given the ego-syntonic, self-defeating, and pervasive nature of these patterns, it is not surprising that they might also interfere with the effective delivery of psychotherapeutic interventions for Axis I problems.

Case Example #1

A never-married woman in her 70s had been suffering from major depression and dysthymia for most of her life. She met DSM-IV (*Diagnostic and Statistical Manual of Mental Disorders,* 4th ed.) criteria for several personality disorders, including borderline, narcissistic, and paranoid personality disorder. She came to me seeking cognitive therapy for her depressive symptoms. After much discussion, the client agreed to a medication consultation. However, she refused to see the psychiatrist I recommended, later admitting that she hadn't wanted to give me too much "power" over her. She disliked the psychiatrist she chose, and quickly discontinued her medication after developing some side effects. She agreed to read a cognitive therapy self-help book for depression. However, after quickly scanning the first chapter, she declared that there was "nothing in it" for her. She found the approach superficial and irrelevant to her problems. When I shifted the focus to the therapy relationship, including her devaluing and mistrustful attitudes toward me, the client became much more engaged in the treatment. Thus, the client's personality pathology rendered more traditional treatment approaches for her depressive symptoms including psychopharmacological and cognitive behavioral interventions ineffective. On the other hand, an approach that directly confronted the client's maladaptive personality traits proved more successful.

Schema Therapy Conceptual Model

Early Maladaptive Schemas

The considerations in the forgoing case suggest that some clients with personality disorders may respond poorly to standard cognitive and behavioral therapy approaches for Axis I problems, unless their personality disorders are addressed. I will now describe a psychotherapeutic approach, schema therapy (Young et al., 2003), which was developed to treat complex, difficult cases, including clients with personality disorders and chronic Axis I conditions, such as treatment-resistant anxiety and mood disorders.

Schema therapy is an integrative form of cognitive therapy that combines cognitive, behavioral, psychodynamic object relations, and experiential-humanistic approaches (Young et al., 2003). The basic unit of analysis in the schema therapy conceptual model is the *early maladaptive schema* (EMS). Early maladaptive schemas are lifelong, repetitive, self-defeating themes or patterns that originated in childhood through the interplay of early temperament and aversive environmental conditions. Young (Young et al., 2003) has identified 18 specific EMSs, such as *abandonment, abuse/mistrust, unrelenting standards, and defectiveness* (Table 7.1). For example, the abandonment schema involves the expectation that one will inevitably be abandoned. EMSs are like absolute, unshakable truths or predictions about oneself, other people, and situations. For example, when the abandonment schema is triggered by some event for example, when a boyfriend fails to call at a predetermined time the prospect of abandonment seems imminent and absolute (e.g., "I knew that he was going to leave me!").

EMSs act as cognitive filters that systematically bias or distort incoming information (Young et al., 2003). These cognitive processes are largely nonconscious (i.e., implicit) and automatic, and therefore outside of the individual's awareness. EMSs are also self-perpetuating and self-reinforcing. They cause individuals to selectively focus attention on information that confirms preexisting beliefs, and ignore information that disconfirms them (e.g., someone with an unrelenting standards schema focuses only on his or her mistakes or failures, and not on his or her successes). Moreover, EMSs are self-reinforcing in that they cause self-fulfilling prophecies. For example, someone with an abandonment schema may drive other people away with his or her clinging, dependent, or controlling behavior, confirming and reinforcing the belief that others will inevitably leave him or her.

Table 7.1 The 18 Early Maladaptive Schemas Grouped by Schema Domain

Domain I. Disconnection and Rejection

1. Abandonment/Instability — The expectation that one will inevitably be abandoned.

2. Mistrust/Abuse — The expectation that one will be abused, harmed, attacked, or humiliated by others.

3. Emotional Deprivation — The expectation that others will not meet one's needs for nurturance, empathy, or protection.

4. Defectiveness/Shame — The belief that one is profoundly flawed, unlovable.

5. Social Isolation/Alienation — The belief that one is alone in the world, alienated from any group.

Domain II. Impaired Autonomy and Performance

6. Dependence/Incompetence — The belief that one is unable to handle everyday responsibilities.

7. Vulnerability to Harm or Illness — The fear that catastrophe can strike at any time.

8. Enmeshment/Undeveloped Self — Over-involvement with significant others at the expense of normal self- or social development.

9. Failure — The expectation that one will inevitably fail, or is inadequate in the area of achievement.

Domain III. Impaired Limits

10. Entitlement/Grandiosity — The belief that one is superior to other people, and therefore entitled to special treatment.

11. Insufficient Self-Control/Self-Discipline — Inadequate self-control and frustration tolerance.

Domain IV. Other Directedness

12. Subjugation — The surrender of control to other people because one feels coerced.

13. Self-Sacrifice — Excessive focus on meeting the needs of other people, at the expense of one's own needs.

14. Approval Seeking/Recognition Seeking — Excessive emphasis on gaining the approval or recognition of other people.

Domain V. Overvigilance and Inhibition

15. Negativity/Pessimism — Pervasive focus on the negative aspects of life.

16. Emotional Inhibition — Excessive inhibition of spontaneous action, feeling, or communication.

17. Unrelenting Standards/Hypercriticalness — The belief that one must strive to meet very high internal standards, usually to avoid criticism.

18. Punitiveness — The belief that people should be punished harshly for making mistakes.

Source: Adapted from Young, Klosko, & Weishaar, 2003. With permission.

Finally, EMSs have their origins in adverse childhood events, occurring at a time when neuronal plasticity is at its peak (Cicchetti & Walker, 2003). Research shows that traumatic childhood events, such as child abuse, can lead to lifelong changes in brain structure and function (Anand, Coskun, Thrivikaman, Nemeroff, & Plotsky, 1999; Brambilla, Soloff, Sala, Nieoletti, Keshavan, & Soares, 2004). As of yet, there is no research on the neurobiological basis of EMSs. However, it seems plausible that these patterns reflect lifelong brain alterations stemming from a combination of adverse childhood events, especially chronic ones (e.g., chronic child abuse or neglect, traumatic losses, exposure to family violence) and genetic vulnerabilities (Caspi et al., 2002). As a result, such patterns may be highly entrenched and resistant to change.

Schema Coping Responses

When people or situations trigger EMSs, intense, disruptive effects are produced. According to Young (Young et al., 2003), there are three typical ways in which people cope with the disruptive effects of schematic activation: schema avoidance, schema surrender, and schema overcompensation. Schema avoidance involves avoiding people or situations that might trigger a schema. For example, someone with an abandonment schema might avoid getting close to people, either avoiding relationships altogether or by choosing superficial relationships that were "just about sex" to avoid true feelings of intimacy. He or she might also flee relationships when they threaten to become too close.

Schema surrender means giving into the schema. For example, someone with an abandonment schema might (unconsciously) seek out relationships with partners who are emotionally unavailable or unpredictable, because such relationships have a comfortable, yet painful, familiarity. In fact, he or she may find that he or she has a high degree of sexual or romantic "chemistry" with the very people who are the worst for him or her, partners who cannot make a commitment to him or her. By surrendering to the schema, his or her worst fears about abandonment are confirmed and reinforced.

The final coping style is schema overcompensation: doing the opposite of the schema. For example, one client with an abandonment schema always chose partners who formed an infantile type of dependency on him. Because of their (perceived) weakness and helplessness, he felt that they would never leave him. Alternatively, someone with an abandonment schema might try to "turn the tables" on his or her romantic partners by always threatening to leave them, or by behaving in an aloof, inconsistent, or unpredictable manner. In this way, he or she leaves his or her partners in a perpetual state of uncertainty about his or her commitment to the relationship. In effect, he or she is saying, "I'm not worried about your leaving me; you should be worried about my leaving you!" Many people with personality disorders utilize all three coping styles: schema avoidance, surrender, and overcompensation. However, typically one or two of the coping styles predominate. Like EMSs, schema coping responses are largely automatic mechanisms that operate outside of conscious awareness.

Schema Modes

Schema modes are the final component of the schema therapy conceptual model (Young et al., 2003). Unlike EMSs and coping responses, which are enduring or traitlike entities, schema modes are transient state-related phenomena. Schema modes combine EMSs and coping responses and typically also involve intense affective responses (an exception is the *detached protector mode*, which involves emotional "numbing," or the blocking of emotional responses). Schema modes can also be thought of as aspects of the personality that may predominate at a given moment. For example, someone with an abandonment schema may exhibit a variety of schema modes, which may fluctuate from moment to moment. When the abandonment schema is triggered, he or she may experience intense and painful feelings of despondency, helplessness, loneliness, or neediness (abandoned child mode). However, this mode may alternate rapidly with other ones, such as feelings of rage (angry child mode), the blocking out of painful feelings by engaging in self-soothing, self-numbing activities (e.g., by binge eating, drug or alcohol abuse, or self-mutilation) (detached protector/self-soother mode), or attacking or intimidating his or her partners (e.g., by stalking them) (bully and attack mode).

In clients with more severe personality disorders, these modes can fluctuate rapidly. Because a healthy adult mode is poorly developed in severe personality disorders, schema modes are relatively dissociated from each other. They function in a largely unintegrated manner that the client is unable to bring under conscious, deliberate control. Thus, when a client with borderline personality disorder is threatened with abandonment, either perceived or real, he or she may spend hours or days fluctuating between states of despair, rage, and numbness, with little ability to put his or her experience into a more objective perspective, or engage in healthier, more adaptive ways of coping (i.e., healthy adult mode).

Schema Therapy Treatment Approach

Assessment Phase

Schema therapy is an integrative form of treatment that combines cognitive, behavioral, psychodynamic object relations, and humanistic/existential approaches (Young et al., 2003). Schema therapy is a moderate to long-term treatment approach, because long-standing, otherwise intractable problems are its focus. Treatment usually lasts for 1 to 2 years, or longer in cases of severe personality disorders. The treatment proceeds in two phases, an assessment and case conceptualization phase, and a schema change phase. In the first phase, which can take several sessions, the goal is to help identify the client's prominent EMSs, schema coping responses, and modes. The therapist explains the schema therapy model to the client in accessible, nontechnical language so that client and therapist share a common "road map" for exploring the client's self-defeating patterns. Young and colleagues have developed several self-report questionnaires to obtain information regarding clients' early adverse parenting experiences (Young Parenting Inventory, Young, 1994), EMSs (Young Schema Questionnaire, Young & Brown, 2001), and coping responses (Young-Rygh Avoidance Inventory, Young & Rygh, 1994; Young Compensation Inventory, Young, 1995). More broad-based life history questionnaires (e.g., Multi-modal Life History Inventory, Lazarus, 2002) are also used to obtain information about clients' complaints and significant life events. Imagery exercises are used to access schemas that may be outside of the client's awareness. For example, clients may be asked to close their eyes and describe in vivid detail an unpleasant childhood experience involving their mother or their father. Over the course of several sessions, the therapist and client construct a plausible provisional "story" of the client's self-defeating life patterns, using the concepts and language of schema therapy. Many clients find even this initial assessment phase to be therapeutic, because previously troubling but inexplicable life patterns can finally be understood in a manner that is objective, nonjudgmental, and compassionate.

Treatment Phase

Empathic Confrontation. In the treatment phase, which can last for a year or longer, the therapist uses several techniques to ameliorate clients' long-standing maladaptive patterns. The concept of *empathic confrontation* is of central importance (Young et al., 2003). The client must be repeatedly confronted with his or her maladaptive life patterns, but in a manner that is empathic, comprehensible, and nonjudgmental. The schema therapy concepts and language provide a means for doing so. For example, the therapist might say to the client, "Yes, it's true that your boss can be very demanding and critical, but your response to him gets you into trouble. When he treats you like that, your abuse/mistrust and defectiveness schemas get triggered. You feel that he is out to humiliate you, the same way that you did when your father used to make fun of you in front of your older brothers. You feel the same rage and humiliation now that you did then. When you got older, you vowed that no one was ever going to treat you like that again. When someone attacked you, you gave it back to him twice as hard (overcompensation coping response). Now that kind of response causes big problems for you, because people don't know where you're coming from. Your boss has no idea how humiliated he made you feel. He only sees your anger and thinks, "'What's this guy's problem?'" Thus, the therapist's use of schema therapy concepts and terms enables him or her to confront the client's self-defeating patterns, but in an empathic, nonjudgmental manner.

Cognitive Restructuring. Cognitive restructuring plays an important role in schema therapy, particularly early in the schema change phase of treatment (Young et al., 2003). The therapist and client use *collaborative empiricism* to challenge the validity of the client's schemas. For example, a client with a defectiveness/shame schema might be asked to weigh the evidence supporting and contradicting the idea that he or she is completely worthless. Even clients with strong defectiveness schemas are usually able to muster some evidence that they have worth. The goal of these interventions is to help the client achieve some healthy intellectual distance toward his or her schemas. In this way, the client begins to develop a healthy internal voice to rationally challenge the validity of the schemas.

Schema flash cards can be very useful in this early phase of treatment (Young et al., 2003). Flash cards are used to counteract the client's schemas in situations where they become triggered. For example, a client who is feeling panicky because her boyfriend hasn't called her on time might read the following flash card, which she and her therapist have written together:

> Right now I am feeling panicky because my boyfriend hasn't called me. I believe that he is about to break off the relationship. However, I know that I am feeling this way because my abandonment schema has been triggered. I felt this way as a child, because my mother wasn't around when I needed her. However, the healthy adult part of me knows that my boyfriend loves and cares about me, and is usually there for me when I need him. In the

past, when he hasn't called, there has usually been some good reason for it. When I remind myself of this, I usually feel better.

Thus, schema flash cards incorporate evidence contradicting the client's schemas, and remind the client of the schema's childhood origins. In this way, they can help her to gain some rational control over her schemas when they have become activated.

Experiential Exercises

Typically, even after clients can challenge their schemas rationally, they still *feel* as if the schemas are true. For this reason, schema therapy incorporates a number of experiential techniques to lessen the emotional power of the schemas, such as guided imagery and role-playing exercises (Young et al., 2003). Guided imagery exercises can be a highly effective method for challenging the schemas at an emotional level. In one variation on this technique, the client is asked to close his or her eyes and relive in vivid detail a recent situation that is troubling him or her. After having imagined the scene, he or she is then asked to recall an earlier situation from his or her childhood that *felt the same way* as the current situation. Typically, the client's main schemas and coping mechanisms are quite evident in these reimagined scenarios, helping the client to emotionally comprehend the link between the past and the present.

Imaginal rescripting is often used by schema therapists to heal some of the early emotional wounds that the schemas represent. According to Young (Young et al., 2003), EMSs result from unmet or frustrated basic developmental needs, such as the need for affection, protection, guidance, or affirmation. Some of these needs can be met, albeit only in a partial way, using imaginal rescripting. During imagery exercises, clients are asked to replay a painful childhood scene, but to alter some key elements. For example, in imagination, the client might confront his or her abusive or neglectful parent, insisting on his right to be protected or nurtured. Alternatively, the client might ask the therapist to "enter" the scene to help him or her. These imagery exercises are often cathartic, helping the client to release painful emotions. Moreover, the use of rescripting can help to modify or "overwrite" childhood memories to make them less painful, and to help meet some of the client's early developmental needs. For example, a client who had been physically abused by her older brother reported that she felt safer after imagining that a protector had prevented her brother from hurting her. In another case, a man who had been neglected by his narcissistic mother reported that he felt less lonely after imagining a scene in which his therapist confronted the mother, insisting that she give her son the attention that he deserved.

The Therapy Relationship

The therapy relationship is another critical component of the treatment. Through *limited reparenting*, the therapist can provide some of the nurturance, guidance, protection, and acceptance that the client was unable to obtain in childhood (Young et al., 2003). While maintaining appropriate boundaries, the therapist adjusts his or her interpersonal style to help to meet some of the client's basic developmental needs. For example, the therapist may provide advice to a client who did not receive adequate guidance while growing up, or warmth to a client who did not receive adequate nurturing. In this regard, the basic therapeutic stance in schema therapy is quite different from that of traditional psychoanalytic psychotherapy with its emphasis on the therapist's neutrality. In fact, schema therapists emphasize the need to be warm and genuine with clients, a stance that is similar to that of client-centered therapists.

The therapy relationship also provides a unique opportunity to observe and confront client's schemas in the "here and now" of the therapeutic situation itself. Because therapy involves a significant relationship, the client's EMSs, coping responses, and schema modes are activated in the therapeutic situation. For example, the client may experience the therapist as controlling (subjugation schema), withholding (emotional deprivation schema), unreliable (abandonment schema), or abusive (abuse/mistrust schema). Using empathic confrontation, the therapist challenges these perceptions, and helps the client recognize how his or her EMSs and maladaptive coping responses interfere with the therapeutic process. To take the example of the subjugation schema, one client may miss therapy sessions when his or her subjugation schema is triggered (schema avoidance); another may comply with what he or she perceives as the therapist's demands (schema surrender); and a third may behave in a defiant, rebellious manner toward the therapist (schema overcompensation). The schema therapist points out these patterns, drawing parallels to the client's current life situation, while noting the origins of these patterns in childhood experiences. In some cases, the therapist may disclose his or her own reactions to the client's maladaptive behavior, providing the client with feedback about the effect of his or her behavior on other people. Thus, empathic confrontation within the therapy relationship itself may be a powerful mechanism for modifying EMSs, maladaptive coping responses, and schema modes.

Schema Mode Work

Schema modes are of greatest importance in working with clients with severe personality disorders, where clients may rapidly alternate between different modes both within the therapy session itself and in their daily lives (Young et al., 2003). In such cases, helping clients to recognize and label their modes is a critical step toward greater self-integration. Moreover, the schema therapist must become adept at interventions that switch clients from modes that interfere with therapeutic progress to more productive ones. For example, when a client is in detached protector mode, little therapeutic progress can occur, because the client is blocking out his or her emotional responses. Young et al. (2003) have developed a number of interventions for moving clients out of unhealthy modes and into ones in which emotions are more accessible, such as abandoned child mode or healthy adult mode. For example, using a technique drawn from gestalt therapy, the therapist can ask the client to play the role of the detached protector, and carry out a dialogue between the detached protector and the therapist. The therapist asks the detached protector to explain the purpose he or she serves in the client's life (e.g., "I exist to protect Sam from pain and disappointment."). By carrying out a dialogue with this part of the client, the therapist helps the client become more cognizant of this self-protective schema mode and the vulnerability that lies beneath it.

Behavioral Interventions

Behavioral interventions are a final, but critically important, step in breaking long-standing self-defeating patterns. Because self-defeating behaviors are usually "schema driven," they can be quite resistant to change. For this reason, in schema therapy, cognitive and experiential interventions typically precede behavioral ones (Young et al., 2003). After clients have achieved some rational and emotional distance toward their schemas, behavioral changes become easier to implement. Behavioral interventions usually focus on clients' maladaptive coping mechanisms: schema avoidance, surrender, and overcompensation.

For example, avoidant clients can be given assignments to help them gradually reduce their avoidant behavior. One client had been unable to make friends because of his strong feelings of defectiveness. Although he felt sad and lonely, he was certain of being rejected, and therefore avoided social interactions. After challenging the client's schemas with cognitive and experiential interventions, the therapist prescribed the following behavioral intervention. The client was told to arrive a few minutes early to the religious service he regularly attended, and sit next to someone who looked interesting. He was then to turn to the person and introduce himself, being sure to smile and make eye contact. This behavior was first rehearsed during the therapy session. In the next session, the client reported that the exercise had gone well; in fact, he and the person sitting next to him had chatted amicably for a few minutes. As a next assignment, the client was told to introduce himself to someone interesting at the social gathering that followed the religious service. In this step-by-step manner, the client surmounted some of his social avoidance, and was eventually able to form a friendship with one of his fellow congregants.

Case Example #2

Following is a case example that illustrates schema therapy case conceptualization and treatment techniques. In this case, I used primarily standard schema therapy methods and made less use of schema mode work, which is more central to working with more severe personality disorder clients (e.g., borderline or narcissistic personality disorders).

Anna, a divorced woman in her 40s with two grown children, had suffered from periodic episodes of major depression throughout her adulthood. She also met DSM-IV criteria for dependent personality disorder. Despite being bright, attractive, and outgoing, she often felt inferior to other people, whom she saw as more competent, likable, and successful than herself (dependence/incompetence, defectiveness/shame, and failure schemas). Because she was emotionally needy (emotional deprivation schema), and felt incompetent to make decisions on her own (dependence/incompetence schema), she formed intense, dependent relationships with other women (schema surrender coping style). She needed an excessive amount of advice and reassurance from her friends, even over minor matters, and often chose friends who dominated her. Rather than standing up for herself, she complied with her friends' demands, fearing that otherwise they would abandon her (abandonment schema). In fact, she bent over backward to please her friends, going out of her way to win their approval (approval seeking schema), and making sacrifices for them at the expense of her own happiness (self-sacrifice schema).

She had recently plunged into a severe depressive episode, one of the worst she had ever experienced. She had been relatively stable for several years, seeing a psychodynamic psychotherapist, and taking antidepressant medication. However, she had recently discontinued her medication due to side effects, precipitating a downward spiral. She frantically tried several new medications recommended by her psychiatrist, but discontinued each of them after experiencing side effects, without giving any of them an adequate trial. She sought cognitive behavioral therapy with me, blaming her previous therapist for not intervening actively enough during her downward course.

Anna had been divorced several years earlier, and was upset about ongoing conflicts with her children, who were in their early 20s. They "walked all over her," just as her friends did. Because they were having problems in their personal lives, and were treating her badly, she felt that she had been a failure as a mother (failure schema). Her own mother was a cold, distant, critical, and emotionally unpredictable parent (emotional deprivation schema). She saw the world as a dangerous place (vulnerability to harm schema), where things rarely worked out well (negativity/pessimism schema) a view that Anna had internalized. Her father, who was deceased, had been more loving, but was often away on business. Anna had been a "parentified" child, who had been put in charge of taking care of her younger siblings, establishing a pattern of sacrificing excessively for others (self-sacrifice schema).

Recently, Anna's feelings of abandonment and deprivation had intensified due to the death of a beloved uncle, and her feelings of alienation from her children. In our first session, she cried bitterly over how lonely she felt. She had also grown more resentful of her friends, whom she felt were mistreating her, and was disillusioned and bored with her job as a city employee. She also felt hopeless about recovering from her depression, fearing that no medication would help her, but was willing to give cognitive therapy a chance.

My initial treatment goal was to actively intervene to counteract the EMSs that were contributing to Anna's depression and impeding her recovery. Specifically, I wished to promote feelings of hopefulness and self-efficacy about her depression by challenging her negativity/pessimism schema; support her in pursuing an adequate trial of antidepressant medication; provide her with sufficient therapeutic contact and emotional support to lessen her feelings of loss and loneliness (abandonment and emotional deprivation schemas); and promote feelings of worthiness by countering her self-denigrating thoughts (defectiveness/shame, failure, and dependence/incompetence schemas), and focusing on her strengths.

Beginning with cognitive interventions, I used thought records to counter her pessimism about her ability to overcome her depression (and about the efficacy of medication), and her feelings of defectiveness and failure as a mother. For example, after weighing the evidence, she recognized that she had always been able to recover from previous depressive episodes; that medication had helped her in the past, and might again in the future; and that she was now pursuing a form of therapy (i.e., cognitive-behavioral therapy) with proven efficacy for depression. Similarly, she was able to recognize that her children's problems were not all her fault, and that she deserved to be treated in a respectful and decent manner by them.

To counter Anna's long-standing feelings of abandonment, deprivation, and defectiveness, I adopted an approach involving warmth, acceptance, empathy, availability, and guidance (i.e., limited reparenting). I temporarily increased our therapeutic contact from once to twice per week, and encouraged Anna to contact me between sessions, should she need to. I also made an audiotape "flashcard" for her to listen to every morning, when her depressive symptoms were at their worst. The audiotape, which followed the format described earlier, was designed to counter her feelings of defectiveness, hopelessness, deprivation, and abandonment, which frequently plagued her in the morning hours. The audiotape also helped her to feel comforted by the sound of my voice at the time of the day when she felt the loneliest.

After a few weeks, Anna reported that she was feeling more hopeful about her prospects of recovery, but was still experiencing severe depressive symptoms. She agreed to see her psychiatrist again, and try a new antidepressant medication. Despite some initial side effects, she was able to tolerate the new medication, and after a few weeks began to experience some therapeutic benefits, including less depressed mood, improved concentration, and more energy.

Taking an empathetic but also firm stance (i.e., empathic confrontation), I began pointing out some of the self-defeating patterns that were keeping her "stuck," that is, unable to meet her own basic emotional needs and therefore contributing to her depression. For example, her dependent behavior toward female friends reinforced a view of herself as defective and incompetent, impeding her ability to make her own decisions and initiate important life changes (e.g., looking for a new job, forming an intimate connection with a man). Similarly, her self-sacrificing and approval seeking focused excessive attention on the needs of other people, rather than focusing on her own unfulfilled needs for intimacy and self-worth. As she came to understand these patterns, she took some important steps to alter them: dropping friends she considered too controlling or demanding, and placing limits on her own self-sacrificing behavior.

Her difficult relationship with her children was a source of considerable pain for her. When she got depressed, she longed for the intimacy with her children that she no longer had, envied her friends' intimacy with their children, ruminated about her failures as a mother, and fulminated bitterly about her children's ungrateful and abusive behavior toward her. Although it was true that her children behaved badly toward her, some of the longing and rage she felt stemmed from her emotional deprivation and abandonment schemas. She had used her children to fill an inner emptiness created by her own cold, critical, and emotionally volatile mother. When her children felt smothered and controlled by her neediness, and rebelled against her, she felt rejected, reopening her early wounds of deprivation and abandonment. Through empathic confrontation, she was able to recognize these patterns, and curtail some of her intrusive behavior. At the same time, we used role-playing exercises to help her place firmer limits on her children's demanding and abusive behavior. Through these changes, her relationship with her children gradually began to improve.

Guided imagery exercises also played an important role in the treatment. On several occasions, I asked Anna to close her eyes and recall early painful experiences involving her parents and siblings. In one session, for example, she recalled a frightening episode from childhood in which her younger sister had been lost in the woods. Her mother had become paralyzed with fear, and, crying hysterically, had insisted that Anna, who was about 10 years old at the time, lead the search for her missing sister. Although Anna had eventually found the missing sister, the entire experience had been terrifying. In this episode, the childhood origins of Anna's abandonment schema, i.e., her mother's childlike helplessness and neediness in times of stress, were evident. Using imaginal rescripting, I asked Anna to replay the episode. Following my instructions, Anna had her adult self ("Healthy Adult Anna") enter the image to confront the mother, insisting on young Anna's right to be soothed and protected during this frightening experience. After such guided imagery exercises, Anna invariably reported feeling calmer and less fearful. Thus, through the use of imaginal exposure and rescripting, early traumatic experiences were reprocessed in a way that lessened their pathogenic effects.

After 6 months of treatment, Anna's depression had remitted considerably, although she reported still experiencing better and worse days. She was less self-critical about herself as a mother, and felt better about herself overall. She had learned to set better limits with her children, and her relationship with them gradually improved. She became more assertive with her friends, and less dependent on them. She resumed dating, and began to date one man regularly. She decided on a career change, and started her own business. She felt more hopeful about the future and less lonely. After 1 year of treatment, she no longer experienced significant depressive symptoms. Moreover, she had managed to modify some of her lifelong maladaptive patterns (e.g., abandonment, emotional deprivation, defectiveness/shame, and dependence/incompetence schemas) and maladaptive coping responses (e.g., "surrendering" to her schemas by engaging in overly dependent behavior), increasing her chances of meeting her needs for healthy intimacy, as well as for fulfillment in her career.

Summary

Schema therapy is an integrative form of cognitive therapy that holds considerable promise for treating personality disorder clients with comorbid Axis I psychopathology. Schema therapy is currently the only treatment for personality disorders that has demonstrated efficacy for reducing both personality pathology and Axis I symptoms in a randomized clinical trial (Giesen-Bloo et al., 2004). The relationship between personality disorders and the outcome of Axis I treatment is undoubtedly complex. However, for many clients with personality disorders, schema therapy may prove to be a more effective alternative to standard cognitive and behavioral interventions for Axis I disorders.

References

Anand, K., Coskun, V., Thrivikaman, K., Nemeroff, C., & Plotsky, P. (1999). Long-term behavioral effects of repetitive pain in neonatal rat pups. *Physiology and Behavior, 66*, 627–637.

Brambilla, P., Soloff, P., Sala, M., Nicoletti, M., Keshavan, M., & Soares, J. (2004). Anatomical MRI study of borderline personality disorder patients. *Psychiatric Research: Neuroimaging, 131*, 125–133.

Caspi, A., McClay, J., Moffitt, T., Mill, J., Martin, J., Craig, I., et al. (2002). Role of genotype in the cycle of violence in maltreated children. *Science, 297*, 851–854.

Cicchetti, D., & Walker, E. (Eds.). (2003). *Neurodevelopmental mechanisms in psychopathology.* New York: Cambridge University Press.

Dreessen, L., & Arntz, A. (1998). The impact of personality disorders on treatment outcome of anxiety disorders: Best-evidence synthesis. *Behavior Research and Therapy, 36*, 483–504.

Giesen-Bloo, J., Arntz, A., van Dyck, R., Spinhoven, P., & van Tilburg, W. (2004, November). *Schema focused vs. transference focused psychotherapy for borderline personality disorder: Results of a multicenter trial.* Paper presented at the 2nd European Congress for Psychotherapy, Amsterdam, The Netherlands.

Lazarus, A. (2002). The multimodal assessment therapy approach. In F. Kaslow (Ed.), *Comprehensive handbook of psychotherapy: Integrative/eclectic* (Volume 4) (pp. 241–254). New York: John Wiley & Sons, Inc.

Muller, R.T. (2002). Personality pathology and treatment outcome in major depression: A review. *American Journal of Psychiatry, 159*, 359–371.

Persons, J., Burns, D., & Perloff, J. (1988). Predictors of drop out and outcome in cognitive therapy for depression in a private practice setting. *Cognitive Therapy and Research, 12*, 557–575.

Reich, J. (2003). The effect of axis II disorder on the outcome of treatment of anxiety and unipolar depressive disorders: A review. *Journal of Personality Disorders, 17*, 387–405.

Ross, S., Dermatis, H., Levounis, P., & Galanter, M. (2003). A comparison between dually diagnosed inpatients with and without axis II comorbidity and the relationship to treatment outcome. *The American Journal of Drug and Alcohol Abuse, 29*, 263–279.

Taft, C., Murphy, C., Musser, P., & Remington, M. (2004). Personality, interpersonal, and motivational predictors of the working alliance in group cognitive-behavioral therapy for partner violent men. *Journal of Consulting and Clinical Psychology, 72*, 349–354.

Vaglum, P., & Ravndal, E. (2003, May). *Personality disorders predict completion of substance abuse treatment.* Paper presented at the annual meeting of the American Psychiatric Association, San Francisco, CA.

Yoemans, F., Clarkin, J., & Kernberg, O. (2002). *A primer of transference-focused psychotherapy for the borderline patient.* Northvale, NJ: Jason Aronson.

Young, J. (1994). *Young parenting inventory.* New York: Cognitive Therapy Center of New York.

Young, J. (1995). *Young compensation inventory.* New York: Cognitive Therapy Center of New York.

Young, J., & Brown, G. (2001). *Young schema questionnaire: Special edition.* New York: Schema Therapy Institute.

Young, J., Klosko, J., & Weishaar, M. (2003). *Schema therapy: A practitioners guide.* New York: Guilford Press.

Young, J., & Rygh, J. (1994). *Young-Rygh avoidance inventory.* New York: Cognitive Therapy Center of New York.

CHAPTER **8**

Chronic Depression and Personality Disorders

KENNETH R. SILK AND DANIEL MAYMAN

Key Teaching Points

- Models by which we can understand how Axis I and Axis II disorders affect each other are
  - The variant or alternative clinical form (spectrum or subclinical) model
  - The common cause model
  - The vulnerability or predisposition (pathoplasty or exacerbation) model
  - The complication or scar model
  - The psychobiological model
  - The independence model

- While depression has often been thought to be most frequent in borderline personality disorder, it is actually more frequent in cluster C personality disorders.
- The presence of a personality disorder does not prevent recovery from the symptoms of a major depressive episode.

- Depression in patients with personality disorders is frequently marked by emptiness, loneliness, negativity in the face of high expectations, low self-esteem, and pessimism.
- Chronic depression needs to be distinguished from depressive personality disorder and treatment-resistant depression or persistence of a major depressive episode.
- Many symptoms of chronic depression in patients with personality disorders are not very responsive to psychopharmacologic agents and the best treatment approach is one that combines and integrates psychopharmacologic and psychotherapeutic interventions.

Introduction

The consideration of chronic depression and personality disorders involves addressing an interaction between Axis I and Axis II disorders. The interaction between an Axis I mood disorder and an Axis II personality disorder has been looked at from many different points of view, but in general studies have explored the interaction or overlap between major depressive episodes and the specific personality disorder, borderline personality disorder (BPD). In this chapter, we will briefly explore and try to understand the relationship of the Axis I condition that here is referred to as "chronic depression" to the general group of personality disorders and not just to BPD, even though most of the data have been generated from studies involving BPD. In fact, in the early 1980s, soon after the publication of DSM-III (*Diagnostic and Statistical Manual of Mental Disorders,* 3rd ed.), there was a flurry of papers declaring that BPD was actually a variant of an affective disorder (Akiskal, 1981; Akiskal, Chen, Davis, Puzantian, Kashgarian, & Bolinger, 1985a; Akiskal, Yerevanian, Davis, King, & Lemmi, 1985b; Carroll et al., 1981; Liebowitz & Klein, 1981). We make note that this chapter does not review the overlap of depression and personality, a topic that has been dealt with, though not resolved, in many papers in the literature (Akiskal, Hirschfeld, & Yerevanian, 1983; Fava, Alpert, Borus, Nierenberg, Pava, & Rosenbaum, 1996; Gold & Silk, 1993; Gunderson & Elliott, 1985; Gunderson & Phillips, 1991; Hirschfeld, Klerman, Clayton, Keller, McDonald-Scott, & Larkin, 1983; Klein, Kupfer, & Shea, 1993; Pilkonis & Frank, 1988; Ramlint & Ekselius, 2003; Shea et al., 1990; Widiger, 1993). Rather, this chapter tries to understand the nature of what *chronic* depression is or may be in the context of patients with personality disorders.

Models of Axis I-Axis II Co-Occurrence

A number of different models have been put forth to explain the co-occurrence of Axis I and Axis II disorders. These models look at the relationships between Axis I and Axis II disorders particularly in situations where there seems to be an unusually high amount of overlap, that is, high frequency of co-occurrence, of specific Axis I disorders with the personality disorders in general, and sometimes with a specific personality disorder. High co-occurrence has never been defined. We will briefly review the possible models below.

Axis II disorders can, in one model, be considered as a *variant or an alternative clinical form* of an Axis I disorder; and this variation in clinical presentation is one of the possible reasons for the overlap between certain Axis I disorders and certain Axis II disorders. This can also be conceived of as the *spectrum or subclinical model*. This model implies that one disorder is a milder form of another disorder, though both are subsumed under the larger disorder. Thus schizotypal personality disorder can be viewed as falling within the schizophrenic spectrum, and borderline personality disorder, perhaps in one line of thinking, can be viewed as falling into the impulsive disorders spectrum. Both disorders in this spectrum or alternative clinical variant model, however, are thought to have close relationships with each other in terms of etiology and possible mechanisms of action (Akiskal, 1981).

Other possible explanations for Axis I/Axis II overlap or comorbidity can be explained by *a common cause model* where the etiologies of the two disorders are not merely related but are the same. In this model, while there is a difference in phenotypic presentation, the belief is that both the Axis I and Axis II disorder share the same genotype (Lyons, Tyrer, Gunderson, & Tohen, 1997).

There is also the *vulnerability or predisposition model*. This model suggests that the presence of one disorder increases the chances or makes the patient more vulnerable to the other disorder. Certainly, chronic untreated or treatment-resistant depression (TRD) can lead to a negative, pessimistic, hopeless, angry person who may be or grow to be very dependent, while at the same time denying or resisting dependency wishes (Hirschfeld et al., 1983). This may then lead to or take on the clinical appearance of a cluster B or cluster C personality disorder. Conversely, a person with BPD who is angry, demanding, manipulative, and has tenuous and very ambivalent object relationships, may increase his or her vulnerability to depression by repeatedly driving people away. These people do experience rejection quite often, and they also experience the affective sequela of such rejection. While in this model the disorders are thought of as distinct entities, they nonetheless have a relationship based upon the presence of one leading to or facilitating the chance to develop the other. The *pathoplasty or exacerbation model* is a variant on the vulnerability model in that the presence of one may influence the clinical presentation of the other.

The *complication or scar model* suggests that the presence of one disorder can lead to a second disorder, and even when the first disorder remits, the second disorder persists. This model is a variation on the vulnerability model and was explored in a recent paper from the Collaborative Longitudinal Personality Disorders Study (CLPS) (Gunderson et al., 2004).

There can also be *psychobiological models* that suggest that there may be common biological underpinnings of both the Axis I and Axis II disorder. This model can also be viewed as both disorders having common psychobiological causes, and thus it is a variant of the common cause or the spectrum model. The most well-known of these biological models is by Siever and Davis (1991), though Cloninger's model should also be considered here (Cloninger, Svrakic, & Przybeck, 1993).

Finally there is the *independence model* that suggests that the two disorders are independent. In the independence model, it is only by chance, or by sharing presenting symptoms which are nonspecific and common to both disorders, that such overlap occurs (Dolan-Sewell, Kreuger, & Shea, 2001).

These various theories can be collapsed into a few larger groupings. One idea is that the disorders are independent of each other and that comorbidity occurs either by chance or because of an artifact that leads to the two disorders sharing a number of nonspecific but overlapping criteria. The second concept is that having one disorder makes the patient vulnerable to the other disorder, and this may be because the presentation of one disorder makes a person, especially in interpersonal situations, quite vulnerable to the other disorder. The complication or scar model, the vulnerability or predisposition model, and the pathoplasty model fit here. The third concept implies that some common genetic or constitutional predisposition has different or varying expressions clinically, but it is this constitutional commonality that links the two disorders. Certainly, the psychobiological model, the variant or alternative clinical form (spectrum) model, and the common cause model will fit well here (Gunderson & Elliott, 1985; Gunderson & Phillips, 1991; Gunderson et al., 2004; Koenigsberg, Anwunah, New, Mitropoulou, Schopick, & Siever, 1999).

The Depression-Personality Disorder Overlap

The overlap between depression and personality disorder was first studied between BPD and major depression. At first it was thought that there was a significantly greater comorbidity of major depression with BPD but not necessarily with the other personality disorders (Gunderson & Elliott, 1985; Gunderson & Phillips, 1991). However, that idea has not held up. In a recent report from the CLPS study, it was shown that mood disorders are more common in personality disorders other than BPD. In this study, while there was a 37% co-occurrence of BPD with MDD and a 44% co-occurrence of BPD with any mood disorder, avoidant personality disorder had a 51% co-occurrence with MDD and a 58% co-occurrence for any mood disorder. Obsessive-compulsive personality disorder had a 39% co-occurrence for major depressive disorder (MDD) and a 41% co-occurrence with any mood disorder (Skodol et al., 1999). In the study of BPD from the McLean Study of Adult Development, Zanarini et al. (1998) found that 83% of BPD patients endorsed an episode of major depression and 96% endorsed any mood disorder; in their "other" personality disorders group, 67% endorsed an MDD episode and 72% endorsed any mood disorder.

A number of studies reveal that mood disorders are probably more common in cluster C disorders than in cluster B disorders (Fava et al., 2002). Conversely, when the prevalence of personality disorders among depressed patients is explored, Keller et al. found that while 48% of depressed patients had a personality disorder, it was avoidant personality disorder at 21% and obsessive-compulsive personality disorder at 13% that were the most common personality disorders among these depressed patients (Keller et al., 1998). In a recent review, Mulder found that the most common personality disorders in depressed patients are avoidant, borderline, and possibly paranoid and obsessive-compulsive (Mulder, 2004).

There are a number of methodological and conceptual issues that need to be raised about all these studies. The first is the issue of the definition of a mood disorder, which is often, but not always, the definition of major depressive episode in DSM III or IV. Also, when these studies evaluate co-occurrence of a mood and a personality disorder, there is often the question of over what time period is the co-occurrence being measured. The studies that examine the comorbidity of a personality disorder during a depressive episode are simultaneous, so to speak, cross-sectional measurements. Those studies are measuring the presence or absence of both disorders at a specific given point in time. However, the studies that examine the presence of a mood disorder or mood symptoms in patients with personality disorders are often examining whether or not a person has had an episode of a mood disorder some time in the immediate past. This immediate past can span anywhere from 6 months to 2 years (Perry, 1985).

Other questions also arise. Should dysthymia also be included? It is in some, but not all, studies. Should depression as part of a bipolar I or a bipolar II disorder also be included? Where does depressive personality disorder fit into the picture?

Certainly, depressive personality disorder might meet the definition of chronic depression occurring within a personality disorder, and an argument could be made for considering chronic depression and personality disorder as a comorbidity between two axis II disorders with one of them being depressive personality disorder (Ryder & Bagby, 1999). But in this chapter, we are viewing the chronic depression as part of a mood disorder on Axis I rather than as part of a personality disorder, though we will soon make the argument that perhaps what is viewed as chronic or nonresponsive depression may indeed be aspects of depression that are not responsive to medications, and may be more characterological, if not in origin, then in persistence over time.

Chronic Depression and Treatment-Resistant Depression

What might be considered to fall under the clinical condition of chronic depression? Certainly dysthymia as well as depressive personality disorder could be considered as chronic depression. But there are a number of conditions that are probably more appropriate to label, or perhaps are more commonly thought of, as chronic depression. People with chronic depression often assume the label of treatment-resistant depression (TRD), but there is no real operationalized set of criteria that defines TRD. There are various statements that up to 30% of depressed patients do not respond adequately to treatment (whether psychological or psychopharmacological), but there remains the question as to how many treatments must a patient fail before he or she is declared treatment resistant (Souery et al., 1999). Paykel (1994) found that up to 20% of depressed patients remain ill after 2 years, and arguments have been made that up to 10% of patients remain ill despite multiple treatment attempts (Nirenberg & Amsterdam, 1990).

While there is no current reliable or acceptable definition of TRD, we can suggest that chronic depression and TRD may, in many instances, overlap. However, we would suggest further that the chronic depression found in patients with personality disorders may differ from the chronic depression found in TRD. While there have been no studies comparing how these two types of depression may be different, we propose that the chronic depression in patients with personality disorder often resembles certain elements of the provisional diagnosis of depressive personality disorder (DPD). On the one hand, in its clinical criteria, people with DPD are chronically unhappy; they have low self-esteem and are pessimistic. They are often brooding and moody and feel worthless and may or may not be critical toward others as well as toward themselves (Phillips, Gunderson, Hirschfeld, & Smith, 1990). On the other hand, while patients with chronic depression and personality disorder may at some time or other fall into a major depressive episode, these are not people whose depression is marked by significant appetite or sleep disturbances. If a sleep disturbance is present, it is often a difficulty in falling asleep but not a difficulty in staying asleep problem, and while there may be some early morning awakening, these patients often complain more about not having restful sleep than repeated awakenings with difficulty resuming sleep. These are not people who are anhedonic, and they usually do not have an appetite disturbance. These patients are often viewed as partially treated depression. Partial treatment of depression in this group implies that some of the psychophysiological signs of depression have improved, (i.e., sleep, appetite, anhedonia), but the cognitive constructs and pessimism and low self-esteem in interpersonal interactions remain. In this respect, these chronic depressions can resemble DPD.

However, these patients may have neither partially treated depression nor TRD. In a few studies, patients with BPD appear to experience depressive effect that is qualitatively different from what we usually think of as "major" depression. Kurtz and Morey (1998) studied the frequencies of negative evaluations and judgments in 40 MDD patients, 20 of whom had comorbid BPD. Using a word stimuli paradigm by Kaplan (1972), it was found that patients with comorbid BPD gave less "like" responses to words classified as neutral or ambivalent when compared with the MDD subjects as well as the controls. This difference did not appear to be related to BPD impulsivity in that the reaction times in the BPD patients followed the reaction times of the MDD subjects and the controls quite closely. In a similar vein, our group found that on the Adjective Check List (Gough & Heilbrun, 1983), borderlines rated their parents, especially their fathers, not only as more unfavorable on negative scales than depressed subjects or normal controls, but also rated them as less favorable on positive scales than the comparison groups. We concluded that patients with BPD had a great tendency to view the world in negative, malevolent ways, certainly a posture or attitude that could be viewed as depressive (Baker, Silk, Westen, Nigg, & Lohr, 1992).

Rogers, Widiger, and Krupp (1995) developed a measure to examine what they determined to be 11 aspects of depression gleaned from reviewing a number of self-rated scales that measure depression. The authors identified boredom, emptiness, abandonment fears, self-condemnation, self-destructiveness, cognitive dysfunction, hopelessness, guilt, sense of failure, somatic complaints, and helplessness as the 11 aspects. Depressed patients with BPD more frequently endorsed self-condemnation, abandonment fears, emptiness, self-destructiveness, and hopelessness than did the depressed patients without BPD. Boredom was not identified more frequently by patients with BPD, but emptiness, "meaninglessness or emotional void," seemed to be an important parameter in BPD patients (Rogers et al., 1995, p. 270).

Our group also examined a group of borderline patients with (N = 16) and without (N = 17) major depression and compared them to patients with major depression without BPD (N = 14) on the quality of their depressive experiences. Using Blatt's Depressive Experiences Questionnaire (Blatt, Quinlan, Chevron, McDonald, & Zuroff, 1982), a questionnaire that distinguishes between an interpersonally oriented anaclitic depression and introjective self-critical depression, it was found that borderline patients scored high on both types of depression. But more importantly, borderline patients, even when they were not depressed, evidenced "depressive" qualities marked primarily by emptiness, loneliness, desperation in attachments, and a labile, diffuse negative affectivity (Westen, Moses, Silk, Lohr, Cohen, & Segal, 1992).

In Gunderson and Phillip's review of the interface between BPD and unipolar depression (Gunderson & Phillips, 1991), they suggest characteristics of depression that are unique to unipolar depression, characteristics that appear to be unique to BPD, and characteristics that appear to be shared between the two conditions (Figure 8.1). They suggest that the depression in unipolar depression is marked by guilt and remorse, a withdrawn or agitated state, and suicidality without suicidal gestures. While these unipolar people are concerned with defeat and failure, they have stable relationships and welcome caregiving by others. In contrast, depression in BPD is often marked by emptiness and loneliness as well as behavior that is both angry and needy. Suicide gestures appear to be part of the clinical picture, and concerns are not about defeat or failures but rather about interpersonal loss, separation, or what is perceived as abandonment. Relationships are hostile dependent rather than stable, and caregiving is not readily accepted in the face of their superficial self-sufficiency. Both unipolar depressed as well as BPD patients seem to share a sustained effect that has an early onset as well as feelings of worthlessness and hopelessness. Both have a fragile self-esteem (more readily admitted to by the unipolars), and have dependency needs and a hunger for others.

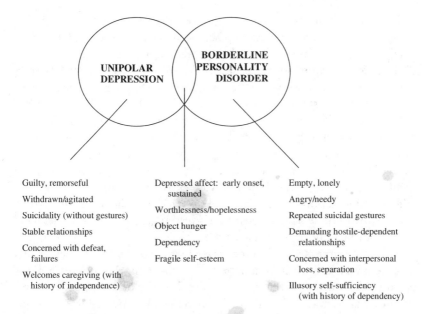

Figure 8.1 Shared and unshared characteristics of unipolar depression and borderline personality disorder. From Gunderson & Phillips (1991). With permission.

In a review, Mulder (2004) concluded that early onset sustained depression may predispose people to develop personality psychopathology (Ramlint & Ekselius, 2003; Rothschild & Zimmerman, 2002; Russell et al., 2003). Whether this is the result of the scar or the complication model as stated previously, in that early onset depression predisposes a person to develop personality disorder that persists even after the depression is resolved, or whether this may be the product of both disorders (depression as well as personality disorder) sharing a high predisposition to neuroticism (Eysenck, 1987; Kendler, Neale, Kessler, Heath, & Eaves, 1993), remains unclear. One might want to consider a model not dissimilar to the one proposed by Gunderson and Sabo, where, in discussing PTSD, they argue that chronic PTSD can be the scar for the later development of BPD when the trauma is so early and persistent that the reaction to the trauma becomes generalized and embedded in a chronic way into how the individual "normally" reacts to the world. In this way, the emotion attached to the reaction to the trauma becomes part of the personality and becomes generalized across a number of situations and not just situations that are specifically related to memories of the trauma. This can then be distinguished from acute reactions to the trauma and the specific reminders of the trauma that occur in PTSD (Gunderson & Sabo, 1993).

It is difficult not to keep coming back to BPD because it is with that disorder that most of the research has been done, even though we again need to make note that the overlap between depression and personality disorder is not limited to the specific personality disorder of BPD. We can, from the summary above, make a number of statements, generalizing from BPD to personality disorders as a whole. Personality-disordered patients are often lonely, dependent upon others to whom they can become attached in pathological ways, but who view the world and relationships (even those upon whom they depend) in negative terms. These people probably struggled with some form of chronic depression early on in adolescence, and this led them to view most situations, even neutral or ambivalent situations or relationships, as negative. The overriding cognitive posture of these people toward the world suggests disappointment and lack of satisfaction (Akiskal et al., 1980).

These descriptors are often the ways in which patients with personality disorders view the world. If a patient has true comorbid depression and personality disorder, and not personality disorder or personality characteristics that seem to fade with the improvement of depression (Fava et al., 2002; Griens, Jonker, Spinhoven, & Blom, 2002), there is growing evidence that the personality disorder does not limit or slow down the improvement from the depression, or impact the response to pharmacotherapy (Mulder, 2002, 2004; Russell et al., 2003). If these recent studies by Mulder and Russell et al. are supported by others, then we can say that the chronic depression seen in patients with personality disorder is not the result of the personality disorder pathology preventing the psychopharmacologic intervention from being effective. The biological aspects of the depression respond to the psychopharmacologic treatment whether or not there is a comorbid personality disorder present. However, the comorbid personality psychopathology may be, in some part, responsible for the persistent negative, pessimistic, empty, and lonely effects and cognitions of the patient even after the depression has been substantially resolved through psychopharmacology. In this model, the personality pathology is in some part responsible for the persistence of some residue that may be labeled chronic depression but may, in actuality, be the enduring posture of the personality pathology.

Perhaps what is really being viewed here as chronic depression in patients with personality disorders may not be depression in the DSM sense at all, or at least may not be a depression that is medication responsive. It is important to note that the symptoms that we consider the essential part of major depression today are based very much on depression as defined in the Hamilton Rating Scale for Depression (HRSD)

(Hamilton, 1960). Hamilton's definition of depression was primarily a biological, somatic definition of depression, and while it did include constructs such as psychic anxiety and guilt, it did not incorporate emptiness or loneliness or fear of abandonment into its criteria set. In fact, an argument could be raised that Hamilton's definition of depression was based upon the clinical response of depressed patients who were initially exposed to imipramine (Kuhn, 1958). This is a far cry from the depression described by Freud in "Mourning and Melancholia" (Freud, 1914 [1957]) or as elaborated upon by Jacobson (1972 [c 1971]), a depression that was attributed to ambivalently felt introjects turned upon the self. This is not to say that Hamilton was wrong, but we must not forget that there is a greater variety of symptoms that we would think would relate to depression than merely those listed in the HRSD. Much of what is perceived of as chronic depression such as the emptiness and loneliness and negativity suggested previously in personality disordered patients are not descriptors found in the HRSD. These particular symptoms or manifestations of depression are not inherently responsive to medications, and hence can be considered as chronic if one agrees that they are descriptors of depression.

Personality disordered patients often have a different set of expectations than nonpersonality-disordered patients. It is not uncommon for personality-disordered patients not only to consider neutral or ambivalent words as negative (Kurtz & Morey, 1998), but to experience neutral and/or ambivalent situations as negative as well. While this propensity may fall under the realm of cognitive distortions and pessimistic world view, it is not uncommon for personality-disordered patients, at least those with BPD, to view neutral events as negative (Nigg, Lohr, Westen, Gold, & Silk, 1992). For many of us a day that goes along fairly close to what has been planned, with only minimal disruptions and only minor crises, can be viewed as an "OK" or a neutral day, while patients with BPD will view a similar day as negative, not neutral. In fact, from a clinical point of view, it is very difficult, in our experience, for many personality disorder patients to view any given day or situation as neutral, neither good or bad, but just "OK." And preliminary work from our PET studies of induced sadness suggests that borderline patients are always defending biologically against depression or negative effect, even when there is little negative effect present (Silk, Zubieta, & Koeppe, 2004).

This is not an insignificant issue since if we try to medicate such patients we will often come upon what we call treatment resistance. Further, too much enthusiasm on the part of the therapist/psychiatrist to try to medicate these more characterological symptoms of depression can lead to frustration on the part of the pharmacologist, a frustration that can lead to more and more complex combinations of medications (Main, 1957). But none of the medications work very well because the symptoms they are allegedly targeting are not, at least with the medications and expertise that we currently possess, responsive to psychopharmacologic agents (Silk & Heap, 2002).

Questions to Be Answered

There are many assumptions in the previous statements and much speculation. There is speculation because there is little data to explicate the issue of chronic depression in personality disorders. There are a number of issues that need to be clarified if we are to make progress in understanding what is chronic depression in personality disorders and what is the best way to approach or treat this chronic depression. Some questions or issues that come to mind include:

1. What is the definition of chronic depression in personality disorders? Does the form that the symptoms of chronic depression takes differ depending upon the specific personality disorder? For example, if more patients with cluster C personality disorders appear to have chronic depression than patients with cluster B personality disorder, then is the residual or chronic depression that persists in cluster C patients different from the residual or chronic depression in cluster B patients?
2. Given what is stated in the first issue, might we expect the chronic symptoms of depression in cluster C patients to respond to different psychopharmacologic agents than the chronic symptoms of depression might respond to in cluster B patients?
3. What is treatment resistance? Is treatment resistance the failure of specific symptoms known to be responsive to medications not responding to a series of different antidepressant medications or medication strategies? Or is treatment resistance the persistence of some residual symptoms of depression that are not very responsive in most instances to pharmacologic intervention?
4. Given the definition decided upon in item 3, then what can be realistically expected in terms of the treatment response of all the symptoms of depression to antidepressant medication(s) in patients with personality disorders? What is defined as a good outcome with respect to depressive symptoms in a patient with personality disorder and depression?

If we do not unravel these four questions, it will be very difficult for us to proceed and clarify the nature of what we are here calling chronic depression. Clarification can help lead to clearer, more homogenous categories of depression and depression subgroups both within groups of patients with personality disorders as well as among patients with chronic depression who do not appear to have personality disorders. We could then proceed to appreciate what may be more proper and more specific psychopharmacologic treatment for depression, as well as to recognize how to classify these chronically depressed personality disordered patients both biologically and phenotypically (clinically). This could then lead us to define more specific endophenotypes that might lead us closer to understanding the genetic similarities or differences between personality disordered patients with chronic depression and depressed patients who are defined as treatment resistant. Further, it would allow us to appreciate better cognitive, emotional, and psychological similarities and differences that could inform the selection of specific psychosocial interventions.

Clinical Issues

While we struggle to solve some of these issues, we are nonetheless left with patients who have personality disorders and who suffer from chronic depression. How then are we to approach this issue clinically? What strategies might we use to appreciate better the nature and then perhaps the responsivity of these chronic symptoms of depression?

The clinical evaluation of depression in a patient with a personality disorder needs to begin with a careful consideration of the patient on both Axis I and Axis II. What is the nature of the Axis I disorder and what is the nature of the Axis II disorder? If the patient complains of depression, does the depression meet the criteria for a major depressive episode? Are there distinct disturbances of sleep, appetite, ability to enjoy, ability to concentrate? How persistent or consistent are these symptoms of depression or do they vary from day to day, that is, do the depressive symptoms seem to wax and wane with environmental and/or life events even if they never really elevate to the positive side of "neutral"? Does the depression seem fairly stuck and immune to life events? How long has the depression been present? Has it been treated pharmacologically, and if so, has it improved at all? Are we dealing with residue of a major depressive episode, or are we dealing with persistent depressive and negative effects that do respond to interpersonal situations better than medications, even if the improvement doesn't last? Are pessimism, negativity, anger, and loneliness and emptiness part of the picture?

When collating the symptoms that are present, we must ask ourselves whether we can expect these symptoms to respond to psychopharmacologic intervention (Silk, 2004). If there are symptoms that clearly can be considered to be ones known to be medication responsive, then has the patient been treated long enough with sufficiently high enough doses of antidepressant medications to reach improvement? If that is so, then antidepressant augmentation strategies should be employed, the details of which are not in the scope of this paper but which are reviewed in many different places (Barbee, Conrad, & Jamhour, 2004; Dording, 2000; Marangell, 2000). It is important to note that it is very difficult for patients to accurately report what augmentation strategies have been applied, even if they have been quite accurate in reporting the history of which medications have been used in monotherapy (Posternak & Zimmerman, 2003). Therefore, it is very important that information about combinations of medications that have been used in the past be solicited from people who have treated the patient before and used those strategies. If, on the other hand, multiple augmentation strategies have been used, and in fact, even if they have not been employed, a careful review of nonpharmacological treatment should be done as well. There is increasing evidence of the success of nonpharmacological strategies combined with psychopharmacologic agents in depressed patients (Keller et al., 2001; Kool, Dekker, Duijsens, de Jonnghe, & Puite, 2003; Silk, 1999), particularly strategies that use cognitive-behavioral approaches.

All depressions, even when there is no personality disorder, are not the same (Akiskal et al., 1980, 1985a, 1985b; Liebowitz & Klein, 1981; Parsons et al., 1989), and all depressions experienced by patients with personality disorders are not the same (Soloff, George, Nathan, & Schulz, 1987; Westen et al., 1992). Further, not all depressions are equally responsive to medications (Parsons et al., 1989). The evaluation and treatment of chronic depression in patients with personality disorders asks no more of us than the treatment of any psychiatric patient asks of us: a thorough evaluation leading to a diagnosis or a number of diagnoses, an hypothesis as to how the two disorders may or may not be linked, and a strategic treatment plan that employs careful and thoughtful initiation of comprehensive treatment that draws from the best of what we understand about both psychopharmacologic as well as psychotherapeutic approaches to the disorder(s) uncovered.

Conclusions

There is much work that remains to be done in order to understand the relationship between chronic depression and the personality disorders. There is no common definition as to what chronic depression is, and we need to understand how chronic depression and treatment-resistant depression are similar to as well as different from each other. Further, we need to determine whether chronic depression is different from the characterological or persistent negativity and pessimism and general loneliness and emptiness about which patients with personality disorders often complain.

Yet while there are many answers that need to be uncovered, these patients continue to show up in treatment settings and request respite from the pain of these persisting negative affects. A thorough history and evaluation followed by an integrated treatment plan that addresses psychopharmacologic as well as psychotherapeutic strategies that are designed to minimize biologically responsive symptoms and maximize coping skills and ego strength provides the most comprehensive and empathic approach that we can currently offer these individuals.

References

Akiskal, H. S. (1981). Subaffective disorders: Dysthymic, cyclothymic and bipolar II disorders in the "borderline" realm. *Psychiatric Clinics of North America, 4,* 25–46.

Akiskal, H. S., Chen, S. E., Davis, G. C., Puzantian, V. R., Kashgarian, M., & Bolinger, J. M. (1985a). Borderline: An adjective in search of a noun. *Journal of Clinical Psychiatry, 46,* 41–48.

Akiskal, H. S., Hirschfeld, R. M., & Yerevanian, B. I. (1983). The relationship of personality to affective disorders. *Archives of General Psychiatry, 40,* 801–810.

Akiskal, H. S., Rosenthal, T. L., Haykal, R. F., Lemmi, H., Rosenthal, R. H., &. Scott-Strauss, A. (1980). Characterological depressions. Clinical and sleep EEG findings separating subaffective dysthymias from character spectrum disorders. *Archives of General Psychiatry, 37,* 777–783.

Akiskal, H. S., Yerevanian, B. I., Davis, G. C., King, D., & Lemmi, H. (1985b). The nosologic status of borderline personality: Clinical and polysomnographic study. *American Journal of Psychiatry, 142,* 192–198.

Baker, L., Silk, K. R., Westen, D., Nigg, J. T., & Lohr, N. E. (1992). Malevolence, splitting, and parental ratings by borderlines. *Journal of Nervous and Mental Disease, 180,* 258–264.

Barbee, J. G., Conrad, E. J., & Jamhour, N. J. (2004). The effectiveness of olanzapine, risperidone, quetiapine, and ziprasidone as augmentation agents in treatment-resistant major depressive disorder. *Journal of Clinical Psychiatry, 65,* 975–998.

Blatt, S. J., Quinlan, D. M., Chevron, E. S., McDonald, C., & Zuroff, D. (1982). Dependency and self-criticism: Psychological dimensions of depression. *Journal of Consulting and Clinical Psychology, 50,* 113–124.

Carroll, B. J., Greden, J. F., Feinberg, M., Lohr, N., James, N. M., Steiner, M., et al. (1981). Neuroendocrine evaluation of depression in borderline patients. *Psychiatric Clinics of North America, 4,* 89–99.

Cloninger, C. R., Svrakic, D. M., & Przybeck, T. R. (1993). A psychobiological model of temperament and character. *Archives of General Psychiatry, 50,* 975–990.

Dolan-Sewell, R. T., Kreuger, R. F., & Shea, M. T. (2001). In W. J. Livesley (Ed.), *Handbook of personality disorders. Theory, research, and treatment* (pp. 84–104). New York: Guilford.

Dording, C. M. (2000). Antidepressant augmentation and combinations. *Psychiatric Clinics of North America, 23,* 743–755.

Eysenck, H. J. (1987). The definition of personality disorders and the criteria appropriate to their definition. *Journal of Personality Disorders, 1,* 211–219.

Fava, M., Alpert, J. E., Borus, J. S., Nierenberg, A. A., Pava, J. A., & Rosenbaum, J. F. (1996). Patterns of personality disorder comorbidity in early-onset versus late-onset major depression. *American Journal of Psychiatry, 153,* 1308–1312.

Fava, M., Farabaugh, A. H., Sickinger, A. H., Wright, E., Alpert, J. E., Sonawalla, S., et al. (2002). Personality disorders and depression. *Psychological Medicine, 32,* 1049–1057.

Freud, S. (1914/1957). Mourning and melancholia. In *The Standard Edition of the Complete Psychological Works of Sigmund Freud, Volume XIV,* (pp. 243–258). London: The Hogarth Press.

Gold, L. J., & Silk, K. R. (1993). Exploring the borderline personality disorder-major affective disorder interface. In J. Paris (Ed.), *Borderline personality disorder: Etiology and treatment* (pp. 39–66). Washington, DC: American Psychiatric Publishing, Inc.

Gough, H. G., & Heilbrun, A. B. (1983). *The Adjective Check List manual* (1983 ed.). Palo Alto, CA: Consulting Psychologists Press.

Griens, A. M., Jonker, K., Spinhoven, P., & Blom, M. B. (2002). The influence of depressive state features on trait measurement. *Journal of Affective Disorders, 70,* 95–99.

Gunderson, J. G., & Elliott, G. R. (1985). The interface between borderline personality disorder and affective disorder. *American Journal of Psychiatry, 142,* 277–288.

Gunderson, J. G., Morey, L. S., Stout, R. L., Skodol, A. E., Shea, M. T., McGlashan, T. H., et al. (2004). Major depressive disorder and borderline personality disorder revisited: Longitudinal interactions. *Journal of Clinical Psychiatry, 65,* 1049–1056.

Gunderson, J. G., & Phillips, K. A. (1991). A current view of the interface between borderline personality disorder and depression. *American Journal of Psychiatry, 148,* 967–975.

Gunderson, J. G., & Sabo, A. N. (1993). The phenomenological and conceptual interface between borderline personality disorder and PTSD. *American Journal of Psychiatry, 150,* 19–27.

Hamilton, M. (1960). A rating scale for depression. *Journal of Neurology, Neurosurgery and Psychiatry, 23,* 56–62.

Hirschfeld, R. M. (1999). Personality disorders and depression: Comorbidity. *Depression and Anxiety, 10,* 142–146.

Hirschfeld, R. M., Klerman, G. L., Clayton, P. J., Keller, M. B., McDonald-Scott, P., & Larkin, B. H. (1983). Assessing personality: Effects of the depressive state on trait measurement. *American Journal of Psychiatry, 140,* 695–699.

Jacobson, E. (1972). *Depression: Comparative studies of normal, neurotic, and psychotic conditions.* New York: International Universities Press.

Kaplan, K. J. (19172). On the ambivalence-indifference problem in attitude theory and measurement. *Psychological Bulletin, 77,* 361–372.

Keller, M. B., Gelenberg, A. J., Hirschfeld, R. M., Rush, A. J., Thase, M. E., Kocsis, J. H., et al. (1998). The treatment of chronic depression, part 2: A double-blind, randomized trial of sertraline and imipramine. *Journal of Clinical Psychiatry, 59,* 598–607.

Keller, M. B., McCullough, J. P., Klein, D. N., Arnow, B., Dunner, D. L., Gelenberg, A. J., et al. (2001). A comparison of nefazodone, the cognitive behavioral-analysis system of psychotherapy, and their combination for the treatment of chronic depression. *New England Journal of Medicine, 342,* 1462–1470.

Kendler, K. S., Neale, M. C., Kessler, R. C., Heath, A. C., & Eaves, L. J. (1993). A longitudinal twin study of personality and major depression in women. *Archives of General Psychiatry, 50,* 853–862.

Klein, M. H., Kupfer, D. J., & Shea, M. T. (Eds.). (1993). *Personality and depression: A current view.* New York: Guilford.

Koenigsberg, H. W., Anwunah, I., New, A. S., Mitropoulou, V., Schopick, F., & Siever, L. J. (1999). Relationship between depression and borderline personality disorder. *Depression and Anxiety, 10,* 158–167.

Kool, S., Dekker, J., Duijsens, I. J., de Jonnghe, F., & Puite, B. (2003). Changes in personality pathology after pharmacotherapy and combined therapy for depressed patients. *Journal of Personality Disorders, 17,* 60–72.

Kuhn, R. (1958). The treatment of depressive states with G22355 (imipramine hydrochloride). *American Journal of Psychiatry, 115,* 459–464.

Kurtz, J. E., & Morey, L. C. (1998). Negativism in evaluative judgments of words among depressed outpatients with borderline personality disorder. *Journal of Personality Disorders, 12,* 351–361.

Liebowitz, M. R., & Klein, D. F. (1981). Interrelationship of hysteroid dysphoria and borderline personality disorder. *Psychiatric Clinics of North America, 4,* 67–87.

Lyons, M. J., Tyrer, P., Gunderson, J., & Tohen, M. (1997). Heuristic models of comorbidity of axis I and axis II disorders. *Journal of Personality Disorders, 11*, 260–269.

Main, T. F. (1957). The ailment. *British Journal of Medical Psychology, 30*, 129–145.

Marangell, L. B. (2000). Augmentation of standard depression therapy. *Clinical Therapeutics, 22*, Suppl A, A25–38 (discussion A39–41).

Mulder, R. T. (2002). Personality pathology and treatment outcome in major depression: A review. *American Journal of Psychiatry, 159*, 359–371.

Mulder, R. T. (2004). Depression and personality disorder. *Current Psychiatry Reports, 6*, 51–57.

Nierenberg, A. A., & Amsterdam, J. D. (1990). Treatment-resistant depression: Definition and treatment approaches. *Journal of Clinical Psychiatry, 51*, 39–47.

Nigg, J. T., Lohr, N. E., Westen D., Gold, L. J., & Silk, K. R. (1992). Malevolent object representations in borderline personality disorder and major depression. *Journal of Abnormal Psychology, 101*, 61–67.

Posternak, M. A., & Zimmerman, M. (2003). How accurate are patients in reporting their antidepressant treatment history? *Journal of Affective Disorders, 75*, 115–24.

Parsons, B., Quitkin, F. M., McGrath, P. J., Stewart, J. W., Tricamo, E., Ocepek-Welikson, K., et al. (1989). Phenelzine, imipramine, and placebo in borderline patients meeting criteria for atypical depression. *Psychopharmacology Bulletin, 25*, 524–534.

Paykel, E. S., (1994). Epidemiology of refractory depression. In W. A. Nolen, J. Zohar, S. P. Roose, & J. D. Amsterdam (Eds.), *Refractory depression: Current strategies and future directions* (pp. 3–18). New York: John Wiley & Sons.

Perry, J. C. (1985). Depression in borderline personality disorder: Lifetime prevalence at interview and longitudinal course of symptoms. *American Journal of Psychiatry, 142*, 15–21.

Phillips, K. A., Gunderson, J. G., Hirschfeld, R. M., & Smith, L. E. (1990). A review of the depressive personality. *American Journal of Psychiatry, 147*, 830–837.

Pilkonis, P. A., & Frank, E. (1988). Personality pathology in recurrent depression: Nature, prevalence, and relationship to treatment response. *American Journal of Psychiatry, 145*, 435–441.

Ramklint, M., & Ekselius, L. (2003). Personality traits and personality disorders in early onset versus late onset major depression. *Journal of Affective Disorders, 75*, 35–42.

Rogers, J. H., Widiger, T. A., & Krupp, A. (1995). Aspects of depression associated with borderline personality disorder. *American Journal of Psychiatry, 152*, 268–270.

Russell, J. M., Kornstein, S. G., Shea, M. T., McCullough, J. P., Harrison, W. M., Hirschfeld, R. M., et al. (2003). Chronic depression and comorbid personality disorders: Response to sertraline versus imipramine. *Journal of Clinical Psychiatry, 64*, 554–561.

Ryder, A. G., & Bagby, R. M. (1999). Diagnostic viability of depressive personality disorder: Theoretical and conceptual issues. *Journal of Personality Disorders, 13*, 99–117.

Shea, M. T., Pilkonis, P. A., Beckham, E., Collins, J. F., Elkin, I., Sotsky, S. M., et al. (1990). Personality disorders and treatment outcome in the NIMH Treatment of Depression Collaborative Research Program. *American Journal of Psychiatry, 147*, 711–718.

Siever, L. J., & Davis, K. L. (1991). A psychobiological perspective on the personality disorders. *American Journal of Psychiatry, 148*, 1647–1658.

Silk, K. R. (1999). Collaborative treatment for patients with personality disorders. In M. Riba & R. Balon (Eds.), *Psychopharmacology and psychotherapy: A collaborative approach* (pp. 221–227). Washington, DC: American Psychiatric Publishing, Inc.

Silk, K. R. (2004). The pharmacotherapy of personality disorders. Logistics and limitations (p. 32). *Syllabus and Scientific Proceedings, 56th Annual Institute on Psychiatric Services.*

Silk, K. R., & Heap, J. (2002). Is chemical imbalance a useful concept in treating personality disorders? *Syllabus and Proceedings Summary, 155th Annual Meeting, American Psychiatric Association*, Philadelphia, May 18–23, p. 31.

Silk, K. R., Zubieta, J. K., & Koeppe, R. A. (2004). A PET study of mu-opioid neurotransmission and affective lability in borderline personality disorder (pp. 196–197). *Syllabus and Scientific Proceedings, 157th Annual Meeting, American Psychiatric Association*, Philadelphia, May 18-23, p.31.

Skodol, A. E., Stout, R. L., McGlashan, T. H., Grilo, C. M., Gunderson, J. G., Shea, M. T., et al. (1999). Co-occurrence of mood and personality disorders: A report from the Collaborative Longitudinal Personality Disorders Study (CLPS). *Depression & Anxiety, 10*, 175–182.

Soloff, P. H., George, A., Nathan, R. S., & Schulz, P. M. (1987). Characterizing depression in borderline patients. *Journal of Clinical Psychiatry, 48,* 155–157.

Souery, D., Amsterdam, J., de Montigny, C., Lecrubier, Y., Montgomery, S., Lipp, O., et al. (1999).
Treatment resistant depression: Methodological overview and operational criteria. *European Neuropsychopharmacology, 9,* 83–91.

Westen, D., Moses, M. J., Silk, K. R., Lohr, N. E., Cohen, R., & Segal, H. (1992). Quality of depressive experience in borderline personality disorder and major depression: When depression
is not just depression. *Journal of Personality Disorders, 6,* 382–393.

Widiger, T. A. (1993). Personality disorder and axis I psychopathology: The problematic boundary of axis I and axis II. *Journal of Personality Disorders, 17,* 90–108.

Zanarini, M. C., Frankenburg, F. R., Dubo, E. D., Sickel, A. E., Trikha, A., Levin, A., et al. (1998).
Axis I comorbidity of borderline personality disorder. *American Journal of Psychiatry, 155,*
1733–1739.

CHAPTER 9

Family Intervention in the Treatment of Personality Disorder and Issues of Compliance[1]

IRA D. GLICK AND BLAIR MULLEN

Key Teaching Points

- Individual symptoms of personality disorder are in part related to the family system dynamics.
- Families do not cause personality disorders, but they can exacerbate the genetic vulnerability.
- Family psychoeducation and intervention, pharmacotherapy, as well as individual therapy are necessary for many patients to improve their long-term outcome.
- The family may play a decisive role in treatment compliance as well as treatment success or failure.

---

[1] Adapted in part from Glick, I. D., & Loraas, E. L. (2001). Family treatment of borderline personality disorder. In M. M. MacFarlane (Ed.), *Family therapy and mental health* (pp. 135–150). Binghamton, NY: Haworth Clinical Practice Press.

Introduction and Overview

Although personality disorders (PDs) have long been a focus of individual psychotherapists, only recently have family therapists turned their attention to the illness (Allen, 2004; Magnavita & MacFarlane, 2004). Despite extensive study, the etiology of this disorder remains unclear, and effective treatments are still in the developmental stage. To date, most treatment approaches have focused on the patient with the disorder, with only secondary interest in the family or significant others.

The most common clinical situation for the family therapist arises when one member of a couple enters couples' therapy with complaints about the relationship. As therapy evolves, it becomes apparent that the relationship difficulties are inextricably linked with one or both partner's basic character structure or personality. Often the relationship was initially functional, but difficulties emerge when one or both partners are unable to adjust to developmental changes in the family life cycle (e.g., birth of a child, death of parent, etc.) or an acute crisis in the family such as the loss of a job (see Carter & McGoldrick, 1988, for a description of family life cycle stages and the impact of various stressors on the family system). The core issue is that an individual's ability to adapt in the family unit is limited by their basic personality or character structure.

Effective treatment of PD must address the complex interplay between relationship dynamics, character structure, and developmental crises and life stages. When PD is viewed and treated with a relationship focus, it is sometimes possible to help family members master life-cycle changes and tasks, adapt to the character styles of their partners, and move on to live happier and satisfying lives.

Definition of Borderline Personality Disorder (BPD)

PDs are grouped separately from Axis I disorders because they usually have symptoms extending back into early development. Another group develops a personality disorder secondary to an Axis I disorder like bipolar disorder. Both represent maladaptive patterns of coping (in contrast to classical signs and symptoms), which often manifest primarily in social situations and interactions. They have less predictive value than the Axis I disorders.

By way of example, let us define one type of personality disorder and then examine how an individual symptom has interpersonal implications. The DSM-IV (*Diagnostic and Statistical Manual of Mental Disorders*, 4th ed.) lists nine criteria for the diagnosis of PD (American Psychiatric Association, 1994). Interestingly, seven of these nine criteria have obvious and clinically important interpersonal implications. The first relates to the issue of abandonment, which relates to situations in which family members are either perceived as, or actually are, unreliable or abandoning. The second criterion has to do with unstable interpersonal relationships. The patient does not have a sense of permanence or consistency in his/her relationship with others (e.g., family members). The third deals with identity disturbance where the patient experiences a shifting sense of who he/she is, and therefore, a lack of consistency and reliability within relationships. The fourth is impulsivity, which results in impulsive, destructive behaviors that can cause destabilization of the family. The fifth criterion is suicidality and our sense is that this type of behavior stems not only from the emotional pain associated with the illness, but in part, from conscious and unconscious attempts to control family behavior by use of the threat of suicide. The sixth criterion is affective instability which is related to the first criterion and directly undermines family emotional consistency. The seventh, and a related problem, is anger. The patient is a potential powder keg waiting to explode and the family may serve to ignite the patient. Each of these criterion and their interpersonal implications will be elaborated later.

Etiology

Understanding the Family in Context of Personality Disorder

Again, by way of example, we will focus on BPD. Data suggest that BPD may have, in part, a genetic etiology (Siever & Davis, 1991). There is a suggestion of familial transmission (Silverman et al., 1991). As we begin to know more about life course, we see there is biologic dysfunction and symptoms typically beginning early, perhaps preadolescence, which reach their full expression during the individual's 20s and 30s, resulting in (at least) 2 decades of intense symptoms, and problems, for patients and their families. What is most fascinating is that the intensity of symptomatology levels off (i.e., lower levels with less peaks) in the 40s and 50s, but there is evidence of a lower resultant functional level than prior to the illness. (Paris, 2003a, p. 75). It should be noted that there are very few medical illnesses that fit this model (in psychiatry, one subset of patients with schizophrenia have this life course, and in internal medicine there are some similarities to regional enteritis) again raising the perplexing question of BPD etiology.

Biological Data

For several decades, clinician researchers, including Klein (1968) and others, have suggested that there may be a biological contribution to PD.

The evidence was mostly anecdotal and empirical, that is, based on use of antidepressants, mood stabilizers, and neuroleptics which improved some symptoms. Research into the biological correlates of behavioral and personality traits have provided data that there is a heritable, biological component to some selected personality and behavioral traits (Siever & Davis, 1991). Specifically, there may be familial transmission of the hallmark borderline-related personality characteristics, an area reviewed by Coccaro and Siever (1995). Further,

> twin studies suggest that genetic rather than environmental factors are responsible for the covariation among traits delineating the borderline pattern. Although environmental factors exert a considerable influence they appear to operate to consolidate genetic influences and modulate the way specific traits are expressed rather than change the trait structure of personality. (Livesley, Jang, & Vernon, 1998)

These familial problems (i.e., the dysfunctional personality characteristics) in combination with cognitive impairments in perception and abstract thinking in BPD patients, presents a situation with high potential for misunderstanding in both patients and their families (Burgess & Zarconi, 1992). More recently, in clinical psychopharmacologic trials, medication has been associated with global improvement in some patients with BPD (Schatzburg, Cole, & DeBattista, 2003). This empirical finding suggests (but does not prove) that a part of the etiology of the disorder is "biological": likewise, prescribing a medication by itself cannot resolve the multiple intrapsychic and interpersonal issues.

Family Pathology; Lack of Social Support for the Borderline Disorder

As Clarkin, Marziali, and Munroe-Blum (1991) note, the data on family pathology has been mostly correlational, (in contrast to causal) and relate to issues involving a complex interplay between inborn vulnerability and developmental trauma. Kagan's work (Kagan, Rezneck, Snidman, & Gibbons, 1988) demonstrates that a vulnerable individual in a severely dysfunctional family may produce the symptoms we associate with BPD. Similarly, Stone (1988) has proposed a "psycho-biological model of the borderline conditions that explores the role of a hyperirritability that may either antedate parent-child interaction or stand apart from traditional developmental stages" (p. 3). The model suggests that "one pathway towards this hyperirritability is the traumatic effect of abuse, which may alter the neuroregulatory response system in ways that cannot be accounted for in purely developmental models" (Stone, 1988). Sholevar and Schwoeri have formulated this as follows:

> The premise of family and marital therapy is that personality and character constrictions are rooted in early developmental failures and lead to marital characteristics that are an extension of personality dysfunction. The interactional and marital disorder creates a relational and social context that perpetuates the intrapsychic conflicts and hinders the forward movement of the couple and their children. (Sholevar & Schwoeri, 2003, p. 716)

MacFarlane has summarized the dynamics as follows:

> The relevance and impact on family members of a borderline patient cannot be overstated. In the family system, all members experience family events within a context peculiar to their roles. Each family member is impacted by the actions and behaviors of the others. Every family unit embodies a unique developmental history that evolves as the family members grow and change. A new marriage, the birth of a child, adolescent turbulence, separating offspring, death of a spouse, or other external events, such as illness or job loss, can produce conflict and difficulty in adapting. The healthiest families are those that can withstand and adapt to these stresses. When one or more members exhibit borderline pathology, the reverberations are experienced throughout the family unit. (MacFarlane, 2004, p. 121)

Parental Pathology

When examining parental pathology in relation to BPD, it has been found that parents of borderline patients have a low incidence of schizophrenia and a high incidence of affective disorder (Soloff & Millward, 1983). In borderline patients with a comorbid history of major depression, the incidence of parental affective disorders is especially high (Pope, Jonas, Hudson, Cohen, & Gunderson, 1983). Families of borderline patients have a higher incidence of the same behaviors found in BPD patients (Loranger, Oldham, & Tulis, 1982) which include alcoholism (Loranger & Tulis, 1985), antisocial personality disorder (Soloff & Millward, 1983), and other cluster B personality disorders (Pope et al., 1983; Zanarini, Gunderson, Marino, Schwartz, & Frankenberg, 1990). Goldman, D'Angelo, and DeMaso (1993) reported higher rates of psychopathology among family members of patients with BPD compared to a control group with other psychiatric disorders. The nature and extent of parental pathology may be related to disruptive environmental events, such as increased risk of early loss or separation, physical and sexual abuse, and nonintact parental marriage (Links, Boigo, Huxley, Steiner, & Mitton, 1990). In summary, "familial transmission" of various characteristics of borderline personality disorders seems likely, and such transmission may result from combinations of genetic, nongenetic biological, and epigenetic factors.

Borderline Couples

While there is a substantial amount of literature on patients with BPD, this is not the case for *borderline couples*. Up until recently, little was written on adults in a relationship or in a family with a borderline-identified patient. There are two obvious reasons for this: First, most psychotherapy of patients with BPD has been psychoanalytically oriented, where the focus is on the dynamics of the individual. Second, family therapists usually have not been interested in an individual family member's diagnosis, but rather on the effects of the illness on the families. In addition, much of what has been published in the family literature is anecdotal. Of note, in 2004, MacFarlane edited the first book on the family treatment of personality disorders.

PD symptoms and personality characteristics often play an integral role in relationship dynamics and are a source of considerable stress. Partners often play a homeostatic or regulating role with respect to PD interpersonal patterns. When one partner becomes angry, the other soothes; when one partner feels hurt and rejected, the other shows great affection. As a result, therapy with the "borderline couple" must include treatment of both the individual with the disorder and the partner in order to fully address these relationship dynamics (Koch, 1985). When both spouses in the marriage have a personality disorder, the therapist must provide an empathetic environment with delineated boundaries. This is often termed the *holding environment,* and it allows the patient to develop trust and a sense of object constancy, which is often underdeveloped in borderline patients. Once the holding environment is established, the therapist becomes the *manager of the holding environment,* allowing the couple to better focus on the sources of their distress (McCormack, 1989).

In summary, it can be said that when it comes to etiology of personality disorders, *hard* data are accumulating that there *are* disturbed biological substrates in the patient (Siever & Davis, 1991), and probably in family members as well (Silverman et al., 1991). There is *suggestive* evidence that disturbed biology in combination with a disturbed *bad-fit* family is etiologic in borderline disorder and that the issues of (1) parental pathology, (2) physical and sexual abuse, and (3) neglect and overprotection are related to the development and/or maintenance of what we now label as BPD. There is no evidence that pathologic family relationships *alone* can cause borderline disorder. On the other hand, researchers agree that a family can cause a genetically vulnerable, identified patient great distress, and a very ill identified patient can certainly cause the family great burden.

Evaluation and Family Assessment

Evaluation and treatment of the PD patient and his/her family may occur in a number of settings. Because of the explosive and crisis-like nature of borderline pathology, many therapists quickly jump from the initial interview directly into treatment. However, we strongly urge a careful evaluation of the PD patient and his/her family *before* plunging into treatment (regardless of modality). A therapist should take the time to (1) evaluate the strengths and weaknesses of the family system; (2) ask the question of whether (and how) the patient and family affect each other, especially in regard to family burden and *expressed emotion*, that is, the coping mechanism of family members as they live with a chronic mental illness like a chronic PD, specifically high hostility and overinvolvement; and (3) evaluate the nature and severity of family members' psychopathology and their relationships to the patient's. Finally, when a patient with PD is hospitalized (now rare), it is mandatory to identify both prehospital and (the anticipated) posthospital family behavior that is associated with the patient's psychopathology (Clarkin et al., 1991).

Treatment

By way of introduction, it is important to state that there are no controlled trials of family treatment for any one type or cluster of personality disorders. As in the MacFarlane book (2004), all family intervention models are based on anecdotal experience with family intervention (Crits-Christoph & Barber, 2002).

As we have discussed, our model is based on the belief that patients with borderline personality disorder (BPD) are biologically derived from, and psychosocially (i.e., interactionally) inseparable from the family. Our understanding of the literature dealing with etiology of PD suggests that in some cases, family psychopathology preexists the birth of a vulnerable *identified patient* (IP), thus producing impaired relationships amongst family members in an already fragile family structure. In families where preexisting function is *within normal limits*, families can become dysfunctional with the addition of an impaired child, significant other, or parent. If these assumptions are correct, we believe a change from the current working *family therapy models* are indicated.

In our judgment when the family is available and motivated, we believe that the treatment of choice is family psychoeducation with family (systems or dynamic) intervention where possible in combination with pharmacotherapy and/or individual psychotherapy as needed. This prescription may put us at variance with many psychopharmacologists as well as psychotherapists of different schools, but in our experience, this may lead to the best long-range function, not only for the family, but for the patient.

In our model, the focus of treatment is not either patient or family, but rather both. The goals of our treatment are as follows:

1. To educate the family unit on the nature of the disorder.
2. To help the family assess and implement the degrees of both practical support (e.g., financial, shelter) and emotional support that might be planned and carried out.
3. To reduce negative expressed emotion if present.
4. To improve overall family and marital function (including sexual function), rather than focusing family life on patient psychopathology.
5. To decrease enmeshment, and by extension, to decrease the rescue fantasies (of a spouse or parent).
6. To support patient compliance with other modalities: for example, hospitalization medication and/or individual psychotherapy.
7. To help the patient (regardless of age) individuate, and associated with that goal, respect the boundaries of the family.

Enabling Factors

In order to accomplish treatment, we believe that certain *enabling factors* must be present. Essential are a motivated family or significant others. In order for the treatment process to work, the family must have some ability to regulate affect, tolerate anxiety, control projection, and not denigrate treatment. In some situations, the presence of an active psychosis or severe depression in one (or more) members may make family treatment impossible. We are well aware that there are many patients who do not want their families involved in their treatment. Likewise, many families refuse involvement. Nevertheless, we encourage therapists to contact families to evaluate the extent of a family's motivation; never take the identified patient's judgment without contacting the significant others.

Strategies

In our judgment we see family intervention as part of a treatment package. This includes medication, when indicated, for certain target symptoms, such as depression (in the biological sense of the word, not the lay use of the term) or psychotic symptoms (Cornelius, Soloff, Perel, & Ulrich, 1993). Of course, individual therapy may also be a part of the treatment if it is clinically judged that the patient has the capacity to do the cognitive work necessary to benefit from such an approach. In some cases, family therapy, marital therapy, and individual therapy are thought to be needed concomitantly.

If both family and individual therapies are deemed appropriate for a patient, we frequently suggest that family therapy be started before individual therapy. Family therapy allows the therapist and the family to set the stage for and to work together to achieve individuation (rather than the family fighting against the patient to prevent it). In other cases, however, it might be necessary to establish a therapeutic alliance with the patient before starting therapy. While there is no evidence to indicate that one "school" of family therapy is more efficacious than another, we suggest a mixture of dynamic, psychoeducational, and systems models for family therapy depending on the needs of the family members. (Glick, Berman, Clarkin, & Rait, 2000, pp. 241–259).

In our experience, with large numbers of inpatients as well as very impaired outpatients, the family therapist preferably should do the individual therapy. The rationale is that there is more to be gained than lost with one versus two therapists. Due to the severity of the illness, often patients have difficulties in trusting therapists. It is our belief that once a patient finds one therapist they can trust, it is very hard for them to transfer trust to another therapist, even a colleague of the initial therapist (but hard data on this belief are lacking).

Family Techniques

One way to conceptualize family interventions is to divide them into psychoeducational, systems, and dynamic interventions. The role of the family therapist is to review with both the patient and family, the symptoms, diagnosis, treatment, and prognosis of borderline personality disorder (Schultz, Schulz, Hamer, Resnick, Friedel, & Goldberg, 1985). Especially emotionally loaded issues include individuation, blame, and sexual function. The list also includes suicidality and violence or the fear of emotional blackmail often manifested by suicidal threats on the part of the borderline patient. We always recommend a frank discussion of suicide risk with families in the presence of the patient. It is important for families to know patients may commit suicide despite a family's good intentions and despite good therapy. The family should understand that overprotection of an adult patient to prevent suicide is often counterproductive. Often a core question is, "Who is guilty?" of causing the illness. The answer of course is, "No one," and as families increasingly understand the nature and origins of the illness, this helps moderate volatile family interactions and decrease expressed emotion. Finally, in this context, Linehan's cognitive behavior program may contain relevant material to include in a psychoeducation program for families (Linehan, 1999). It includes components of (1) psychoeducation, (2) balancing polarities between a couple (with the aim of a new synthesis, and flexibility arising out of opposing positions), (3) improving problem-solving strategies, (4) increasing communication, and (5) using case-management strategies for very impaired families (Linehan, Armstrong, Suarez, & Allmon, 1991).

As to systemic family therapy, the first issue is to *join* with the family. This is a delicate operation, which involves issues of control and power. The next step is to *reframe*. This involves positive connotation of the symptoms in the light of the family's efforts to help. There are obviously different approaches if the patient is a spouse versus a young adult. The therapist must walk a fine line between siding with the younger versus older generation. The task of the therapist is to help the patient and the family to achieve maximum function. The usual problem in terms of boundaries is that the marital coalition is usually undermined by mutual blaming around the pathology of the young adult. Also, the young adult (as the identified patient) is sometimes in a "parental role" because of a weakened marital dyad.

Gunderson (1989, p. 2751) has described two patterns of family involvement and their management, which also speaks to these issues:

> One pattern is characterized by over involvement. Borderline offspring of such families are often actively struggling with dependency issues by denial or by anger at their parents. Whether denied or reviled, these needs for dependency are often being actively gratified by the family (Shapiro, 1989). Such a family requires active, ongoing family participation in treatment. To exclude the family from involvement in the index borderline person's treatment leads the parents to withhold support and, moreover, causes the patient to feel as if participation in therapy is disloyal to the parents and will lead to abandonment.

Borderline patients also come from families characterized by abuse (violent or incestuous) or neglect. In this pattern, the parents are likely to be angry at their offspring for having either solicited or been sent for treatment. These parents will be overtly resentful of treatment efforts that require their involvement in an examination of the family interactions. Meetings with the parents alone may be required in order to solicit their support for the borderline person's treatment. In such meetings, it is useful to be formally educative about the nature of the offspring's illness and to attempt to reassure the parents that the treatment is directed toward helping the patient develop more independence and, specifically, that it is not directed at blaming them.

In terms of dynamic family therapy, one of the central problems is the issue of transference. Transference is unusually intense and varied, ranging from "*very idealized*" to *devaluing*, both of which often exist simultaneously. Countertransference problems are especially difficult and are often reflected in family myths. For example, a common problem is that the therapist "sides" with one group (or spouse) versus the other. Slipp (1981) has done an excellent job in outlining 12 guidelines for therapists working psychoanalytically with couples where one or both have borderline personality disorder. Unfortunately, space does not permit a detailed outline of these guidelines; however, readers are encouraged to examine this work in more detail.

It is important to emphasize that the techniques we are recommending are not unique to BPD. They can be found in contemporary family approaches to schizophrenia and mood disorders including bipolar illness. These techniques are also commonly and centrally utilized in the group therapy field. Namely, powerful reality testing is provided by the group (family) members, such that regression and intense transference distortions are minimized; group (family) members assume responsibility for their actions and for changing behaviors, and come to expect the same of the identified patient; and the sessions can serve as a positive holding environment (Yalom, 1985).

Integration with Other Modalities

Until now, for personality disorders, there has not been controlled research that systematically compares the various treatment modalities and their efficacy. As we mentioned, the first book to focus on family therapy is the *Family Treatment of Personality Disorders* (MacFarlane, 2004), and several chapters focus on "interaction." It is important to emphasize that when the treating mental health professional is a psychiatrist, he or she should be attentive not only to psychotherapy, but also to the potential value of medications. When the treating mental health professional is not a psychiatrist, he or she should always work closely with a psychiatric cotherapist so that additional opportunities to help these patients with medication should not be missed. Situations where BPD requires medication include depressive and anxiety symptoms, psychotic symptoms, and breaks in reality testing. Obviously, use of medication may impact family treatment in that taking a pill by a family member suggests (to the family) that the individual is sick (which has negative connotations). On the other hand, medication for the PD patient (or family) often allows access to psychotherapy.

Compliance

A prominent motivation for treatment is to receive the support these individuals were deprived of in childhood (Masterson, 1981, p. 152). Individuals with BPD typically come to treatment with an erratic, inconsistent, and unpredictable pattern of problems including unstable relationships, labile mood, impulsivity, and identity confusion. Variability is the hallmark of BPD; no single feature or pattern is invariably present. However, long-term compliance with treatment is almost always a problem.

Difficulties Achieving Successful Treatment

At one point, BPD was believed to be caused by faulty parenting, and many families felt unfairly blamed. As we mentioned earlier, our current understanding is that BPD has a strong biological component, and that it results from a combination of genetic and environmental factors (Livesley et al., 1998). Recent research suggests that individuals suffering from BPD have imbalances in the neurotransmitters that regulate emotion and impulse control. Serotonin is one neurotransmitter believed to play a significant role in BPD. When individuals suffer from this type of an imbalance, life stresses can easily overwhelm their coping abilities. Therefore, successful treatment requires several components.

Having a Motivated Family or Significant Other

It is true that ingrained personality traits are not easy for people to change, but behavior that has been learned can be unlearned. Having the support of family members or significant others is imperative to the treatment process. Family members often feel mystified and exhausted by their relative's illness. The intense mood swings and anger outbursts can be frightening and disruptive. Impulsive acting out in areas such as spending, substance abuse, or sex can be a major source of marital conflict. Relatives are often overwhelmed with worry regarding their loved one's safety following repeated suicide attempts or acts of self-mutilation. At times, partners and family members feel manipulated by these suicidal or self-destructive behaviors, and are torn between reaching out to their loved one and setting personal limits and boundaries. It is not unusual for relatives and spouses of PD individuals to feel depressed themselves, and to struggle with feelings of guilt, shame, and helplessness. This is why it is imperative that the family be a part of the treatment plan and learn to regulate affect, tolerate anxiety, control projection, and be supportive of the treatment process. The difficulty with this is that many patients do not want their families involved in their treatment. Additionally, many families refuse involvement.

Establishing a Therapeutic Alliance

Most patients with personality disorders have difficulty in trusting therapists. So it is difficult for them to allow involvement of their family or significant others. To overcome the debilitating aspects of the disorder, it is necessary that the missing aspects of the core identity be felt, recovered, and integrated into a solid whole. However, due to the hypersensitivity issue, the therapist's feedback may be rejected. When boundaries are out of awareness, sometimes the only way to discover them is by an inadvertent testing. When this occurs, it can trigger paranoia and a negative transference towards the therapist. Unfortunately, for both patient and therapist, the end result is a no-win situation with the patient generally terminating the therapy prematurely. When such a situation does occur, it is in the best interest of both parties to process their interaction and discover the etiology of the hypersensitivity to control. It is our belief that once a patient finds one therapist they can trust, it usually is very hard for them to transfer to another therapist (but hard data on this belief are lacking).

Financial Constraints

Another problem is that many insurance plans won't cover treatment in part because (a) treatment can take from several months up to several years and (b) the persistent myth that treatment rarely works. This acts as a barrier for clinicians to learn about state-of-the-art PD treatments. Clinicians then rely on outdated information, misleading statements, and erroneous information about PD they have heard from their associates.

Stigma

The name PD is confusing. It imparts very little relevant or descriptive information, and reinforces the existing stigma. Although the term *border-line* was once thought to be on the border of schizophrenia, BPD is now believed to be more closely related to (or comorbid with) mood disorders such as depression, or possibly to impulse control disorders like attention-deficit hyperactivity disorder. The term BPD is inaccurate in that it suggests that the whole person (and the personality) is flawed, that is, "bad." As we discussed, the cause of the disorder is not a flawed personality but rather a biologically based brain disorder, specifically a dysfunction of the limbic system of the brain (Drake, Phillips & Pakalnis, 1991). Families need to learn all they can about PD so that they can advocate for appropriate treatment for their loved ones. Informed families are then better able to deal with the stigma often encountered from both mental health professionals and other family and friends.

Misconception of Medication

Psychotropic medication may be useful for individuals with PD depending on the presenting symptoms. However, over time, for some patients, medication may be problematic as personality issues confound the medication issues. Problems in medicating PD include noncompliance, demands for frequent changes in the dose or type of medication, overdosing, and failure to accurately report change, for example, reporting feeling worse when apparently doing better (Sperry, 1995, p. 75). Comorbidity with alcohol and drug abuse and addictive behavior is also a concern in using medication. Alcohol and others drugs can potentiate prescribed medication and heighten chances for an accidental overdose, or individuals with PD may decide to use prescribed medications in combination with alcohol and other drugs to attempt suicide (Layden, Newman, Freeman, & Morse, 1993, p. 111–112).

Effects of Treatment Refusal

It is crucial that those who have BPD are treated. The consequences of a lack of treatment affects not only the person with BPD, but also their family members and significant others. Tumultuous relationships are inherent to the disease. If medication is used, it will (may) have side effects. For some patients, such symptoms serve as a rationale to discontinue all treatment. In some cases, this may be appropriate, in others not, that is, it is a compliance issue that needs discussion among patient, family, and physician.

Summary

This review of etiology, evaluation, and treatment has led us to a number of final points. We believe PD can be managed over time, but it is difficult. Along with data supporting the notion of crucial genetic-biological underpinnings, there are suggestions of family psychopathology, which may be related to etiology. As a result, the patient's behavior affects the family and vice versa. Therefore, successful treatment of personality disorder should involve a family therapy component.

Having said that, it must be noted that long-term prognosis for BPD families is better than thought (Paris, 2003b). Presumably the families, like their patient-members, get better (level out) after 2 decades of great difficulty, but definitive information is lacking. In this context, the issue of "survival" for the family of the patient with BPD needs to be addressed. Families need to be educated about the illness of the patient; although it may have genetic roots, it is not their fault, that is, they are not to blame. Consumer support groups like the National Alliance for the Mentally Ill (NAMI) are invaluable for providing support, psychoeducational material, and other help. Furthermore, the symptoms of PD have the potential to cause great family distress and burden. Therefore, the family has to be careful not to exacerbate a difficult situation by blaming the patient for symptoms of functional difficulties the patient is unable to control (a similar dilemma for families with bipolar disorder or with schizophrenia). Finally, the family must be prepared for the fact that these conditions are often lifelong, and plan for the costs of therapy, estate planning, and so forth accordingly.

In conclusion, in thinking about personality disorders and the family, we agree with what Lacey & Price (2004) have written about eating disorders and the family:

> Family dysfunction is only one paradigm of the etiology of eating disorders; it is not essential for the development of these conditions but is a significant factor in a proportion of sufferers. Families, their dynamics, and pathologies, may also be of importance to the recovery process. There is robust evidence for the efficacy of family therapy in eating disorders of early onset and short duration. Family therapy need not be restricted to the task of addressing family dysfunction, should it exist; it is a forum in which the affected individual and the family may prepare for change: the return to the family system of a newly autonomous person. The importance of engaging the family, together with the patient, in treatment cannot be overstated. In most individual

clinical circumstances, to alienate the family is to undermine the possibility of therapeutic gain. A supportive, educational, and noncritical approach, together with family therapy where indicated, is more likely to reap benefits.

References

Allen, C. (2004). Borderline personality disorder: Towards a systemic formulation. *Journal of Family Therapy, 26*(2), 126–141.

American Psychiatric Association (1994). *Diagnostic and statistical manual of mental disorders* (4th ed.). Washington, DC: Author.

Burgess, J., & Zarconi, V. (1992). Cognitive impairment in dramatic personality disorders. *American Journal of Psychiatry, 149*, 136.

Carter, B., & McGoldrick, M. (1988). *The changing family life cycle: A framework for family therapy* (2nd ed.). New York: Gardner Press.

Clarkin, J., Marziali, E., & Munroe-Blum, H. (1991). Group and family treatments for borderline personality disorder. *Hospital and Community Psychiatry, 42*, 1038–1043.

Cornelius, J., Soloff, P., Perel, J., & Ulrich, R. (1993). Continuation pharmacotherapy of borderline personality disorder with haloperidol and phenelzine. *American Journal of Psychiatry, 150*, 1843–1848.

Coccaro, E., & Sieve, L. (1995). The neuropsychopharmacology of personality disorders. In F. Bloom & D. Kupfer (Eds.), *Psychopharmacology: The fourth generation of progress* (pp. 1567–1580). New York: Raven.

Crits-Christoph, P., & Barber, J. P. (2002). Psychological treatments for personality disorders. In P. E. Nathan & J. M. Gorman (Eds.), *A guide to treatments that work* (2nd ed., pp. 611–623). New York: Oxford University Press.

Drake, M. E., Phillips, B. B., & Pakalnis, A. (1991). Auditory evoked potentials in borderline personality disorder. *Clinical Electroencephalogram, 22*(3), 188–192.

Glick, I. D., Berman, E. M., Clarkin, J. F., & Rait, D. S. (2000). *Marital and family therapy* (4th ed.). Washington, DC: American Psychiatric Publishing, Inc.

Goldman, S., D'Angelo, E., & DeMaso, D. (1993). Psychopathology in the families of children and adolescents with borderline personality disorder. *American Journal of Psychiatry, 150*, 1832–1835.

Gunderson, J. (1989). Borderline personality disorder. In *American Psychiatric Association: Treatments of psychiatric disorders: A task force report of the American Psychiatric Association* (pp. 2749–2759). Washington, DC: American Psychiatric Association.

Kagan, J., Rezneck, J., Snidman, N., & Gibbons, J. (1988). Childhood derivatives of inhibition and lack of inhibition to the unfamiliar. *Child Development, 59*, 1580–1589.

Klein, D. (1968). Psychiatric diagnosis and a typology of clinical drug effects. *Psychopharmacology, 13*, 359–386.

Koch, A. (1985). The treatment of borderline personality disorder within a distressed relationship. *Journal of Marital & Family Therapy, 11*, 373–380.

Lacey, J. H., & Price, C. (2004). Disturbed families, or families disturbed? *British Journal of Psychiatry, 184*, 195–196.

Layden, M. A., Newman, C. F., Freeman, A., & Morse, S. B. (1993). *Cognitive therapy of borderline personality disorder.* Boston: Allyn and Bacon.

Linehan, M. M. (1999, September). *Update on DBT.* Paper presented to the International Society for the Study of Personality Disorders, Geneva, Switzerland.

Linehan, M. M., Armstrong, H., Suarez, A., & Allmon, D. (1991). Cognitive-behavioral treatment of chronically parasuicidal borderline patients. *Archives of General Psychiatry, 49*, 1060–1064.

Links, P., Boigo, I., Huxley, G., Steiner, M., & Mitton, J. (1990). Sexual abuse and biparental failure as etiologic models in borderline personality disorder. In P. Links (Ed.), *Family environment and borderline personality disorder* (pp. 105–120). Washington, DC: American Psychiatric Publishing, Inc.

Livesley, W. J., Jang, K. L., & Vernon, P. A. (1998). Phenotypic and genetic structure of traits delineating personality disorder. *Archives of General Psychiatry, 55*(10), 941–948.

Loranger, A., & Tulis, E. (1985). Family history of alcoholism in borderline personality disorder. *Archives of General Psychiatry, 42*, 153–157.

Loranger, A., Oldham, J., & Tulis, E. (1982). Familial transmission DSM-III borderline personality disorder. *Archives of General Psychiatry, 39*, 795–799.

MacFarlane, M. M. (2004). *Family treatment of personality disorders: Advances in clinical practice.* Binghamton, NY: Haworth Clinical Practice Press.

Magnavita, J. J., & MacFarlane, M. M. (2004). Family treatment of personality disorders: Historical overview and current perspectives. In M. M. MacFarlane (Ed.), *Family treatment of personality disorders* (pp. 3–32). Binghamton, NY: Haworth Clinical Practice Press.

Masterson, J. F. (1981). *The narcissistic and borderline disorders, An integrated developmental approach.* New York: Brunner/Mazel.

McCormack, C. (1989). The borderline/schizoid marriage: The holding environment as an essential treatment construct. *Journal of Marital & Family Therapy, 15*, 299–309.

Nathan, P., & Gorman, J. (2002). Psychological treatments for personality disorders: A guide to treatments that work (2nd ed., pp. 548–611). New York: Oxford University Press.

Paris, J. (2003a). Long-term outcome of personality disorders. In *Personality disorders over time precursors, course, and outcome* (pp. 69–75). Washington, DC: American Psychiatric Publishing, Inc.

Paris, J. (2003b). *Personality disorders over time precursors, course, and outcome.* Washington, DC: American Psychiatric Publishing, Inc.

Pope, H., Jonas, J., Hudson, J., Cohen, B., & Gunderson, J. (1983). The validity of DSM-III borderline personality disorder. *Archives of General Psychiatry, 40*, 23–30.

Schatzburg, A. F., Cole, J. O., & DeBattista, C. (2003). Diagnosis and classification. In *Manual of clinical psychopharmacology* (4th ed., p. 30). Washington, DC: American Psychiatric Publishing, Inc.

Schultz, P., Schulz, S., Hamer, R., Resnick, R., Friedel, R., & Goldberg, S. (1985). The impact of borderline and schizotypal personality disorders on patients and their families. *Hospital and Community Psychiatry, 36*, 879–881.

Shapiro, E. (1989). Family and couples therapy. In *American Psychiatric Association: Treatments of psychiatric disorders: A task force report of the American Psychiatric Association* (pp. 2660–2666). Washington, DC: American Psychiatric Association.

Sholevar, G. P., & Schwoeri, L. D. (2003). Family therapy with personality disorders. *Textbook of family and couples therapy* (pp. 715–723). Washington, DC: American Psychiatric Publishing, Inc.

Siever, L. J., & Davis, K. L. (1991). A psychobiological perspective on the personality disorders. *Psychiatry, 148*, 1647–1658.

Silverman, J., Pinkham, L., Horvath, T. B., Coccaro, E. F., Klar, H., Schear, S., et al. (1991). Affective and impulsive personality disorder traits in the relatives of patients with borderline personality disorder. *Psychiatry, 148*, 1378–1385.

Slipp, S. (1981). Marital therapy for borderline personality disorders. In A. Gurman (Ed.), *Questions and answers in the practice of family therapy* (pp. 258–259). New York: Brunner/Mazel.

Soloff, P., & Millward, J. (1983). Developmental histories of borderline patients. *Comprehensive Psychiatry, 24*, 547–588.

Sperry, L. (1995). *Handbook of diagnosis and treatment of the DSM-IV personality disorders.* New York: Brunner/Mazel.

Stone, M. (1988). Towards a psychobiological theory of BPD: Is irritability the red thread that runs through borderline conditions? *Disassociation, 1*, 2–15.

Yalom, I. (1985). *The theory and practice of group psychotherapy* (3rd ed.). New York: Basic Books.

Zanarini, M., Gunderson, J., Marino, M., Schwartz, E., & Frankenberg, F. R. (1990). Psychiatric disorders in the families of borderline outpatients. In P. Links (Ed.), *Family environment and borderline personality disorder* (pp. 67–84). Washington, DC: American Psychiatric Publishing, Inc.

CHAPTER **10**

Toward DSM-V: Questions and Controversies

KENNETH R. SILK

Key Teaching Points

- The DSM is an iterative process.
- The DSM originally was general in structure and psychodynamic in its theoretical posture.
- DSM-II, and particularly DSM-III, moved away from the psychodynamic posture to become more empirical and atheoretical.
- In DSM-III and DSM-IV, personality disorders were placed on a separate axis, Axis II, to attempt to get clinicians to pay attention to the personality traits and personality disorders in the patients who were presented to them.
- Personality disorder diagnoses became prototypic and categorical beginning in DSM-III.
- There are problems with the categorical approach to personality and personality disorders as presented in DSM-III, and clinicians and patients may be better served through a dimensional or blended dimensional-categorical approach to personality and personality disorders in DSM-V.

- The dimensions in DSM-V could describe the degree of presence of specific character traits.
- The dimensions in DSM-V could describe levels of functioning.
- The dimensional system may convey more accurate and more overall information about patients, their character, and their functioning than a purely categorical system provides.

Introduction: Setting the Stage with DSM-I and DSM-II

DSM-I (*Diagnostic and Statistical manual. Mental Disorders* [1st ed.]) had two large categories for personality disorder classification. The first was "personality disorders" defined as "disorders of psychogenic origin or without clearly defined tangible cause or structural change" (American Psychiatric Association, 1952, p. 7), where structural change implied an organic origin. The other large category that addressed personality disorders was a grouping called "transient situational personality disorders," a concept that some symptom patterns or behaviors that can be viewed as part of a personality disorder may be the result of symptoms that are present because of a comorbid Axis I disorder or because of a situation so overwhelming to the patient that symptoms or defensive posture is mistaken for a personality disorder (Reich, 2002; Reich, Noyes, Hirschfeld, Coryell, & O'Gorman, 1987). As the situation or comorbid condition remits, then the patient no longer appears to have a personality disorder (Reich & Hoffman, 2004).

Personality disorders in DSM-I were defined as "developmental defects or pathological trends in personality structure, with minimal subjective anxiety, and little or no sense of distress. In most instances, the disorder is manifested by a lifelong pattern of action or behavior, rather than by mental or emotional symptoms" (American Psychiatric Association, 1952, p. 34). Personality disorders were further divided into "personality pattern disturbance(s)" that were thought to "rarely if ever be altered in their inherent structures by any form of therapy. Their functioning may be improved by prolonged therapy, but basic change is seldom accomplished" (American Psychiatric Association, 1952, p. 25). In fact, the personality disorders in this subgrouping were thought to be so severe that patients had little maneuverability except perhaps into psychosis. Inadequate, schizoid, cyclothymic, and paranoid were the personality disorders listed here.

A different subgrouping, "personality trait disturbance," was reserved for people who easily fell out of equilibrium, even with minor stress. This vulnerability was attributed to "disturbances in emotional development" resulting in a "fixation and exaggeration of certain character and behavior patterns" in some and "a regressive reaction to environmental or endopsychic stress" in others (American Psychiatric Association, 1952, p. 36). Emotionally unstable, passive-aggressive, and compulsive personality fell into this subgrouping.

A third subgrouping was called "sociopathic personality disturbance," an illness defined "primarily in terms of society and conformity with prevailing cultural milieu, and not only in terms of personal discomfort and relations with other individuals" (American Psychiatric Association, 1952, p. 38). Antisocial and dissocial reactions as well as sexual deviation and addiction were listed under this heading.

By the time DSM-II was published in 1968, personality disorders were put together into a single large category of "deeply ingrained maladaptive patterns of behavior ... [that generally were] life-long" (American Psychiatric Association, 1968, p. 42). Paranoid, cyclothymic, schizoid, antisocial, inadequate, and passive-aggressive remained in the group. Compulsive had become obsessive-compulsive, and explosive, hysterical, and asthenic were added. Emotionally unstable was removed but was to reappear in DSM-III (American Psychiatric Association, 1980), in a somewhat different form, under the label of "borderline personality disorder (BPD)."

The process of diagnosis includes both the undertaking of the process of naming as well as the end result, that is, arriving at the name. Thus, diagnosis involves a detailed description of characteristics related to a specific condition for taxonomic purposes as well as the process that one undergoes in order to identify and name a disease given the signs and symptoms that present clinically. In this process, we are also utilizing a third concept of diagnosis, which is the act of discriminating and distinguishing one set of symptoms and/or signs from another set. Then we are able to provide identifying labels for each of the different "diagnoses."

Diagnosis is not reality but rather, a theoretical construct (First et al., 2002). To physicians, a disease represents whatever the physicians of a particular time and place define as a disorder or disease. Today we think of it is a label put forth to identify a group of patients who present with similar clinical pictures, that is, phenotypes. We make the assumption not only that the phenotype may be related to a particular genotype, but also that another set of patients with a different phenotypic presentation or diagnosis has a different genotype underlying it. But, of course, genes are not organized along disease models or diagnoses. Genes most probably define vulnerabilities and susceptibilities such as emotional lability, variations in cognitive processing, or the level, expression, or inhibition of anxiety (Auerbach et al., 1999; Caspi et al., 2002).

The DSM-I was followed in 1968 by DSM-II (American Psychiatric Association, 1968), and while there were some differences in the two manuals, the most important difference was an epistemological one. In the DSM-I, the emphasis was on reactions, in that, for example, the category of schizophrenia was called schizophrenic reactions, and the concept of manic depression was listed within affective reactions. In the DSM-II, these reactions became disorders so that we now had schizophrenic and/or major affective disorders. This was not simply a change in word usage; rather it reflected a movement away from the psychodynamic or psychoanalytic concepts that suggested that psychiatric symptomatology resulted from psychological reactions to stressors or conflicts or developed in the process of compromise formation. The authors of DSM-II preferred disorders as a term "that by and large did not imply a particular theoretical framework for understanding the non-organic mental disorders" (American Psychiatric Association, 1980, p. 2).

DSM-III

All this was to change much further with the publication of DSM-III in 1980 (American Psychiatric Association, 1980). The DSM-III was very different in its overall structure from the two preceding iterations of the DSM. Where in DSM-I and II disorders were described in paragraph form and in quite general descriptive terms, in DSM-III a diagnosis was met if patients fulfilled all or a number of very specific criteria that were published in list (some say checklist) form. The DSM had now moved completely away from the psychodynamic/psychoanalytic framework to become what was described as neo-Kraepelinian, that is, to depend upon specific signs and symptoms that were translated into inclusion and exclusion criteria (Blashfield, 1984). DSM-III was a clear attempt at categorical diagnoses and was based upon defining the prototypic patient within each of the diagnostic groupings. By using DSM-III, it was felt that there was a much greater chance that two or more clinicians or researchers could reach agreement as to whether any given patient met or did not meet each of the specific criteria, and thus there would be greater reliability in diagnoses. In this manner, clinical presentation and information could not only be more accurately and reliably assessed, but also that the continued presence or absence of the diagnosis could be followed more accurately over time. DSM-III was promoted as being substantially more scientific than its predecessors (which indeed it was) because more of the diagnoses and the specific criteria that lay behind the diagnoses had been arrived at and supported by empirical data and research. Thus, there was the belief that the diagnoses as defined in DSM-III had greater validity than the diagnostic constructs in the previous editions of the DSM.

A number of developments began to take hold in the late 1960s, that expanded during the 1970s, that impacted the form and structure of DSM-III (Houts, 2002; Stone, 1997). Empirical data exploring psychiatric diagnoses began to be collected during the late 1960s; this pursuit was led by a group of psychiatrists primarily from the Department of Psychiatry at Washington University in St. Louis (Feighner et al., 1972; Robins & Guze, 1970). These psychiatric diagnostic empiricists began by trying to develop a set of Research Diagnostic Criteria (RDC) (Spitzer, Endicott, & Gibbon, 1978) so that researchers in different investigative sites could utilize a diagnostic system that would allow similar patients to be identified as falling into a specific diagnostic grouping despite being diagnosed by different clinicians. These RDC criteria were developed in the form that DSM-III was later to adopt: a list of specific criteria, the presence or absence of which (inclusion and exclusion criteria) could not only be reliably determined but could also then lead to a reliable and specific psychiatric diagnosis. Greater diagnostic reliability and homogeneity would allow better research to be conducted because all members within the cohort being studied would have met at least a number of similar specific diagnostic criteria.

There were other events that transpired during this period that also helped shape the ultimate form of DSM-III. Academic psychiatry was no longer ruled or under the strong and powerful direction of the psycho-analytic movement. By 1980, the number of psychoanalysts who were also chairs of major departments was few. Psychiatric symptoms or disorders were no longer thought of as being overwhelming reactions to specific events or related to id impulses overtaking a weakened or inadequate ego. While the promoters and developers of the DSM-III would argue that DSM-III had no specific theoretical point of view save for the point of view of looking for support through the examination of empirical data, others would argue that, in truth, it was the principles of biological psychiatry and genetics which drove DSM-III into its specific form. In addition, psychiatry needed empirical evidence, rigorously collected, to promote the idea that in psychiatry there were real diseases and in a good number of instances with empirical data to back it up. DSM-III was structured to do just that.

The idea of real diseases took on a life of its own, and psychiatrists and especially psychiatric trainees, who would be the psychiatrists and the psychiatric teachers of the future, began to believe that the diagnoses, as enumerated in DSM-III, were in fact real diseases that could be scientifically studied and delineated from other psychiatric diseases. These DSM-III diagnoses were, in fact, still hypothetical constructs, and more study needed to be conducted before we could determine that they were distinct diseases. If distinct diseases could be delineated, then answers to some questions that had been plaguing psychiatry for decades might be more close at hand (Carroll et al., 1981).

Although DSM-III has helped us through its diagnostic guidelines and diagnostic processes to answer many questions that could never have been answered using older diagnostic systems, it also raised a number of important and perplexing issues. For instance, it was initially felt that major depression was a distinct and separate disorder from the anxiety disorders, and by using the DSM-III appropriately, we could easily sort patients between those two diagnostic categories. But 25 years later we are still perplexed by the large number of patients who do not easily fall into one or the other of these two diagnostic groups. It appears that if one has depression for long enough, then he or she will eventually develop anxiety symptoms as well, or that chronic anxiety or panic can also lead to a clinical picture that has many elements of what we would attribute to major depression (Kendler, 1996). The DSM-III diagnoses were supposed to represent phenotypes that could lead us to uncover specific genotypes or at least endophenotypes that would provide biological or psychophysiological support to the distinctions that separated one diagnostic entity from another. Yet we now know that many of the medications that are effective in reducing and or eliminating depressive symptoms also provide relief from anxiety and panic. The distinct division between anxiety and depression, so hoped for in the early days of DSM-III, did not easily fall out, either biologically or descriptively (Kendler & Gardner, 1998; Tyrer, Seivewright, & Johnson, 2003).

Another idea was that the DSM-III, in its process of leading us to diagnose "true disorders," would lead to diagnoses that would remain stable over time. While in some respects that is true, in a not insignificant number of patients, diagnoses are not stable. In these instances patients seem to move from one diagnosis to another over time (Rabinowitz, Slyuzberg, Ritsner, Mark, Popper, & Ginath, 1994; Shean, 2003). Before the Internet, where enormous amounts of information are available to anyone willing to access it, most patients did not read the DSM before coming to us. Also, many patients in clinical settings do not as easily fit the DSM-III categories as DSM-III predicted, and as we had hoped they would (Fennig et al., 1994).

DSM-III and Axis II

Beginning with DSM-III, the personality disorders were relegated to an "axis," Axis II, different from the axis on which all the other psychiatric diagnoses were based, Axis I (American Psychiatric Association, 1980; First et al., 2002). This last statement is true for DSM-IV as well; however, in DSM-III and DSM-III-R specific developmental disorders were also included on Axis II. While the decision to have an Axis II was probably more of a political decision than a decision based upon empirical data, Axis II did separate off and create personality disorders as a distinct entity that was worthy of scientific study (Stone, 1997). With the creation of a second axis in DSM-III, and with the relegation of personality disorders to that second axis, there began to develop a strong interest in studying these disorders (Blashfield & Intoccia, 2000).

DSM-III states that Axis II was created to ensure "that consideration is given to the possible presence of disorders that are frequently overlooked when attention is directed to the usually more florid Axis I disorder" (American Psychiatric Association, 1980, p. 23). What is also of interest is that DSM-III suggested that traits could also be described or noted on Axis II (though not given a numeric diagnostic code) even when the full criteria for a personality disorder had not been met.

On the one hand, diagnoses are extremely useful and convey an enormous amount of information within them. Diagnoses are an important device in moving the field forward in that they allow us to identify relatively homogeneous groups of patients for genetic and pharmacologic studies. It would be hard to think of practicing psychiatry without diagnoses and a diagnostic scheme, but again we need to remind ourselves that at the current time using diagnoses is more of a tool of communication than an exact naming of a group of patients who share an underlying genotype or identical biological processes (First et al., 2002; Robins & Guze, 1970). The latter idea of psychiatric diagnoses being synonymous with specific genotypes may turn out to be true some time in the future, but it is certainly not true at the present time. Thus, any diagnostic schema is only as good as it is until the next iteration comes along. If diagnoses and the diagnostic criteria that support them stop being an iterative process, then neither psychiatry nor our understanding of psychiatric diseases will grow (Kendell, 2002).

On the other hand, we need to make sure that we do not allow a diagnostic system to get between us and our patients. Psychiatry remains profoundly interpersonal, and when a patient says that he is depressed, we should say, "Tell me about your depression," or "How do you understand how your depression came about," long before we begin to review the DSM checklist pertaining to sleep, appetite, anhedonia, and/or fatigue (Tasman, Riba, & Silk, 2000).

The DSM and Personality Disorders: From Categories to Dimensions

From DSM-III forward, personality disorders have been considered as disorders that cause significant impairment in social or occupational functioning because of strong, inflexible, personality traits which are defined as enduring patterns of perceiving, relating to, and thinking about the world and oneself (American Psychiatric Association, 1980). There were 12 personality disorders listed in DSM-III, and 11 are listed in DSM-IV. Passive-aggressive was eliminated in DSM-IV. The specific criteria that built toward a diagnosis changed somewhat from DSM-III to DSM-IV, and some criteria have been added and some criteria taken away. In addition to the removal of passive-aggressive personality disorder in DSM-IV, cyclothymia was moved to Axis I and was no longer considered a personality disorder but found a home in affective disorders on Axis I (American Psychiatric Association, 1994). The personality disorder diagnoses that remained from DSM-II were antisocial, paranoid, schizoid, obsessive-compulsive, and passive-aggressive (this latter to be eliminated in DSM-IV as mentioned previously). The personality disorders inadequate, asthenic, and explosive were removed in going from DSM-II to DSM-III. Hysterical could be viewed in many ways as being renamed histrionic, but schizotypal, borderline, narcissistic, dependent, and avoidant were added. In each of the sets of diagnostic criteria for each of the diagnoses, there was an attempt to translate and codify the "enduring patterns of perceiving, relating and thinking about oneself and the world" into specific criteria that formed the foundation for meeting the diagnosis of a specific personality disorder.

Another change in DSM-III was that the specific personality disorders were grouped into three clusters. One cluster included odd patients such as those with paranoid, schizoid, and schizotypal personality disorders. Another cluster contained dramatic or emotional or labile patients such as those with antisocial, borderline, histrionic, and narcissistic personality disorders. The third cluster contained patients who were anxious and/or inhibited, those patients with obsessive-compulsive, dependent, and avoidant (and passive-aggressive) personality disorders.

Yet, even with further revisions that took place in DSM-III-R (American Psychiatric Association, 1987) and DSM-IV (American Psychiatric Association, 1994), there were still problems with the diagnosis of personality disorders. First, it was rare, especially when utilizing structured interviews, for a patient to meet the criteria for only one personality disorder. In some instances, almost 50% of the patients met criteria for four or more personality disorders (McGlashan et al., 2000; Oldham, Skodol, Kellman, Hyler, Rosnick, & Davies, 1992; Widiger, Frances, Harris,

Jacobsberg, Fyer, & Manning, 1991), though Westen (1997) would argue that in clinical practice, clinicians only gave a single personality disorder diagnosis to any given patient. The clinicians in Westen's study did not rely on the DSM Axis II criteria to diagnose the patient; rather, they were making the Axis II diagnosis based upon how the patient related to them in the office setting. Westen used this information to argue against the categorical model currently in use and for a dimensional model, in his opinion, that utilized a prototype-matching method that combines both dimensional and categorical approaches (Westen & Shedler, 2000).

But Westen is not the only person to argue for a dimensional model for the diagnosis of personality disorder. Many of what we view as personality traits can be considered in their milder forms to be useful characteristics for a person to possess, and the argument has been raised repeatedly that the traits that become disorders in Axis II are merely variants of normal traits (Livesley, Jackson, & Schroeder, 1992; Widiger & Corbitt, 1994). The DSM-III states that it is only when these traits become persistent and enduring and lead to impairment, that they become disorders, but the boundary of when a trait becomes pathological is unclear (Clark, 1992). For example, conscientiousness is a useful trait, but too much of it can lead to an obsessive-compulsive personality disorder. On the one hand, a person can display a trait so strongly that it causes severe impairment; on the other hand, there can be degrees of a trait that are quite prominent and dictate many aspects of a person's interpersonal style, but fall short of full impairment and thus fall short of meeting criteria for a personality disorder. A dimensional model that emphasizes the degree of a trait's presence without qualifying for a full disorder not only may be a useful construct but also may, because of its prominence, be worth mentioning in a diagnostic evaluation. A dimensional model would be able to accomplish this recognition of a trait that falls short of developing into a disorder (Livesley, Jang, & Vernon, 1998; Oldham & Skodol, 2000; Widiger & Costa, 1994).

Dimensional models of personality include Eysenck's three-factor model (Eysenck, 1991); Costa and McCrae's Five-Factor Model (Costa & McCrae, 1992); Livesley's Dimensional Assessment of Personality Pathology (DAPP [Livesley et al., 1998]); Cloninger et al.'s Temperament and Character Inventory (TCI [Cloninger, Svarkic, & Pryzbeck, 1993]); Clark's Schedule for Nonadaptive and Adaptive Personality (SNAP [Clark, 1993]); Benjamin's Interpersonal Circumplex (Structural Analysis of Interpersonal Behavior [SASB (Benjamin, 1993)]); and the Shedler and Western Assessment Procedure (SWAP-200 [Westen and Shedler, 1999a, 1999b]). Each of these dimensional schemes has been empirically tested against the current DSM-IV personality disorders, and various combinations of the different dimensions in the different schemas do show some support for building personality disorder diagnoses upon trait dimensions rather than the inclusion and exclusion prototypic categorical model currently in place.

These dimensional schemes may in fact convey more information about any given patient than a categorical system. For example, five of nine criteria are needed to meet the diagnosis of borderline personality disorder (BPD). In a categorical schema, if someone met only four criteria, then there would be no information provided on Axis II. In a similar way, no information or diagnosis would be provided on Axis II if a patient met no or only one criterion for BPD. Yet the patient who meets four of nine criteria of BPD is probably "closer" in terms of behavioral and interpersonal functioning to patients actually meeting DSM-IV criteria for BPD than to patients who meet no or only one criterion. How then is that difference conveyed? A dimensional system can, in these instances—and instances like these are far from rare—provide information on the degree to which a patient comes close to meeting an Axis II diagnosis.

A mixed dimensional/categorical system could wind up recording more traits and dimensions of traits than actual diagnoses. In the world of dimensional diagnoses, then, a patient could have a personality disorder diagnosis with paranoid and histrionic traits, or personality disorder (not further subdivided as it is today) with traits of emotional instability and impulsivity. Impulsivity and/or paranoia could be refined further by being "scored" on a three-point scale from mild to moderate to severe. Another mixed dimensional/categorical approach could employ the current categorical diagnostic groupings, but instead of giving an "official" diagnosis dependent solely upon whether or not a patient met or did not meet "full" criteria for a given disorder, there could be something like "Personality disorder, probable: type borderline: criteria 4 of 7 with impulsivity and anger most prominent."

Beyond Dimensions to DSM-V

Dimensional Functionality

In 2000, Oldham and Skodol raised a number of issues that should be considered with respect to personality disorders as we plan for DSM-V. One of the issues they raise is the one just discussed. Should the current categorical system be replaced by a dimensional system? But Oldham and Skodol also suggest that perhaps a dimensional system need not only be descriptive, but especially with regard to the personality disorders, it could also be employed to address functionality (Oldham & Skodol, 2000). As emphasized previously, in order to meet criteria for a personality disorder, there needs to be significant impairment, and Oldham and Skodol suggest that the degree of impairment be evaluated and recorded. One might consider the many famous people from sports or cinema who would certainly meet criteria for narcissistic personality disorder save for the fact, as best as we can tell, that their functionality is not significantly impaired. As we become more sophisticated about biological processes that underlie some of the dimensions of psychopathology found in patients with personality disorders, perhaps a dimensional biological system, such as proposed by Siever and Davis (1991), may be appropriate to employ.

Oldham and Skodol identify other questions and controversies to be considered as we plan for DSM-V. Should we move personality disorders to Axis I? Should we adopt, as suggested above, a different way of dealing with whether or not a person meets criteria for a personality disorder by collapsing diagnostic categories and stratifying them according to whether or not any given patient is above or below the diagnostic threshold or above or below ratings on specific traits that have been identified as relating to that diagnostic category?

Eliminating Axis II

The developers of DSM-III wanted to place personality disorders on a separate axis so that personality disorder (or perhaps personality) would be considered on every patient, and the severity of Axis I pathology or symptomatology would not "crowd out" consideration of the presence or absence of personality traits. Certainly an argument can be made always to consider personality styles (traits) that are present in all patients, and Axis II has provided a way for clinicians to be reminded to consider these styles on all patients. If we eliminated Axis II and rolled all diagnoses into Axis I, would clinicians avoid considering the patient's personality? At the present time, many clinicians defer making any diagnosis or comment on Axis II.

Another reason why the personality disorders were placed (some might say relegated) to an axis different from the other disorders beginning with DSM-III, may relate to the growing evidence of significant biological (and by extension genetic or constitutional) underpinnings for many of the Axis I disorders. At the time of the publication of the DSM-III, the personality disorders or Axis II disorders were believed to be most effectively treated through psychotherapeutic rather than psychopharmacologic matters because they were believed to result more from the nurture of upbringing than from the nature of biological abnormalities (Silk, 1994, 1998). The different axes then could be thought of as having been created for disorders that were treated primarily via biological versus nonbiological methods (Auchincloss & Michaels, 1983).

We are well aware that this division as to etiology of nature versus nurture is not relevant today (Gabbard, 2004; Paris, 1999; Rutter, 2002), and the assumptions behind this Axis I–Axis II division are merely myths. These myths, according to Gunderson and Pollack (1985), were divided into the myth of etiologic primacy (biology vs. environment or nature vs. nurture), the myth of distinctiveness or discontinuity (episodic vs. lifelong disorders), the myth of treatment specificity (medications vs. psychotherapy), and the myth of severity (that disorders on one axis are more severe than those on the other axis). In reading these today, it might be difficult to know which axis occupies which of the dichotomies in each of these distinctions. These assumptions that were made between Axis I and Axis II disorders have not really withstood the test of time (Silk, 1996). Yet, nonetheless, there still may be a good reason to keep personality disorders on a different axis in order to remind clinicians to consider the personality if not the possible personality disorder of each of the patients who present to them. After all, in considering the personality of each of our patients, we are in actuality asking, who is the *person* behind this patient, a question we in psychiatry should never take lightly.

There are a number of arguments as to why Axis II should continue to exist. People are currently familiar with its use, and it is quite important that clinicians pause and consider the personality (or the personality disorder) of the patient who presents to them. Axis II has clustered together a group of disorders that has generated a good deal of research. Research in many respects is much easier from a categorical point of view where there are allegedly clear boundaries and greater reliability in deciding who is in the cohort and who is not. For example, it allows us to study the impact of Axis II upon Axis I and vice versa. Many people have staked their academic careers on studying Axis II, and where would they turn if the axis were eliminated?

The other side of the argument is that most of the current individual personality disorder diagnoses do not have a substantial amount of empirical research to back them up. Antisocial, borderline, and schizotypal have a reasonable amount of research sustaining the categories. The Collaborative Longitudinal Personality Disorders Study (CLPS) is providing us with some data for avoidant and obsessive-compulsive personality disorders (Gunderson et al., 2000), and there is a smattering of research into narcissistic personality disorder (Ronningstam, 1998). The current categories may not reflect epidemiological reality, and probably do not reflect what we are learning about the biological dimensions of personality.

Yet, before we move from categories to dimensions, we need to remind ourselves that many of the dimensions that we consider with respect to personality disorders have been established by the self-report of patients who are purported to have a personality disorder. These are the very people who externalize their symptoms, see them as ego dystonic, and have difficulty understanding social cues in many circumstances. So we are asking people with terrible judgment and poor insight into their own behavior to judge themselves and rate their behavior. It is upon such judgments that many dimensional models are based.

Diagnostic Categories

There will probably be a reworking of which diagnoses remain under the personality disorders if the personality disorder diagnoses remain categorical. Will schizotypal personality disorder (STPD) remain as a personality disorder or will it be moved under the schizophrenic disorders since in essence the criteria for the diagnosis of STPD are very similar to the prodromal symptoms of schizophrenia (Kendler, Gruenberg, & Kinney, 1994; Siever & Davis, 2004)? Will avoidant personality disorder (AVPD) remain a separate personality disorder or will it be rolled up into social phobia? While many in the United States would consider that AVPD is a form of social phobia "begun early" (Reich, 2000; Reich, Noyes, & Yates, 1989; Schneier, Spitzer, Gibbon, Fyer, & Liebowitz, 1991), people in the Scandinavian countries, especially Norway where the prevalence of AVPD is quite high, would object to it being viewed simply as a form of social phobia (Torgersen, Kringlen, & Cramer, 2001). Will BPD remain under its current name or will the term "emotionally unstable personality disorder," which was in DSM-I, be reintroduced in an attempt to reduce the stigma that is now attached to the BPD label (Skodol, Gunderson, Pfohl, Widiger, Livesley, & Siever, 2002)? Will histrionic and dependent remain as separate and distinct personality disorders? Will the idea of sociopathy be reincorporated into or subdivided within the antisocial personality disorder category?

Discussion

Clearly there are no answers but many interesting questions. Progress is made when new findings create more interesting questions for us which further refine our understanding. DSM-V, whatever its ultimate form, will simply be another iteration in the progression of the various editions of the DSM. I hope it will be well informed and move us forward not only in refining psychiatric diagnosis but also in getting us closer to the endophenotypes that will lead us to the constitutional, genetic, and biophysiological under-pinnings of personality.

As we go forward toward DSM-V, and as we suggest changes, we need to ask ourselves whether the changes will be facilitative to patients, to clinicians, and to researchers. Kendell suggests that to improve upon the current DSM, the next edition needs to "be more comprehensive, be easier to use, deal better with issues of 'clinical significance', have higher reliability, or have higher validity" (Kendell, 2002, p. 3). Certainly, if these improvements can occur, the next iteration will be a better and more useful document for us all.

While prediction is always a difficult process in psychiatry, Blashfield and Fuller (1996), employing a bit of a tongue-in-cheek, used regression estimates based on prior editions of the DSM to predict some aspects of DSM-V. They predict a volume of over 1,000 pages and over 400,000 words. They predict it will have close to 400 diagnoses and 1,800 unique diagnostic criteria. Further, they reviewed the color of the various volumes from the gray of DSM-I to the gold of DSM-II, the green of DSM-III, the blue of DSM-III-R, and the red of DSM-IV. Based upon the basic colors that are recognized across cultures, they predict that the cover DSM-V will be brown. But to put the power of the predictions in context, their prediction for the date of publication of DSM-V ranged from 1998 to 2007.

Closing Summary

The DSM-V will provide us an opportunity to correct and refine diagnoses and diagnostic categories as they now exist in DSM-IV. One of the areas deserving of attention in that refinement is Axis II, the axis that contains the personality disorders. There seems to be a great deal of evidence pointing toward a reworking of the categorical diagnoses on Axis II into a more dimensional or a combined dimensional-categorical system. Such a change through adding a dimensional aspect to the diagnostic system for personality disorders should bring the diagnostic process closer to clinical reality and would hopefully convey, through that revised process, more relevant and useful information about these patients' character, character traits, and level of functioning.

References

American Psychiatric Association. (1952). *Diagnostic and statistical manual. Mental disorders.* Washington, DC: Author.

American Psychiatric Association. (1968). *Diagnostic and statistical manual of mental disorders* (2nd ed.). Washington, DC: Author.

American Psychiatric Association. (1980). *Diagnostic and statistical manual of mental disorders* (3rd ed.). Washington, DC: Author.

American Psychiatric Association. (1987). *Diagnostic and statistical manual of mental disorders* (Rev. 3rd ed.). Washington, DC: Author.

American Psychiatric Association. (1994). *Diagnostic and statistical manual of mental disorders* (4th ed.). Washington, DC: Author.

Auchincloss, E. L., & Michaels, R. (1983). Psychoanalytic theory of character. In J. P. Frosch (Ed.), *Current perspectives on personality disorders* (pp. 2–27). Washington, DC: American Psychiatric Publishing, Inc.

Auerbach, J., Geller, V., Lezer, S., Shinwell, E., Belmaker, R. H., Levine, J., et al. (1999). Dopamine D4 receptor (D4DR) and serotonin transporter (5-HTTLPR) polymorphisms in the determination of temperament in 2-month-old infants. *Molecular Biology, 4*, 369–373.

Benjamin, L. S. (1993). *Interpersonal diagnosis and treatment of personality disorders.* New York: Guilford.

Blashfield, R. K. (1984). *The classification of psychopathology: Neo-Kraepelinian and quantitative approaches.* New York: Plenum.

Blashfield, R. K., & Fuller, K. A. (1996). Predicting the DSM-V. *Journal of Nervous and Mental Disorders, 184*, 4–7.

Blashfield, R. K., & Intoccia, V. (2000). Growth of the literature on the topic of personality disorders. *American Journal of Psychiatry, 157*, 472–473.

Carroll, B. J., Feinberg, M., Greden, J. F., Tarika, J., Albala, A. A., Haskett, R. F., et al. (1981). A specific laboratory test for the diagnosis of melancholia. Standardization, validation, and clinical utility. *Archives of General Psychiatry, 38*, 15–22.

Caspi, A., McClay, J., Moffitt, T. E., Mill, J., Martin, J., Craig, I. W., et al. (2002). Role of the genotype in the cycle of violence in maltreated children. *Science, 297*, 851–854.

Clark, L. A. (1992). Resolving the taxonomic issues in personality disorders. *Journal of Personality Disorders, 6*, 360–378.

Clark, L. A. (1993). *Manual for the schedule for nonadaptive and adaptive personality.* Minneapolis, MN: University of Minnesota Press.

Cloninger, C. R., Svrakic, D. M., & Przybeck, T. R. (1993). A psychobiological model of temperament and character. *Archives of General Psychiatry, 50*, 975–990.

Costa, P. T., & McCrae, R. R. (1992). *Revised NEO Personality Inventory (NEO-PI-R) and NEO Five-Factor Inventory (NEO-FFI) professional manual.* Odessa, FL: Psychological Assessment Resources.

Eysenck, H. J. (1991). Genetic and environmental contributions to individual differences: The three major dimensions of personality. *Journal of Personality, 58*, 245–261.

Feighner, J. P., Robins, E., Guze, S. B., Woodruff, R. A., Winokur, G., & Munoz, R. (1972) Diagnostic criteria for use in psychiatric research. *Archives of General Psychiatry, 26*, 57–63.

Fennig, S., Kovasznay, B., Rich, C., Ram, R., Pato, C., Miller, A., et al. (1994). Six-month stability of psychiatric diagnoses in first-admission patients with psychosis. *American Journal of Psychiatry, 151*, 1200–1208.

First, M. B., Bell, C. C., Cuthbert, B., Krystal, J. H., Malison, R., Offord, D. R., et al. (2002). Personality disorders and relational disorders. In D. J. Kupfer, M. B. First, & D. A. Regier (Eds.), *A research agenda for DSM-V* (pp. 123–199). Washington, DC: American Psychiatric Publishing, Inc.

Gabbard, G. O. (2004, May). Mind, brain, and personality disorders. Paper presented at the 157th annual meeting, American Psychiatric Association, New York.

Gunderson, J. G., & Pollack, W. S. (1985). Conceptual risks of the axis I-II division. In H. Klar & L. J. Siever (Eds.), *Biologic response styles: Clinical implications* (pp. 81–95). Washington, DC: American Psychiatric Publishing, Inc.

Gunderson, J. G., Shea, M. T., Skodol, A. E., McGlashan, T. H., Morey, L. C., Stout, R. L., et al. (2000). The Collaborative Longitudinal Personality Disorders Study: Development, aims, design, and sample characteristics. *Journal of Personality Disorders, 14*, 300–315.

Houts, A. C. (2002). Discovery, invention, and the expansion of the modern Diagnostic and Statistical Manuals of Mental Disorders. In L. E. Beutler & M. L. Malik (Eds.), *Rethinking the DSM: A psychological perspective* (pp. 17–65). Washington, DC: American Psychological Association.

Kendell, R. E. (2002). Five criteria for an improved taxonomy of mental disorders. In J. E. Helzer & J. J. Hudziak (Eds.), *Defining psychopathology in the 21st century. DSM-V and beyond* (pp. 3–17). Washington, DC: American Psychiatric Publishing, Inc.

Kendler, K. S. (1996). Major depression and generalised anxiety disorder: Same genes, (partly) different environments–revisited. *British Journal of Psychiatry, 168* (Supplement 30), 68–75.

Kendler, K. S., & Garner, C. O. (1998). Boundaries of major depression: An evaluation of DSM-IV criteria. *American Journal of Psychiatry, 155,* 172–177.

Kendler, K. S., Gruenberg, A. M., & Kinney, D. K. (1994). Independent diagnoses of adoptees and relatives as defined by DSM-III in the provincial and national samples of the Danish Adoption Study of Schizophrenia. *Archives of General Psychiatry, 51,* 456–468.

Livesley, W. J., Jang, K. L., & Vernon, P. A. (1998). Phenotypic and genetic structure of traits delineating personality disorder. *Archives of General Psychiatry, 55,* 941–948.

McGlashan, T. H., Grilo, C. M., Skodol, A. E., Gunderson, J. G., Shea, M. T., Morey, L. C., et al. (2000). The Collaborative Longitudinal Personality Disorders Study: Baseline Axis I/II and II/II diagnostic co-occurrence. *Acta Psychiatrica Scandinavica, 102,* 256–264.

Oldham, J. M., & Skodol, A. E. (2000). Charting the future of Axis II. *Journal of Personality Disorders, 14,* 17–29.

Oldham, J. M., Skodol, A. E., Kellman, H. D., Hyler, S. E., Rosnick, L., & Davies, M. (1992). Diagnosis of DSM-III-R personality disorders by two structured interviews: Patterns of comorbidity. *American Journal of Psychiatry, 149,* 213–220.

Paris, J. (1999). *Nature and nurture in psychiatry. A predisposition-stress model of mental disorders.* Washington, DC: American Psychiatric Publishing, Inc.

Rabinowitz, J., Slyuzberg, M., Ritsner, M., Mark, M., Popper, M., & Ginath, Y. (1994). Changes in diagnosis in a 9-year national longitudinal sample. *Comprehensive Psychiatry, 35,* 361–365.

Reich, J. (2000). The relationship of social phobia to the personality disorders. *European Psychiatry, 15,* 151–159.

Reich, J. (2002). Clinical correlates of stress induced personality disorder. *Psychiatric Annals, 32,* 581–588.

Reich, J., & Hoffman, S. (2004). State personality disorder in social phobia. *Annals of Clinical Psychiatry, 16,* 130–144.

Reich, J., Noyes, R., Hirschfeld, R., Coryell, W., & O'Gorman, T. (1987). State and personality in depressed and panic patients. *American Journal of Psychiatry, 144,* 181–187.

Reich, J., Noyes, R., Jr., & Yates, W. (1989). Alprazolam treatment of avoidant personality traits in social phobic patients. *Journal of Clinical Psychiatry, 50,* 91–95.

Robins, E., & Guze, S. B. (1970). Establishment of diagnostic validity in psychiatric illness: Its application to schizophrenia. *American Journal of Psychiatry, 126,* 983–987.

Ronningstam, E. F. (Ed.). (1998). *Disorders of narcissism: Diagnostic, clinical, and empirical implications.* Washington, DC: American Psychiatric Publishing, Inc.

Rutter, M. (2002). The interplay of nature, nurture, and developmental influences: The challenge ahead for mental health. *Archives of General Psychiatry, 59,* 996–1000.

Schneier, F. R., Spitzer, R. L., Gibbon, M., Fyer, A. J., & Liebowitz, M. R. (1991). The relationship of social phobia subtypes and avoidant personality disorder. *Comprehensive Psychiatry, 32,* 496–502.

Shean, G. D. (2003). Shifts in diagnostic frequencies during the years 1975–1999. *Journal of Nervous and Mental Disease, 191,* 751–755.

Siever, L. J., & Davis, K. L. (1991). A psychobiological perspective on the personality disorders. *American Journal of Psychiatry, 148,* 1647–1658.

Siever, L. J., & Davis, K. L. (2004). The pathophysiology of schizophrenia disorders: Perspectives from the spectrum. *American Journal of Psychiatry, 161,* 398–413.

Silk, K. R. (Ed.). (1994). *Biological and neurobehavioral studies of borderline personality disorder.* Washington, DC: American Psychiatric Publishing, Inc.

Silk, K. R. (1996). Expert commentary: Axis I-Axis II interactions. *Journal of Psychiatric Research, 30,* 3–7.

Silk, K. R. (Ed.). (1998). *Biology of personality disorders.* Washington, DC: American Psychiatric Publishing, Inc.

Skodol, A. E., Gunderson, J. G., Pfohl, B., Widiger, T. A., Livesley, W. J., & Siever, L. J. (2002). The borderline diagnosis I: Psychopathology, comorbidity, and personality structure. *Biological Psychiatry, 51,* 936–950.

Spitzer, R. L., Endicott, J., & Gibbon, M. (1978). Research diagnostic criteria: Rationale and reliability. *Archives of General Psychiatry, 35,* 773–782.

Stone, M. H. (1997). *Healing the mind: A history of psychiatry from antiquity to the present.* New York: W.W. Norton.

Tasman, A., Riba, M. B., & Silk, K. R. (2000). *The doctor-patient relationship in pharmacotherapy: Improving treatment effectiveness.* New York: Guilford Press.

Torgersen, S., Kringlen, E., & Cramer, V. (2001). The prevalence of personality disorders in a community sample. *Archives of General Psychiatry, 58,* 590–596.

Tyrer, P., Seivewright, H., & Johnson, T. (2003). The core elements of neurosis; Mixed anxiety-depression (cothymia) and personality disorder. *Journal of Personality Disorders, 17,* 129–138.

Westen, D. (1997). Divergences between clinical and research methods for assessing personality disorders: Implications for research and the evolution of Axis II. *American Journal of Psychiatry, 154,* 895–903.

Westen, D., & Shedler, J. (1999a). Revising and assessing Axis II. I: Developing a clinically and empirically valid assessment method. *American Journal of Psychiatry, 156,* 258–272.

Westen, D., & Shedler, J. (1999b). Revising and assessing Axis II. II: Toward an empirically based and clinically useful classification of personality disorders. *American Journal of Psychiatry, 156,* 273–285.

Westen, D., & Shedler, J. (2000). A prototype matching approach to personality disorders. *Journal of Personality Disorders, 14,* 109–126.

Widiger, T. A., & Corbitt, E. (1994). Normal versus abnormal personality from the perspective of the DSM. In S. Strack & M. Lorr (Eds.), *Differentiating normal and abnormal personality* (pp. 158–175). New York: Springer.

Widiger, T. A., & Costa, P. T. (1994). Personality and personality disorders. *Journal of Abnormal Psychology, 103,* 78–91.

Widiger, T. A., Frances, A. J., Harris, M., Jacobsberg, L. B., Fyer, M., & Manning, D. (1991). Comorbidity among Axis II disorders. In J. M. Oldham (Ed.), *Personality disorders: New perspectives on diagnostic validity* (pp. 163–194). Washington, DC: American Psychiatric Publishing, Inc.

Index

The letter t or f following a page number indicates, respectively, either a table or figure.